Anti-Southern Racism and Education in Post-War Italy

This book investigates the racism against Southern Italian children attending North-Western primary schools between the 1950s and the 1970s. Turin serves as the main case study, having become the "third Southern city" after Naples and Palermo during the considered period.

Far from being a new phenomenon, racism against Southern Italians gained renewed prominence in the context of the post-war mass internal migrations, becoming one of the pillars of the process of nation-rebuilding. However, in spite of its relevance, it has not received the attention it deserves.

By drawing on a wide range of sources – printed, archival, photographic, and oral – and situating itself at the intersection of the history of racism, of education, of psychiatry, and of psychology, the book aims to fill this gap and to add to the debate on the borders that nation-states establish to control the access to power of the different groups inhabiting their territories. Its interdisciplinarity makes it suitable for students and researchers across a variety of subject areas.

Grazia De Michele obtained her PhD in Italian history from the University of Reading. She is currently working towards a second PhD at the University of Genoa and is a member of the Centre for the History of Racism and Anti-Racism in Modern Italy (CENTRA).

Routledge Studies in the Modern History of Italy

*Edited by Carlotta Ferrara degli Uberti (University College London),
Marco Mondini (University of Padua and Italian German Historical
Institute-FBK Trent), Silvana Patriarca (Fordham University) and Guri
Schwarz (University of Genoa)*

The history of modern Italy from the late 18th to the 21st centuries offers
a wealth of dramatic changes amidst important continuities. From occupying a semi-peripheral location in the European Mediterranean to becoming
one of the major economies of the continent, the Peninsula has experienced
major transformations while also facing continuing structural challenges.
Social and regional conflicts, revolts and revolutions, regime changes, world
wars and military defeats have defined its turbulent political history, while
changing identities and social movements have intersected with the weight
of family and other structures in new international environments.

The series focuses on the publication of original research monographs,
from both established academics and junior researchers. It is intended as an
instrument to promote fresh perspectives and as bridge, connecting scholarly traditions within and outside Italy. Occasionally, it may also publish
edited volumes. The sole criteria for selection will be intellectual rigour and
the innovative character of the books.

It will cover a broad range of themes and methods – ranging from political to cultural to socio-economic history – with the aim of becoming a reference point for groundbreaking scholarship covering Italian history from
the Napoleonic era to the present.

The Ultimate Italian
Dante and a Nation's Identity
Fulvio Conti

Anti-Southern Racism and Education in Post-War Italy
Grazia De Michele

Debre Libanos 1937
The Most Serious War Crime Suffered by Ethiopia
Paolo Borruso

Anti-Southern Racism and Education in Post-War Italy

Grazia De Michele

Routledge
Taylor & Francis Group

LONDON AND NEW YORK

First published 2023
by Routledge
4 Park Square, Milton Park, Abingdon, Oxon OX14 4RN

and by Routledge
605 Third Avenue, New York, NY 10158

Routledge is an imprint of the Taylor & Francis Group, an informa business

© 2023 Grazia De Michele

British Library Cataloguing-in-Publication Data
A catalogue record for this book is available from the British Library

Library of Congress Cataloging-in-Publication Data
Names: De Michele, Grazia, author.
Title: Anti-southern racism and education in post-war Italy / Grazia De Michele.
Description: Abingdon, Oxon ; New York, NY : Routledge, Taylor & Francis Group, 2023. |
Series: Routledge studies in the modern history of Italy | Includes bibliographical references and index.
Identifiers: LCCN 2022041147 (print) | LCCN 2022041148 (ebook) | ISBN 9780367607920 (hardback) | ISBN 9780367607951 (paperback) | ISBN 9781003100546 (ebook) | ISBN 9781000838695 (adobe pdf) | ISBN 9781000838718 (epub)
Subjects: LCSH: Education, Primary—Social aspects—Italy, Northern—History—20th century. | Children of internal migrants—Education—Italy, Northern—History—20th century. | Discrimination in education—Italy, Northern—History—20th century. | Internal migrants—Italy—History—20th century.
Classification: LCC LC93.I8 D423 2023 (print) | LCC LC93.I8 (ebook) | DDC 370.94509/04—dc23/eng/20221025
LC record available at https://lccn.loc.gov/2022041147
LC ebook record available at https://lccn.loc.gov/2022041148

ISBN: 978-0-367-60792-0 (hbk)
ISBN: 978-0-367-60795-1 (pbk)
ISBN: 978-1-003-10054-6 (ebk)

DOI: 10.4324/9781003100546

Typeset in Sabon
by codeMantra

Contents

Acknowledgements

This book is based on the doctoral dissertation I completed at the University of Reading (UK) in 2013. The list of people I wish to thank is hence quite long.

First, I am grateful to my supervisor, the late Christopher Duggan, for his precious advice and for encouraging me to work on a topic I liked. The decision to focus on racism against post-war Southern migrants in the North-West of Italy grew out of a conversation with John Foot, who provided other useful suggestions. In Turin, Bruno Maida spent hours and hours talking with me about this project and put me in touch with Daniela Marendino, Emiliano Bosi, and all the amazing people of the *Istituto Piemontese per la Storia della Resistenza e della Società Contemporanea 'Giorgio Agosti'*. Daniela introduced me to the heads of several primary schools and followed me in all the dusty school archives I visited. This research would not have been possible without her passion and commitment.

Enrica Capussotti patiently discussed ideas and doubts. Paola Arzenati kindly allowed me to read her MA dissertation. Emma Schiavon taught me the importance of women's history. Leo Goretti has been a loyal friend and a second supervisor. Lucy and Christopher Hudson carefully read the first version of the manuscript. Silvana Palma continues to be the best mentor one may want to have.

I am deeply thankful to Francesco Cassata for motivating me to turn my dissertation into this book, to Guri Schwarz and the editors of the series Routledge Studies in the Modern History of Italy, as well as to Robert Langham for the opportunity to publish it. I am also indebted to Andrea Avalli, Maria Angela De Michele, and Marianna Polverino for their help with secondary sources, to the two anonymous reviewers for their feedback, and to Valter Colle for granting me permission to quote *La Ballata per Ciriaco Saldutto*.

My beloved José has endured years of monologues on the topic of this book and has never stopped holding my hand. Finally, I wish to thank my parents, Lina and Achille, for passing their passion for history on to me, for being a constant source of limitless love, for their sense of humour, and for being two marvellous human beings. This book is dedicated to their unforgettable memory.

Introduction

On 14 October 2008, the Chamber of Deputies – the lower house of Italy's parliament – passed a motion, tabled by the then leader of the Northern League in the chamber Roberto Cota, requiring the government to establish separate classes for foreign migrant pupils who failed an entrance exam to be admitted into Italian schools. Such classes, labelled *classi di inserimento* (insertion classes), would offer a curriculum including Italian and "legality and citizenship education". The aim was to provide pupils with language skills as well as with "(a) understanding of rights and duties (respect for others, tolerance, loyalty, respect for the laws of the host country); (b) support to democratic life; (c) world interdependence; (d) respect for the territorial and regional traditions of the host country, with no ethnocentrism; (e) respect for the moral and cultural diversity of the host country". Cota stressed that the classes were meant "to prevent racism [...] and achieve true integration" of foreign migrant students. The motion itself referred to a system of "transitory positive discrimination, in favour of immigrant minors" as the cornerstone for "reducing the risk of exclusion".[1]

The passing of the motion understandably sparked an outcry. The opposition as well as the Catholic Church, trade unions, associations, and linguists argued against the racist and discriminatory purpose of the scheme. Some highlighted that the new classes were reminiscent of the *classi differenziali*, special education classes that had been abolished in the late 1970s, and used this locution as a synonym of *classi di inserimento*. For example, the then secretary of the Democratic Party, Walter Veltroni, declared that "as an Italian" he found the motion intolerable and wondered whether the Italians "would have tolerated that [their] children ended up in the *classi differenziali* when [they] were the emigrants".[2] Likewise, according to one of the main teachers' trade unions, the measure was "discriminatory [and] brought [the country] back to the 1950s".[3] The Catholic weekly magazine *Famiglia cristiana* published an editorial in which, although claiming that "the problem of foreign students' integration [was] real", it distanced itself from solutions defined as "crypto racist" and likened to the apartheid regime. The article ended by mentioning an important chapter of post-war Italian history: "in the 1960s when children from Naples, Calabria and

DOI: 10.4324/9781003100546-1

Sicily went to school in Novara, nobody ever thought of putting them in a *classe differenziale* in order for them to learn Italian and Northern customs and traditions or to require them to sit an entrance exam".[4]

In fact, in the 1950s and the 1960s, it was common practice for the children of Southern migrants attending primary schools in the cities and towns of the industrialized North-West to be referred to the *classi differenziali*. In spite of its importance and relevance for the historical analysis of the current racism towards foreign migrants and their offspring, this phenomenon has received scant attention by historians as its distorted reappearance in October 2008 shows. The reasons for such lack of interest are multifarious and rooted in certain peculiarities of Italian historiography.

The events that have occurred in Europe since 1989 have dramatically changed the map of the continent. One may think of the implosion of the Soviet Union or of the end of the former Yugoslavia, for example, as events that were followed by an often violent resurgence of nationalism. These events have led scholars to look at the concept of nation in a more critical way. The nation was no longer considered a close and autonomous entity, but the outcome of dialectical relationships between groups perceived as internal or external to it. The main focus thus became the construction of symbolic borders within and without the nation, mainly along the lines of gender, class, race, ethnicity.[5]

The rise of the new approach to the nation has been difficult and is still incomplete in Italy. At the end of the previous century, phenomena such as *Tangentopoli* (Bribesville) and the success of political parties such as the Northern League contributed to promoting the diffusion of a "neo-patriotic stance" among intellectuals.[6] As for historians, according to Michele Nani – among the few to adopt this novel perspective – they have persistently tended to emphasize the distinction between the nation as it was conceived by the liberals in the nineteenth century and the subsequent degeneration into nationalism.[7] As a result, the issue of what Nani refers to as the "nationalization by contrast" has not been introduced into the debate.[8]

A nation – Nani points out – is delimited by external and internal borders. The former keep the nation separated from the foreigners, who can be easily transformed into enemies or peoples to conquer and subjugate; internal borders, on the other hand, are meant to identify particular groups who, depending on the circumstances, can be included or excluded from the national body. These groups can be subaltern classes, women, religious or ethnic minorities, migrants. Historically, in Italy, a portion of the country, identified as the South or the *Mezzogiorno*, and its inhabitants have been constructed as internal 'others' and their belonging to the nation has been – and still is – considered controversial.

The historiography on Italy's South has a long tradition and, since the last decades of the twentieth century, has witnessed a substantial revival. The focus of the investigation has been moved from the historical causes of the presumed backwardness of the *Mezzogiorno* to an analysis of the production of the latter as inherently 'different' from the rest of the country. However, almost all this body of work have focused on the nineteenth and the early twentieth centuries. Fascism and the post-war period have remained untouched. One of the aims of this book is to show how Southern Italians were still seen as internal 'others' in the post-war period, even when they left their places of origin to settle in the most developed areas of the country.

Internal migrations are one of the most conspicuous phenomena of the post-war period. The number of people moving from the countryside to the cities and from one region to another was great. Their social and cultural importance cannot be denied. Still, their history has been, to a large extent, neglected. In his book on Milan, John Foot has lamented the silence of historians on the topic. In his view, "there is a widespread belief [...] that internal immigration during the boom years was absorbed with difficulty, but over time, without enormous problems".[9]

Focusing on the specific case of Milan – but it seems to me that it can be the case for other areas too – Foot has indicated a series of "myths and clichés" surrounding internal migrations. It is commonly believed, for example, that "migration was overwhelmingly from the 'deep' south of Italy to the north [whereas] most immigrants were from Lombardy [and] those from the south and the island only made up 24 per cent of the total immigrants to Milan in 1958".[10] Moreover – in Foot's view – internal migrations are seen as "concentrat[ing] [...] into the five 'peak' years of the miracle (1958–63)". Milan continued, in fact, to witness the arrival of people from all over the country before the First World War, in its aftermath and in the 1930s, as well as after that period.

One would have expected historians – Foot argues – to notice the topicality of post-war internal migrations as a result of the new migrations from foreign countries. Interestingly enough exactly the opposite happened. In the last two decades, internal migrations have been almost completely forgotten. On the other hand, studies on Italian migrations abroad flourished.[11] The issue enjoyed a renewed interest and a general enrichment. The prominence assigned to international migratory flows, however, ended up obscuring internal migrations and opening the field to certain simplifications. The general idea is that Italy transitioned from being a country of *e*migration to a country of *im*migration, whereas the reality is much more complex. In addition, according to Enrica Capussotti, the history of Italian emigration has been assigned a pedagogic role. The negative experience of the Italians abroad is indeed meant to instil 'tolerance' and good sentiments towards foreign migrants living in the peninsula. The latter are thus expected to follow the same path as the Italians, who represent themselves now as fully developed and eventually able to act as models for the newly arrived. Post-war internal migrations are excluded from this narrative. Their history and particularly that of Southern migrants in the North-West could weaken the image of the successful and unproblematic modernization alleged to have taken place between the 1950s and the 1970s.[12]

The scarcity of studies on internal migrations throughout the twentieth century is particularly significant. The pioneering research of Anna Treves on Fascism has not been followed by other monographs until very recently.[13] The post-war period is still to be explored. Women are absent from the few studies available. An exception is the research conducted by Anna Badino analysing, for the first time, the extra-domestic work of Southern women in 1960s Turin.[14] It is a commonplace to think that Southern women did not have extra-domestic jobs as a result of their presumed lack of independence and submission to their husbands. Badino has, however, demonstrated not only the participation of Southern women in the job market but has also investigated its specificities.

Children have not received due consideration. By relying on the way Southern children attending primary schools in the industrialized North-West between the 1950s and the 1970s were constructed as a problem, this book will start to fill this gap. Turin was, among the North-Western cities, the most affected by migrations from the South, and constitutes the main case study. At the beginning of the 1970s, it was the third Southern city after Naples and Palermo.[15] The arrival of the Southerners was not welcomed. The newcomers were seen as a danger to the future of the city. Southern children, in particular, embodied the risk of social and cultural disintegration which Turin was believed to be running. It seemed to me that primary schools could be a privileged point of observation for the analysis of this issue.

Several impediments have made the research carried out for this book more difficult than expected. First of all, I had to deal with the disastrous situation of Italian school archives. It is only since 1999 that Italian schools have been compelled to preserve their documents and to organize their own historical archives.[16] Owing to a chronic lack of funds, though, this legis-lation has remained largely ineffective. Even when, as is the case with some schools, historical archives have been created thanks to the efforts of teach-ers, heads of schools, and archivists, many documents had previously been thrown away. My choice of the schools to consider as case studies was thus influenced by this not irrelevant issue. Luckily, I had the opportunity to be advised by Daniela Marendino, a freelance archivist, who coordinated a pioneering project for the organization of Turin school archives sponsored by the local *Istituto piemontese per la storia della Resistenza e della società contemporanea "Giorgio Agosti"*. After visiting several school archives, I decided to work on the primary school "Margherita di Savoia", located in the populous zone of Lucento, and on the primary school "Gian Enrico Pestalozzi", which was situated in a peripheral neighbourhood known as Barriera di Milano. Both the areas had been affected by migrations from the South in the post-war period.

Another major difficulty was the state of the archive of the former Turin *Provveditorato agli studi*, the local office of the Ministry of Public Instruction, assigned to the Turin State Archive (TSA) charged with making them available to the public. Unfortunately, owing to the lack of funds, the task had not been carried out when I was conducting my research. Researchers were thus forced to rely on a list of the folders – which could hardly be called an inventory – whose inaccuracies further slowed down their work. It was also impossible to locate the post-war documents of the Ministry of Public Instruction which – so I was told – were still kept in a deposit on the outskirts of Rome.

The selection of the primary sources was affected by the state of the archives. I have mostly used class registers and educational periodicals. Other kinds of official documents of interest were found only accidentally. School registers, however, proved to be an exceptional, even though often underestimated, resource. Post-war primary school teachers were compelled to write down in the registers everything concerning their pupils and their work, and these were regularly inspected by the heads of school. They thus offer historians the possibility of access to the classrooms and the benefit of an insider's view. It is important to bear in mind, though, that, as a result of the strict controls to which they were subject, teachers used registers first and foremost to justify their choices and safeguard themselves from possible sanctions.

The state of the Italian archives negatively impacts the history of education as a field of studies. The work of Ester De Fort, author of *A Social History of the Primary School from the Post-Unification Period to Fascism*, and that of Simonetta Soldani, who focused on the role of women and the construction of gender between the nineteenth and the early twentieth centuries, are among the few contributions proposing themes and methodologies going beyond those of institutional history, whose constraints are difficult to evade for the post-war period.[17] The so-called "social history of the classroom", flourishing in other European countries, is still in its infancy in Italy.[18] This book is thus also an attempt to deal with the history of post-war Italian education from this novel perspective. I have tried to consider schools not as detached from the rest of the society, but as places where social conflicts and stratifications find expression. This approach has proved particularly useful with respect to the issue of Southern pupils in Turin primary schools and to the primary sources I relied upon, in particular, class registers. In order to offer a complete analysis of the attitude towards Southern pupils of all the actors involved, it was important to consider and take into due consideration the way in which the presence of Southern families was perceived at a more general level.

Before providing a description of the structure of the book, it is worth clarifying some key concepts constituting its theoretical framework. One of these is the concept of 'otherness'. To put it simply, 'otherness' refers to identity and self, whose construction takes place through the contrast with someone seen as 'different' and defined as 'other'. Post-colonial theory has made great use of 'otherness' to describe the complex process by which Europeans have defined and affirmed their identity in opposition to the image of their colonial subjects. The latter embodied the negation of all the features Europeans attributed to themselves.[19]

Another concept I will make use of, especially for the analysis of school practices put in place to deal with the problem of Southern children, is that of discourse. Following Stuart Hall, it is possible to define discourse as a "system of representation". Relying on the French philosopher Michael Foucault, Hall explains how it is a "group of statements which provide a language for talking about – a way of representing the knowledge about – a particular topic at a particular historical moment". The notion of discourse allows us – Hall continues – to overcome the distinction between language and practice:

> "Discourse [...] constructs the topic. It defines and produces the objects of our knowledge. It governs the way that a topic can be meaningfully talked about and reasoned about. It also influences how ideas are put into practice and used to regulate the conduct of others".[20]

The book is organized as follows. The first chapter discusses the construction of the South and its inhabitants as internal 'others' in the post-war period. The representation of the *Mezzogiorno* as politically, socially, economically, and culturally backward was not a novelty. However, it is important to examine the issue in the context of post-war historical circumstances in order to note continuities and changes. The way in which the South was considered in the aftermath of the Second World War is relevant because, when the Southerners moved towards Northern-Western cities, the image of their place of origin shaped the perceptions of the 'host' societies. Particular attention will of course be devoted to the case of Turin and to the representation of Southern migrants and their children as a threat to the social fabric of the city.

The second chapter focuses on the main topic of this book: how Southern pupils became a burden for Turin educational officials and primary school teachers. The analysis of this issue requires an introduction to the specificities of the post-war Italian education system, which will be carried out in the first section. The second section investigates what can be defined as the educational 'otherness' of the South, that is the inferiority of its schools and the use of the high rates of illiteracy as a signifier of the North/South divide. The last section investigates cases of Southern pupils in Turin primary schools in the 1950s and 1970s.

The third chapter is devoted to the issue of the so-called *classi differenziali*, special education classes to which Southern children attending Turin primary schools were increasingly referred to in the period under consideration. Established at the beginning of the twentieth century, the *classi differenziali* witnessed a *boom* in the post-war period as a result of the increased demand for instruction from subaltern groups. They indeed proved an effective means of perpetuating the exclusion of certain categories of pupils from accessing instruction. In Turin, the majority of children attending *classi differenziali* were born to Southern families. This practice was opposed by protest movements in the 1970s and, at the end of the decade, the *classi differenziali* were dismantled.

The fourth chapter is intended to bring into the discussion the voices of Southern children. It is based on interviews with adults who, as Southern children, attended primary schools in Turin between the 1950s and the 1970s. Through the tools of oral history, the chapter attempts to survey the interviewees' school and childhood narratives.

Notes

1 Camera dei Deputati, *Mozione Cota ed altri n. 1 0003.3*https://leg16.camera.it/410?idSeduta=0066&tipo=documenti_seduta&pag=allegato_a# [last time accessed 22/9/2021]

2 "Classi ponte, cresce l'indignazione: "Intollerabili, incivili, razziste", *La Repubblica*, 15/8/2008 https://www.repubblica.it/2008/10/sezioni/scuola_e_universita/servizi/classi-inserimento/reazioni-classi/reazioni-classi.html [last time accessed: 22/9/2021]

3 "Altro attacco alla scuola da parte della Gelmini!" http://www.flcgil.it/scuola/altro-attacco-alla-scuola-da-parte-della-gelmini.flc [last time accessed: 22/9/2021]

4 "Si dice 'classi ponte'. Leggasi 'classi ghetto'", *Famiglia Cristiana*, 42, 19 October 2008.

5 For an overview of these new approaches see Özkirimli, U., *Theories of Nationalism. A Critical Introduction*, Basingstoke: MacMillan, 2000 and Eley, G., Suny, R. G., (eds), *Becoming National. A Reader*, Oxford: Oxford University Press, 1996.

6 Patriarca, S., "Italian neopatriotism: debating national identities in the 1990s", *Modern Italy*, 6, 1, 2001, p. 30.

7 Nani, M., *Ai confini della nazione. Stampa e razzismo nell'Italia di fine Ottocento*, Rome: Carocci, 2006.

8 Idem, p. 20.

9 Foot, J., *Milan Since the Miracle. City, Culture and Identity*, Oxford: Berg, 2001, p. 38.

10 Idem, p. 42.

11 Sanfilippo, M., *Problemi di storiografia dell'emigrazione italiana*, Viterbo: Settecittà, 2003; Gabaccia, D., *Italy's Many Diasporas*, London: University College of London Press, 2000; Bevilacqua, P., De Clementi, A., Franzina, E., (eds), *Storia dell'emigrazione italiana*, Vol. I *Partenze*, Rome: Carocci, 2001; Id., *Storia dell'emigrazione italiana*, Vol. II *Arrivi*, Rome: Carocci, 2002; Colucci, M., *Lavoro in movimento. L'emigrazione italiana in Europa 1945–57*, Rome: Donzelli, 2008 and Rinauro, S., *Il cammino della speranza. L'emigrazione clandestina degli italiani nel secondo dopoguerra*, Turin: Einaudi, 2009.

12 Capussotti, E., "Sognando *Lamerica*. Memorie dell'emigrazione italiana e processi identitari in un'epoca di migrazioni globali", *Contemporanea*, 4, 2007, pp. 633–46.

13 Treves, A., *Le migrazioni interne nell'Italia fascista. Politica e realtà demografica*, Turin: Einaudi, 1976. Gallo, S., *Il commissariato per le migrazioni e la colonizzazione interna (1930-1940). Per una storia della politica migratoria del Fascismo*, Foligno: Editoriale Umbra, 2015.

14 Badino, A., *Tutte a casa? Donne tra migrazione e lavoro nella Torino degli anni Sessanta*, Rome: Viella, 2008.
15 Ginsborg, P., *A History of Contemporary Italy. Society and Politics, 1943–1988*, Basingstoke: Palgrave, 2003.
16 D.P.R. 8 March 1999 No. 275.
17 De Fort, E., *La scuola elementare dall'Unità alla caduta del Fascismo*, Bologna: Il Mulino, 1996; Soldani, S., (ed.) *L'educazione delle donne: scuole e modelli di vita femminile nell'Italia dell'Ottocento*, Milan: Angeli, 1989; Soldani, S., Turi, G., (eds), *Fare gli italiani. Scuola e cultura nell'Italia contemporanea*, Bologna: Il Mulino, 1993. Important is also the work of historical sociology carried out by Dei, M., *Colletto bianco, grembiule nero. Gli insegnanti elementari italiani dall'inizio del secolo al secondo dopoguerra*, Bologna: Il Mulino, 1994 preceded by the earlier Dei, M., Barbagli, M., *Le vestali della classe media. Ricerca sociologica sugli insegnanti*, Bologna: Il Mulino, 1969. Barbagli is also the author of the important *Educating for Unemployment. Politics, Labor Markets, and the School System. Italy, 1859–1973*, New York: Columbia University Press, 1982.
18 Grosvenor, I., Lawn, M., Rousmaniere, K., *Silences and Images: The Social History of the Classroom*, New York: Peter Lang, 1999; see also Depaepe, M., (ed.) *Order in Progress. Everyday Educational Practice in Primary Schools, Belgium, 1880-1970*, Leuven: Leuven University Press, 2000.
19 For an introduction to the concept in its philosophical implications, see Van Pelt, T., "Otherness", in *Postmodern Culture*, 10, 2, 2000; see also Bhabha, H., "The other question...Homi K Bhabha reconsiders the stereotype and colonial discourse", *Screen*, 24, 6, 1983, pp. 18-36; Spivak, G., "The Rani of Sirmur: an essay in reading the archives", *History and Theory*, 24, 3, 1985, pp. 247–72.
20 Hall, S., "The work of representation", in Hall, S., (ed.) *Representation. Cultural Representations and Signifying Practices*, London: Sage, 1997, p. 44.

1 Post-war South and Southern migrants in Turin

Between imagination and reality

Internal migrations are commonly regarded as among the most notable phenomena characterizing post-war Italian history. The number of people involved was great and they contributed substantially to changing the social and cultural landscape of the country. The impact of the population movements from the South towards the North-Western regions is important for the numbers involved but, above all, for the difficulties that emerged in the encounter between the newcomers and the 'host' society.

In Turin, the arrival of thousands of Southerners was generally perceived as having created a state of emergency, jeopardizing the stability and the well-being of the community. Southern migrant culture and lifestyle became a source of great concern. Southern migrants were constructed as 'others' with the local press playing a substantial part.

This issue is to be seen in the wider context of the post-war revival of the Southern Question. After almost twenty years of silence imposed by Fascism, the birth of the Republic had once again brought the *Mezzogiorno* and its persistent economic, social, cultural, and political backwardness to the centre of the national attention.

The following chapter will first provide an overview of the main topics explored by the new historiography on the South; the second and third sections are devoted to the construction of the South's 'otherness' in the post-war period and its dissemination through weekly magazines. The last section focuses on the representation of Southern migrants in Turin between the 1950s and the 1970s.

1.1 A new history of the South

The history of Italy's South and of its relations with the rest of the country has been deeply rethought since the 1980s by a large group of scholars, both Italian and foreign. The role of the *Istituto meridionale di storia e scienze sociali* (IMES, Southern Institute of History and Social Sciences) founded in 1986 and of the journal *Meridiana* has been crucial in questioning the old approach to the history of the South and in exploring new research paths. A vast array of researchers from several disciplines voiced the need to

DOI: 10.4324/9781003100546-2

consider the *Mezzogiorno* "with all its specificities, an ordinary, one would say 'normal', piece of the world".[1] Important aspects of Southern history have thus been rewritten. The Southern Question itself – generally intended to refer to the problem of the backwardness of Southern Italy – has been readdressed as a "set of controversial historical constructs".[2] The inherent 'difference' of the South and its inhabitants, which had for a long time been considered an objective and indisputable reality, has been viewed as part of a complex system of representations and as a vital constituent of Italian national identity. As Gabriella Gribaudi has tellingly underlined:

> "The South is much more than a geographical area. It is a metaphor which refers to an imaginary and mythical entity, associated with both hell and paradise: it is a place of the soul and an emblem of the evil that occurs everywhere, but an emblem that in Italy has been embodied in just one part of the nation's territory, becoming one of the myths on which the nation has been built".[3]

1.1.1 *The South: an internal 'other'*

The issue of the representation of the South is thus to be understood as a part of Italian nation building. In Italy as well as in other European nation-states, the construction of the nation took place through the establishment of real and symbolic borders and the production of external and internal 'others'.[4] At the same time – as has been noted by Nelson Moe – in the century preceding unification, Italy itself had been symbolically positioned at the margins of a Europe constructing itself as modern, civilized, and bourgeois. During and after unification, the discourse on the backwardness of the Italian peninsula was displaced onto the Southern portion of the country.[5]

Several factors and agents were involved in this process. Marta Petrusewicz, for example, has underlined the importance of the role played in the construction of the Southern Question by the Southern intellectuals who, after the 1848 revolution and the consequent Bourbon repression, found refuge mostly in Piedmont.[6] The long years of exile had changed the relations of the exiles with the host country as well as with their areas of origin: "the more their admiration for the [host] country grew, the more the disdain for their own country grew; the acceptance of the asylum country became refusal of that of origin. [...] Italy became the *alter* of the kingdom of Naples; the refuge countries, all in the North, became the *alter* of the *Mezzogiorno* [which] started to transform itself into a Question".[7]

A further step in the consolidation of Southern 'otherness' was constituted by the events following Garibaldi's landing in Sicily, as the analysis of the correspondence between Camillo Cavour and his emissaries in the South carried out by Moe has revealed. The documents sent to Turin capture the Piedmontese military and political establishment's first encounter with the unknown territories. Even more importantly, though, the descriptions and impressions they contain testify to the need to acquire knowledge of the newly conquered lands in order to rule them. This knowledge was influenced by the course of the events. The disappointment on account of the unwillingness of the Neapolitans to rebel against the Bourbons before Garibaldi's arrival and the need to make sense of their unexpected behaviour sparked a wave of prejudice. "This is not Italy! This is Africa!", Luigi Carlo Farini exclaimed referring to the Neapolitan provinces, described as barbaric and uncivilized lands, requiring military control and rule.[8]

How the construction of the South as a barbaric land served to legitimize the use of force and of repressive measures is even more evident in the issue of brigandage. Brigands – John Dickie has pointed out – were perceived as "black, animal, feminine, primitive, deceitful, evil, perverse, irrational".[9] This view was particularly widespread among the top ranks of the army, which represented "the symbol of the resurgent nation and the principal means of Italianizing its citizens".[10] Brigandage hence contributed to the articulation and differentiation of the national space and to the construction of an "imaginative geography in which the Italian nation is constructed as the opposite of its South".[11] The re-establishment of law and order was to be pursued at all costs and assumed the contours of a civilizing mission. According to Claudia Petraccone, "the identification of the contrast between North and South with that between civilization and barbarism" allowed for no doubt about the use of force. This parallel also entailed the establishment of a conqueror-conquered relation in which the role of Southerners was of "open subordination".[12]

The official birth of the Southern Question was, however, linked to the figures of the so-called *meridionalisti* (meridionalists) – among them Pasquale Villari, Leopoldo Franchetti, and Sidney Sonnino – who initiated the long-lasting tradition of social enquiries into the South. Their approach was largely influenced by positivism.[13] Their works were firmly grounded in the belief that knowledge was essential for tackling the problems that they believed affected the *Mezzogiorno*. They thus collected and analysed an enormous corpus of data regarding the social reality of the South, whose scientificity was subsequently taken for granted, as John Dickie has highlighted.[14] Furthermore, their approach proved to be inadequate for the analysis of social phenomena regarding, for example, Southern middle classes. On the contrary, they interpreted Southern society as sharply divided into landowners and peasants and suggested that it was substantially immobile.[15]

The image of a barbaric and uncivilized South received scientific support from the theories of the school of criminal anthropology, which was founded in the second half of the nineteenth century by Cesare Lombroso and whose members included Giuseppe Sergi, Enrico Ferri, and Alfredo Niceforo. An overall analysis of the circulation and popularization of the theories of Lombroso and his disciples beyond the borders of science and intellectual elites is still lacking. Moreover, the figure of Lombroso and his work has been made the object of a good deal of simplification to the extent that – Daniel Pick has pointed out – he has often been "viewed as a political reactionary, progenitor of a resurgent socio-biology with conservative implications"; his contemporaries, on the contrary, considered him "a progressive figure, bringing evolutionary biology and physical anthropology to bear upon Italy's 'backwardness'".[16]

Lombroso was also deemed an innovator concerning the issue of crime and its causes. He took an active part in the debate on the reform of the penal code which – he advocated – should be based on the principles of criminal anthropology instead of those of the so-called classical school of penology.[17] The pillar of his doctrine has been considered the concept of atavism – a form of arrested development of the individual which produces crime.[18] The latter was not an act of free will – as the classical school of penology sustained – but "the sign of a primitive form of nature within an advanced society".[19]

As for the South, Roberta Passione has underlined how Lombroso changed his view in the course of his career, depending on the general political situation in the country.[20] After his experience in Calabria, where he was sent as a military doctor to assist the army engaged in the repression of brigandage, he insisted on the necessity for the State to intervene and prevent the risk of degeneration of that portion of the country. Passione argues, however, that in the following years and particularly in one of his most renowned works, *L'uomo delinquente* (Criminal Man), republished several times, Lombroso applied "the stigma of atavism and barbarity" to the whole of Southern society, thereby transforming it into a "'monster society', intimately different, inherently anomalous".[21]

It was, however, above all, Alfredo Niceforo's *L'Italia barbara contemporanea* (Contemporary Barbaric Italy) published in 1898, which sparked a bitter controversy on the issue of anti-Southern racism. Niceforo belonged to what Mary Gibson has called the "third generation" of criminal anthropologists.[22] In the early years of his career, on behalf of the *Società romana d'antropologia* (Roman Society of Anthropology) and of the *Società geografica italiana* (Italian Geographical Society), he investigated the diffusion and causes of crime in Sardinia.[23] *L'Italia barbara contemporanea* stands – according to John Dickie – as "almost an inventory of the stereotypes of the South in the late nineteenth century: the *mafia* and the *camorra*; the lottery, brigandage and feudalism; illiteracy, superstition and magic; cannibalism and corruption; Southerners as 'women-people', yet whose society is based on an 'Arabic' oppression of women; Southerners as pathologically individualistic, yet indistinguishable in their teeming masses; dirt and disease as characteristic of the *Mezzogiorno* together with rustic beauty".[24] Barbaric Italy was indeed – according to Niceforo – the *Mezzogiorno*, including Sardinia and Sicily. By using scientific tools and language as well as insisting on the racial difference of Southern populations, Niceforo "reinforced many of the stereotypes and myths already established by the prejudices of meridionalist discourse".[25]

1.1.2 The dissemination of a stereotypical image of the South

Besides analysing the plurality of the actors involved in the production of stereotypical images of the South, scholars have investigated – though to a lesser degree – how these images were disseminated among wider strata of the population. In this regard, the role played by the press was relevant. The issue has been analysed by Dickie, Moe, and Nani.

Dickie and Moe have focused on the magazine the *Illustrazione italiana*. Originally founded in 1873 with the name of *Nuova illustrazione universale*, the *Illustrazione italiana* was a weekly illustrated magazine published in Milan on the initiative of the publisher Emilio Treves. The target readership was the urban bourgeoisie.

As Moe has noted, "for the middle- and upper-class of the Centre-North, increasingly concentrated in the urban centres, the South became the emblem of the rural, traditional and picturesque world that was gradually disappearing from their lives".[26] The position of the South in the imaginary geography of the nation was made evident by the masthead of the magazine. At the centre, there was a statue of a goddess symbolizing Italy, on whose base stood the Capitoline wolf suckling Romulus and Remus. In the background, there were monuments of the most important Italian cities: the Campidoglio, right at the centre, the cathedral of Milan, the Palace of the Signoria in Florence, and others. Interestingly enough, the only reference to the South is to Vesuvius, the volcano – threatening and fascinating at the same time – which dominates Naples. There was no trace of other Southern cities, and the only one which was accorded space was symbolized not by an urban monument, but by a natural element.[27] Dickie, for his part, has stressed how the picturesque representation of the South offered by the magazine "name[d] the South's anomalous position between Italy and the Orient, between the world of civilized progress and the spheres of either rusticity or barbarism".[28]

Nani has, instead, concentrated on the reproduction of the stereotypes of the South in Turinese newspapers at the end of the nineteenth century. In his view, Turinese journalism stands as an important "laboratory […] to follow the evolution of the attitude towards the *Mezzogiorno*", as a result of the leading role played by Piedmont in the process of unification.[29] His analysis of the coverage of the peasant upheaval of the *Fasci Siciliani* offered by newspapers such as the *Gazzetta del Popolo* and the *Gazzetta Piemontese* is particularly interesting. The revolt took place in Sicily between 1893 and 1894 in the context of general and widespread working-class unrest and economic crisis gripping the whole country. The first land occupation and subsequent clash with the forces of public order, occurring in the village of Caltavuturo, did not attract a great deal of attention in Turin, indicating the "persistence of a perception of Sicily widespread in a good portion of the country [as] a far away and extraneous rural reality".[30] In September 1893, when the revolt restarted in a more organized manner, the attitude of the Turinese press changed radically. The phantom of brigandage was evoked and the uprising was interpreted – Nani has pointed out – as the expression of an "irrational collective insanity", thereby denying its political character.[31] Stripped of the recognition of any form of agency, Sicilian peasants were portrayed as barbarians and criminals and the proclamation of state of siege in 1894 was welcomed by the majority of the papers.

Nani has also examined the way in which Niceforo's *L'Italia barbara contemporanea* was received by the Turinese press, thereby suggesting the importance of the dissemination and popularization of the works of criminal anthropologists. The book was praised in the *Gazzetta del Popolo* by Paola Lombroso, Lombroso's daughter, who was a renowned journalist. Niceforo's study – she argues – indicated that the South was still at "the level of the Papuans and the Africans!"[32] *La Stampa* published an article written by Niceforo himself, offering him the opportunity to reply to the sociologist Napoleone Colajanni – who had harshly criticized his work on Sardinia – and to reassert that races did exist and their peculiarities could lead to crime and degeneration.[33]

Another means for the reproduction of Southern 'otherness' was photography. Unfortunately, its heuristic value as a source for historical research has for long been underestimated by Italian scholars. However, the role it played as an instrument of unification was very influential. As Giulio Bollati has remarked, photography "contributed to the creation of a celebratory and didactic national rhetoric, translating into images *topoi* taken from various sources or producing its own".[34] The citizens of the new-born State were inventoried and classified as members of a particular social class or inhabitants of a certain region.

The classificatory function of photography supported the construction of internal and external 'others'. This was the case of the Southerners as well as of colonial subjects. The similarities between the photographic representation of the South – and particularly of Naples – and that of Italy's African colonies have received attention especially from Alessandro Triulzi and Silvana Palma. Naples – Triulzi has pointed out – can be considered the "first national laboratory of representations of otherness".[35] The city, which had previously been a stop-off for the travellers on the Grand Tour, became in the nineteenth century the point of departure for the exploration of the South and, subsequently, of the African continent.[36] It was thus the "Italian threshold of Africa".[37] Some peculiar characteristics of the photographic representation of Naples "anticipated" – according to Triulzi – that of the African colonies. There was no room for workers or industries. Symbols of the city became its natural beauties – Vesuvius or the hill of Posillipo – and its eccentric inhabitants, depicted in absolutely "unreal poses".[38] This was the case of the *mangiamaccheroni* (macaroni-eaters), for example, portrayed with their mouths wide open and holding a bunch of spaghetti in their hands. Likewise, Silvana Palma has tellingly remarked upon the "immanence" which the representation of Neapolitans and Africans had in common. The complex and multifarious realities characterizing Naples and the African continent were serialized and reduced to stereotypes which photographs – widely circulating for commercial purposes – "inflated and disseminated".[39]

1.2 The post-war "rediscovery" of the South

The new historiography on the *Mezzogiorno* has so far focused almost completely on the construction of the South as an internal 'other' up to the end of the nineteenth century. The subsequent periods, including the Fascist regime, have received less attention.

Claudia Petraccone has analysed the unfolding of the debate on the Southern Question in the first half of the twentieth century. However, she has concentrated on the discourse produced by intellectual and political *elites* rather than on its dissemination among larger sectors of the population. The war for the conquest of Libya seemed to close – in her view – the debate between the "two civilizations". The aim of making Libya into a settler colony represented – in her opinion – the nationalist solution to the issue of the economic backwardness of the South, as well as the cure for what was considered the chronic and thorny question of the lack of authentic national unity.[40]

The Fascist regime eventually declared the Southern Question solved. However, the war of aggression against Ethiopia between 1935 and 1936, for example, was depicted by the propaganda as an invaluable opportunity for Southern peasants to expand overseas. The Neapolitan newspaper *Il Mattino* even indicated the latter as the "fittest race to colonize Africa".[41]

The post-war discourse on the South too is still to be investigated through the lens of the renewed historiographical approach. However, a handful of scholars – among whom are Gabriella Gribaudi and Gloria Chianese – have looked at the history of the South during and in the immediate aftermath of the Second World War from a novel perspective. Their works dispel some of the myths concerning, for instance, the failed participation of the South in the Resistance. Furthermore, they suggest that in the post-war period, the South was once more constructed as 'different' from the rest of the country. According to Franco Faeta, old "stereotypes and prejudices resurfaced and, if possible, were reinforced". Even more importantly – Faeta adds – particularly in the immediate aftermath of war, the image of an immobile, reactionary, and corrupt South was mostly conveyed by progressive political forces.[42]

1.2.1 The exclusion of the South from the Resistance

The birth of the Republic can be considered – as Salvatore Lupo and Francesco Benigno have indicated – the crucial moment for the "rediscovery" of the South in the post-war period and for its reappearance on the national stage, after twenty years of "eclipse".[43] The referendum on the Monarchy and the Republic held on 2 June 1946 indeed marked a high "level of real and symbolic polarization between the North and the South".[44] The South had largely voted for the monarchy, which in Naples obtained 80% of votes.[45] This meant, as the Communist Giorgio Amendola commented, that "there [were] large areas of Southern Italy where everything seem[ed] to have remained as it was before, under Fascism".[46] The war had thus passed in vain in the South. However – Gloria Chianese has noted – the South did not vote uniformly for the monarchy. In Campania and Apulia, the latter obtained great support, especially in the provinces of Lecce (85%) and Caserta (83.1%). The situation was extremely varied even within the same region, though. The people of Taranto, an Apulian working-class city, supported the Republic, as did the *braccianti* (landless farm hands) of the province of Foggia.[47] In spite of this heterogeneous situation, the *Mezzogiorno* was depicted as "*in toto* reactionary, extraneous and hostile to the republican democracy".[48]

The conservatism of the South was commonly explained by the fact that it had not participated in the Resistance – in which the population of the North alone was supposed to have been involved. The so-called "wind from the North" – an expression coined by Pietro Nenni to refer to the intimately renovating spirit of the Resistance – was believed not to have reached the South. Over the decades, this assumption has exerted an enduring influence even on historians, regardless of their political orientation. Federico Chabod, for example, in his lessons held in 1950 at the *Institut d'études politiques* of the University of Paris and published by the Italian publisher Einaudi in 1961, was adamant that in the South "we do not find, we cannot find Resistance". There existed too – he acknowledged – the *Comitati di liberazione nazionale* (CLN, Committees for National Liberation), but "they were very different from those of the other regions; here [in the South] the committees were established when by then there was no struggle to be conducted". The opposite had happened in the North, he claimed: "those [the committees] of the North fought instead for two years, many of their members continuously risked their lives, and many indeed died; the populations knew that among them was a group of men assuming the very hard task of leading the struggle".[49]

The traditional historiographic paradigm has been challenged, in the past fifteen years, by the pioneering work of Gabriella Gribaudi which has provided an innovative and groundbreaking analysis of the history of the *Mezzogiorno* during the Second World War.[50] She has taken her cue first from the concept of "total war", a kind of war aimed at the complete annihilation of the enemy, targeting civilians, perhaps even more than the official armies, and characterized by the use of technology to cause death on a mass scale. The Second World War can thus be considered as the total war par excellence. The mass bombings of the civilian populations by the Allies or the brutal Nazi massacres affecting both Southern Italy and other areas of the country represent one of its clearest expressions.[51]

Civilian involvement in war operations, though, also meant civilian resistance. By relying on the studies of Jacques Semelin on unarmed, non-violent civil resistance, Gribaudi shows how the populations of the *Mezzogiorno*, or at least of the portion of it on which she focuses (Naples and the area between the river *Volturno* and the Gustav Line), had not been a passive witness to events taking place elsewhere.[52] In the post-war period, however, their acts of civil disobedience, the help provided to Jews and soldiers whom the Nazis were chasing, and the solidarity with the evacuees, were not acknowledged as forms of resistance. Even when people took up the arms, as was the case of the so-called Four Days of Naples, theirs was not recognized as proper – one might say the right – resistance. The insurrection of Naples against the Nazi occupiers, between 28 September and 1 October 1943, was labelled in the post-war period by politicians and intellectuals as a simple jacquerie. It was most commonly interpreted as the sudden explosion of violence of a hungry populace destitute of any political organization and will. The Communist Party, for example, emphasized the "spontaneous" character of the revolt, whose inner reasons were to be found in the "apolitical and rebellious instinct" of the Neapolitans and not in a firm and politically well-organized anti-Fascist conscience.[53] More generally, what had taken place in Naples – as well as in other areas of the *Mezzogiorno* – did not fit into the dominant and normative model of the Resistance: the struggle conducted by organized military bands mostly comprising men and politically led by the parties of the CLN. It was a masculine model from which women too, with few exceptions, were excluded.[54]

At the end of the conflict, Naples – which had been subject to the protracted Allied occupation between October 1943 and January 1946 – was turned into a symbol of the "degradation produced by the war in the social and civic fabric of the nation".[55] The city was closely identified with the black market, with prostitution and every sort of moral corruption. The presence of the Allies – as Gloria Chianese has pointed out – contributed to a rise in criminality and illicit activities, as a result of the resources the occupants had at their disposal and which the local population, on the contrary, lacked. Theft, robberies, and the black market became a "strategy for survival".[56] This was also the case with prostitution which – Chianese remarks – was at that time State-regulated: "it was repressed only if clandestine", that is not subject to the compulsory medical check-ups, because it could constitute a risk to the "physical integrity" of both Italian men and Allied soldiers.[57] Once arrested, clandestine prostitutes were tested for syphilis and other common venereal diseases and, if positive, were referred to a special ward of the *Ospedale della pace*, under the control of the Prefect. Some medical experiments, such as the use of penicillin to treat syphilis, were conducted on them.[58] The so-called *segnorine* – Chianese adds – became in the local and national imagery the vehicle and the symbol of moral and physical degradation. This image was fixed, for example, by literature. Curzio Malaparte's novel *La Pelle*, was published in 1949 and represented Naples as a devastated female body, plagued by prostitution and invaded by hordes of black American soldiers.[59]

1.2.2 War children

The condition of post-war Neapolitan children also became a powerful trope for the degradation of the city. The issue of war children was a European one. The conflict – it was generally claimed – had had extremely detrimental effects on the younger members of the society and their physical, mental, and moral health had been seriously put at risk when not already permanently damaged. They were thus conceived of as both "endangered and dangerous" and subjected to particular attention.[60] Specific programmes aiming at treating their moral and physical illnesses were set up by governments, doctors, and humanitarian organizations. Their re-education in the broadest sense was deemed crucial for the future well-being of post-war democratic Europe and for preserving the social order.

In Italy, too, the moral panic over war children was strongly felt, especially in the late 1940s.[61] A sense of the way in which the issue was depicted at an institutional level is given by the words of the then Minister of Public Instruction, the Christian Democrat Guido Gonella, used during the speech he delivered at the First National Conference of the *Ente nazionale per la protezione morale del fanciullo* (ENPMF, National Agency for Children's Moral Protection) in September 1946. As will be examined in more detail in Chapter 3, the ENPMF had been established a year earlier by the criminologist Benigno di Tullio and its main focus was to prevent and treat children's corruption. In order to emphasize the timeliness of setting up an agency such as the ENPMF – which indeed was not coincidental – Gonella pointed out:

> "A lugubrious spectre has risen up from the ruin of the war: the face of a child marked with the wrinkles of vice [...] the war has offered [...] the breeding ground for the march of the evil, which devastates the souls, which makes the innocence of children fade and profanes it. [...] The corruption of children is a seismographer recording an underground and wide-ranging earthquake".[62]

The Communist Party also stepped in and organized a "movement of popular solidarity for the rescue of children" – or so it was described about forty years later.[63] Among the first to raise the issue had been Celeste Negarville, during the Second National Council of the Party in April 1945. Referring to the need for "relieving the suffering of the population" through the implementation of welfare policies, he urged action against the "anguishing spectacle of abandoned children awakening our deepest moral anxiety:

city councils can and must do a lot to take the *sciuscià* (shoe-shine boys) away from the street and make of them citizens worthy of a democratic country".[64] A leading role in the setting-up of the movement was played by the *Unione donne italiane* (UDI, Italian Women's Union), the left-wing women's organization. During the winter of 1945–46, thousands of children from Milan and Turin, whose families were in precarious economic conditions, were hosted by better-off families in Emilia. In 1946, the initiative was extended to include the *Mezzogiorno* and particularly areas such as Rome, Cassino, Sicily, and Naples.[65]

In Naples, the *Comitato per la salvezza dei bambini di Napoli* (Committee for the Rescue of the Children of Naples) was established on 19 December 1946. Among its founding members were the Communists Mario Alicata and Maria Antonietta Macciocchi, the criminologist Enrico Altavilla, Extraordinary Commissioner for the local Federation of the *Opera nazionale maternità e infanzia* (ONMI, National Agency for Maternity and Childhood) – founded during Fascism and providing mothers and children with care and assistance – Luigi Auricchio, Director of the University Paediatric Clinic, and the publisher Gaetano Macchiaroli.[66] Between 1946 and 1947, about 12,000 Neapolitan children were hosted by more prosperous families living in Central and Northern Italian regions, such as Liguria, Tuscany, and Emilia.[67] A pamphlet entitled *Let's help the children of Naples*, was sold for twenty liras in order to raise money and awareness. On the cover was a picture of two boys on a train platform: one of them wears a blanket, short trousers and is barefoot; the other is dressed in a ragged shirt and sandals; they both look towards the camera and only the first seems able to smile. They symbolized the poverty and neglect of post-war Neapolitan children, which the movement wanted to bring to public attention.

The way in which the situation of Naples was depicted in the pamphlet shows how intricate was the entanglement of moral panic over war children and the most common *topoi* of the moral degradation of the whole city. The pamphlet focused on what was referred to as the "tragedy of Naples".[68] The spatial extent of this "tragedy" was admitted to be not as wide as that of the whole country. However, the general state of the city was defined as "more intensely horrifying".[69] The condition of children was indicated as particularly worrying: in Naples, owing to a vast array of "particular and sometimes exceptional circumstances", the issue of children had taken on a "feverish rhythm and is so serious that it can actually lead to despair about the destiny of an entire civilization".[70] It was certainly true – the pamphlet went on – that problems such as "the physical and moral degeneration of children, the black market, juvenile crime, vagrancy and begging" were not peculiar to post-war Naples: many other Italian and European cities had been hit by these phenomena. Nevertheless, it was claimed that "in no other place as in Naples do these facts constitute a frightening threat to the whole society".[71] Naples was thus portrayed as an exceptional case at both national and European levels. The recent conflict was claimed only to have worsened an already precarious situation: "the world war in Naples" – it was noted – "has been nothing but the last link in a chain of social misery".[72] Before the outbreak of hostilities, a large portion of the population indeed lived "in narrow alleys, in decrepit and filthy buildings with no basic hygiene facilities".[73] The bombings, as well as the Nazi and the Allied occupation, had done the rest. About 67% of the local factories had been destroyed.[74] Public buildings – such as schools and hospitals – and houses had been bombed or requisitioned. The worst "tragedy", though, was alleged to be that of "work".[75] Many people had lost their jobs because of the war and, in order to get their "daily bread", ended up working for the Allies in conditions of "humiliation and brutishness" which were supposed to have paved the way for "theft and prostitution".[76] The prolonged presence of the Anglo-Americans and the consequent "flooding of *amlire* from the hands of soldiers of any colour" had also increased the "anguishing monster of inflation".[77] In a city already affected by "congenital poverty", the great circulation of money issued by the occupiers had fostered an "illusion of wealth" which had tempted too many people and had created the conditions for the spread of "pimping, brigandage, prostitution".[78]

Children were claimed to have been sucked into the "whirlpool" and forced to live as "strays". A "little army of shrewd and audacious children" had been recruited – so the pamphlet reported – into the ranks of the black market, increasing the profits of those who controlled them.[79] The consequences of the rise in juvenile crime were supposed to affect the "future of a whole generation".[80] The "physical integrity" of Neapolitan children was also considered at risk. Illnesses such as tuberculosis, undernourishment, and anaemia were particularly widespread. In some cases – it was underlined – "health and moral problems overlap". The pamphlet reported an excerpt from the speech delivered by an unnamed "Neapolitan woman" at the first conference of the ENPMF. She had inveighed against the widespread prostitution even among children: "we have seen" – she was reported to have said – "and we have taken Italian journalists to visit the wards of the hospitals [...] and see ten–twelve years old little prostitutes in their spotless beds".[81]

1.2.3 The debate on the *civiltà contadina*

Another important step for the post-war "rediscovery" of the South was represented by the so-called debate on the *civiltà contadina* (peasant civilization) which saw the participation of several intellectuals and politicians, the majority of whom were left wing. The debate was inspired by the movement of land occupation which spread out in various areas of the South in the late 1940s. As Carla Pasquinelli has pointed out, "the struggle for the occupation of land conducted in those years [the immediate aftermath of war] in the *Mezzogiorno* [...] provided the backdrop to a debate involving, together with specialists, politicians and prominent figures of the cultural life of the time".[82]

The movement of land occupation originated – Gloria Chianese suggests – from the experience of the *repubbliche contadine* (peasant republics) occurring in the last months of 1943 in several Southern villages.[83] Their life was quite short and in the end they were dismantled by the authorities. Nonetheless, according to Chianese, their importance should not be underestimated. Among the first republics to be established were Sanza, in the province of Salerno, Maschito, in the province of Potenza, and Calitri, not far from Avellino.[84] The proclamation of the republics was usually accompanied by a popular insurrection, a redistribution of resources and particularly of food, the election of representatives and clashes with Italian and Allied police. Anti-Fascism and egalitarianism as well as rejection of the Monarchy were the main characteristics of the republics, Chianese remarks.

A second wave of land occupations and peasant revolts took place between 1944 and 1947, in the wake of the decrees issued by the then Minister of Agriculture, the Communist Fausto Gullo. As Paul Ginsborg has pointed out, "Gullo's legislation was of great complexity" and contained "Utopian elements".[85] The most important measures included a reform of the contracts between peasants and landowners, in order to guarantee that the former could keep at least 50% of the produce, the creation of the so-called *granai del popolo* (people's granaries), the abolition of any intermediation between peasants and landowners and the opportunity of occupying and cultivating abandoned or semi-abandoned land.[86] The decrees were, however, destined to produce an impressive mobilization among the peasants but poor practical results. Moreover, in July 1946, the Christian Democrat, Antonio Segni, replaced Gullo as Minister of Agriculture and issued new measures weakening the effects of the previous ones.[87]

The movement regained momentum in 1949. In the meantime, the Communists had been excluded from government in 1947, the Christian Democrats had won general elections in 1948 and defeated the *Fronte democratico popolare* (Popular Democratic Front) made up of the Communists and Socialists. It is worthwhile underlining that the social unrest in the countryside was common to almost the whole country and concerned not only peasants without land, but also other categories. For example, in Tuscany, sharecroppers clamoured for a higher share of the crop which was traditionally halved with the landowners.[88] In the Po Valley too, the struggle of farmworkers reached its peak with a strike taking place in May and June and lasting thirty-six days.[89] In Tuscany and in the Po Valley as well as in the South, the repression by the authorities was harsh. Not only were hundreds of protesters arrested, but in many cases, they were killed. One of the most famous killings took place in Melissa, a Calabrian village, where on 29 October three people – two men and a woman – were shot by the police during the occupation of an estate.

The debate on the *civiltà contadina* was first started at the end of the war by the publication of Carlo Levi's book, *Cristo si è fermato a Eboli* (Christ Stopped at Eboli). Levi was a Turinese intellectual, writer, and painter and a member of the anti-Fascist organization *Giustizia e libertà* (Justice and Freedom). As a result of his opposition to the regime, he was exiled in 1935 to Aliano, a Lucanian village in the province of Matera. The book was based on the memories of his experience and was written in Florence between 1943 and 1944.[90] The title referred to a saying which had been reported to Levi by the locals:

> "'We are not Christians,' they say. 'Christ stopped short of here, at Eboli'. 'Christian' in their way of speaking, means 'human being', and this almost proverbial phrase that I have so often heard them repeat may be no more than the expression of a hopeless feeling of inferiority. We're not Christians, we're not human beings; [...] But the phrase has a much deeper meaning and, as is the way of symbols, this is the literal one. Christ stopped at Eboli, where the road and the railway leave the coast of Salerno and turn into the desolate reach of Lucania. Christ never came this far, nor did time, nor the individual soul, nor hope, nor the relation of cause to effect, nor reason nor history. [...] No one has come to this land except as an enemy, a conqueror, or a visitor devoid of understanding".[91]

As Giuseppe Giarrizzo has noted, to Levi, Lucania and particularly the province of Matera, where he had been living, symbolized "the whole peasant South", a world apart, to which his book was meant to provide access.[92] The State itself was perceived by peasants as a remote and incomprehensible entity and an enemy: "to the peasants the state is more distant than heaven and far more of a scourge, because it is always against them".[93] Their reaction to the hostility of the State towards them and the exiles temporarily living in their villages was "resignation", for they were unable to understand what political struggle was:

> "This passive brotherliness, this sympathy in the original sense of the world, as suffering together, this fatalistic, comradely, age-old patience, is the deepest feeling the peasants have in common, a bond made by nature rather than by religion. They do not and cannot have what is called political awareness, because they are literally *pagani*, 'pagans', or country-men as distinguished from city-dwellers. The deities of the state and the city can find no worshippers here on the land, where the wolf and the ancient black boar reign supreme, where there is no wall between the world of men and the world of animals and spirits, between the leaves of the trees and the roots below".[94]

Levi's peasants were thus not part of history and politics but appeared locked into their magic universe isolated from the rest of the world. This representation of an immobile peasant society was criticized, for example, by the Marxist literary critic Carlo Muscetta, as Giarrizzo remarks. According to Muscetta, particularly in those years when the book had been published, peasants were the protagonists of social conflicts breaking their supposedly traditional isolation: "while Levi's poetics tends to make the *Mezzogiorno* appear more distant than India or China, the *Mezzogiorno* today, [...] tends to come out from its immobility, and is politically and socially alive, in unrest and movement to get closer to and be reunited with the «other» Italy".[95]

Levi's book was a source of inspiration for the anthropologist Ernesto De Martino who, until the middle of the 1950s, committed himself to the study of the culture of Southern subaltern classes. De Martino had been trained at the University of Naples and was a pupil of the historian Adolfo Omodeo and of the philosopher Benedetto Croce. In 1941, he took part in the creation of an anti-Fascist committee in Bari and subsequently joined the Socialist Party and, in 1950, the Communist Party.[96] His work has long been debated by scholars who, throughout the years, have highlighted its novelty, complexity, and ambiguity. Among his contemporaries too, his writings sparked a bitter controversy. This was the case of the article *Intorno a una storia del mondo popolare subalterno* (Concerning a History of the Popular Subaltern World), published in 1949 in the left-wing journal *Società*.[97] The article was preceded by an editor's note distancing the journal from De Martino's "thesis and interpretation", though recognizing their importance and topicality.[98] In the article, De Martino referred to Antonio Gramsci, whose *Quaderni dal carcere* (Prison Notebooks) were being published in those years as part of Palmiro Togliatti's cultural and political strategy.[99]

The "popular subaltern world" comprised – according to De Martino – both "colonial and semi-colonial peoples [as well as] the working-class and peasant proletariat of hegemonic nations".[100] In the past, it had been considered by Western-European ethnologists simply as something to be classified, while the understanding of the inner meaning of its cultural practices had been completely neglected. This attitude reflected – De Martino argued – the way in which the popular subaltern world was viewed by "bourgeois society" in the wider political context: "the popular subaltern world constitutes, for bourgeois society, a world of *things* rather than of *persons*, a natural world which is confused with nature itself and is conquerable and exploitable".[101] This approach had been put into crisis since "on a world scale the popular masses are struggling to enter into history, to overthrow the order which keeps them in a subaltern position".[102] What De Martino also referred to as the "bursting of the popular subaltern world into history" posed new problems, though.[103] The masses indeed brought with them "their cultural habits, their ways of struggling against the world, their naïve millenarian faith, their myths and even certain magical attitudes", which he believed caused a "*barbarization* of [traditional high] culture and habits".[104] The main task of traditional high culture was thus to favour the historicization of the cultural forms typical of the popular subaltern world and to use them in a *"progressive"* way.[105] Such strategy would have prevented the culture of the subaltern groups from being instrumental in the reactionary purposes of the dominant classes, as it had been the case with Nazi Germany, and would ultimately have led to their own liberation.

As George Saunders has noted, "De Martino reflects the dilemma of the sympathetic intellectual who wants to help the poor but in fact feels ambivalent at best toward their ideas and values".[106] De Martino's ambivalence towards the 'popular subaltern world' itself went, however, almost completely unnoticed by his contemporaries. Among the then critics of De Martino's stance, it is worthwhile mentioning the Communist Cesare Luporini whose harsh reaction well exemplified the position of many other Communist intellectuals. Luporini accused De Martino of having adopted the old bourgeois perspective in holding that the masses were only then entering into history: as he put it, "the popular masses have never been *out* of history". However, in his view, their active participation in history was the result of the supposed superiority of the working-class over all the other groups of which the popular subaltern world was made up: "what De Martino calls the 'popular subaltern world' is not undifferentiated; [...] there is [in it] a fundamental differentiation, [...] that of the working-class, which is the fruit of civilization and progress, and not of barbarism". Only the working class – Luporini went on – was able "by freeing itself, to wipe out from the face of earth any kind of slavery, exploitation, tyranny and all their *cultural* consequences and to answer to the piercing appeal that for centuries and centuries has come from the depths of the 'popular subaltern world'".[107] Luporini – Stephen Gundle has remarked – not unlike other Italian Communist intellectuals, was firmly convinced that "the forms of popular culture [De Martino was referring to] (folklore, magic, etc.) could never be progressive and were vestiges of the past that should be completely transcended".[108]

The debate was revived and became even more vehement after the post-humous publication of Rocco Scotellaro's writings in 1954. Scotellaro was an intellectual and poet who had died at the young age of thirty in 1953. His life, though short, had been particularly intense. A member of the Socialist Party, in 1946 he had become mayor of his native village, Tricarico, in the province of Matera, and had subsequently moved to Portici, where he had worked with the economist Manlio Rossi Doria at the local *Osservatorio di Economia Agraria* (Observatory of Agrarian Economy). After his death, his poetry and notes concerning an enquiry into the life of Southern peasants on which he was working were published by Carlo Levi and Rossi Doria.[109] This circumstance offered the Communist Mario Alicata the pretext to attack Scotellaro's mentors with an article published in the periodical *Cronache meridionali*, which Alicata himself had founded in that same year. Alicata's main target – as the title of the article *Il meridionalismo non*

si può fermare ad Eboli (Meridionalism Cannot Stop at Eboli) unequivocally indicated – was Levi whom he accused of having misrepresented the
deep transformation that the world of Southern peasants was undergoing
and the rise of their "new conscience".[110] The latter – according to Alicata –
was the result of the "struggle between the rational and critical conception
of the world, to which [peasants] are educated by the daily revolutionary
action of the democratic and social movement, and the old, fossil parts of
their traditional religious, moral and political habits".[111]

Alicata found Levi, Rossi Doria, and Scotellaro guilty of having "idol-
ized the primitive". On the contrary, the "struggle for the redemption of
the *Mezzogiorno*" was to be based on the creation of a vast movement
comprising not only the peasants, but also the intellectuals and the urban
middle classes. Such a struggle, however, could only be successful – Alicata
warned – if the movement "[understood] the need of forming an alliance
with the working-class and of accepting its leadership".[112]

While the intellectuals were discussing the characters and fate of the
civiltà contadina, Southern peasants started – as Claudia Petraccone
has pointed out – to leave the countryside and move to the cities, often
in Central and Northern Italy.[113] Retrospectively, the debate continues
to appear substantially unresolved. Gabriella Gribaudi has noted that on
the one hand, "the idea of the peasant world as an enclosed and uniform
world", which, for example, Levi's book more or less explicitly conveyed,
"is not convincing"; on the other hand, Luporini, Alicata, and their like
harshly criticized Levi, De Martino, and Scotellaro on account of their
conviction that the peasants' world and culture were "an anachronistic
relic and an obstacle to the reawakening of Southern masses [and thus] had
to be rejected totally".[114] According to Franco Gaeta, both sides did not
question – and ended up reinforcing – the "ontological backwardness" of
the South and its inhabitants.[115]

1.3 The South in the weekly magazines

The post-war "rediscovery" of the South in terms of irreducible 'difference'
and backwardness did not concern only politicians and highbrow intellectuals. An important contribution to this process came also, for example,
from weekly magazines.

As David Forgacs and Stephen Gundle have remarked, Italy was usually
considered, at least up to the 1960s, to be a country of "few readers" – for
several reasons, including high rates of illiteracy, poor school attendance,
and the high cost of books. However, "a mass reading public did exist" in
the 1930s for some kinds of publications, such as the sports press, comics,
and illustrated magazines. The readership of weekly magazines – Forgacs
and Gundle add – was much wider than that of newspapers and books,
especially as a result of the more appealing effects obtained by using the
rotogravure technique.[116]

In the post-war period especially, the word *rotocalco* itself became synonymous – according to Nello Ajello – with weekly illustrated current affairs magazines. The first examples of this type of magazine, *Omnibus* and *Oggi*, owned by the publisher Rizzoli, as well as *Tempo*, published by Mondadori, to cite only a few, flourished in the 1930s.[117] In the post-war period, the *rotocalchi* widened their circulation: in 1955, Mondadori's *Epoca*, for instance, sold 500,000 copies while Rizzoli's *Oggi*, one of the most successful, reached the figure of 760,000.[118] One of the main features of these magazines was the wide use of photographs which most commonly accompanied the articles, but which could also be 'read' on their own. For articles concerning social or political issues especially, they stood as documents reproducing an objective reality and were meant to give readers the opportunity – or at least the impression – of acquiring knowledge about it.[119]

The photographic reportages on Naples published in post-war weekly magazines have been – according to Lello Mazzacane – an extremely powerful means of reproducing and fixing a stereotypical image of the city.[120] It might be hypothesized that this applies, more generally, to the whole South, which was repeatedly explored by journalists and photographers who, in different ways and with different approaches (depending also on the magazine for which they were writing), contributed to disseminating old and new stereotypes. It is impossible to offer here a comprehensive and detailed investigation of this issue, which would constitute a research topic on its own. However, a snapshot view can be provided through the analysis of some surveys published between the late 1940s and the 1950s in three prominent magazines, *L'Europeo*, *Epoca*, and *L'Espresso*.

1.3.1 The 1948 survey of *L'Europeo*

L'Europeo was founded in 1945 by the publisher Gianni Mazzocchi and the journalist Arrigo Benedetti. Ajello has pointed out that, in the immediate aftermath of war and at least up to the 1948 elections, the magazine was quite influential and held a dominant position in the market of the *rotocalchi*. Its distinctive trait was the publication of surveys concerning social and political questions and often of investigative reports.[121] Among the latter was the shocking revelation by the journalists Tommaso Besozzi and Nicola Adelfi that the Sicilian bandit, Salvatore Giuliano, had not died during a firefight with the police, as the authorities, including the then Minister of the Interior Mario Scelba, had confirmed, but had been killed by his cousin Gaspare Pisciotta.[122]

Between February and March 1948, *L'Europeo* ran a "survey on the *Mezzogiorno*", carried out by Besozzi, whose declared aim was to bring "the old problem of the *Mezzogiorno*" to the attention of both the "government and the opposition". Southern regions – so the presentation of the survey read – "averse to demagogy, and from ancient experience prone to moderate solutions, seem sometimes resigned to their conditions". The "problem", however, did exist and it was necessary to intervene in order to prevent the "sudden bursts of rebellion and anarchy which from Cerignola to San Ferdinando cost human lives".[123]

Cerignola and San Ferdinando were two towns in the province of Foggia in Apulia. The region had been in turmoil during the period of land occupations. In Cerignola, there had been frequent clashes between local peasants and public order forces, and on 15 November 1947, two people had been killed by the police.[124] In San Ferdinando, not far from Cerignola, on 9 February 1948, four militants of the Communist Party had been attacked and killed during a rally of the *Fronte Democratico Popolare* during the electoral campaign for the general elections to be held in April.[125]

Interestingly enough, neither the two towns, nor Apulia, figured among the places Besozzi visited for his survey. Paradoxically, the two episodes, which were significant in the social and political turmoil of the South in that period, were used as a pretext to offer a representation of the *Mezzogiorno* as immobile, parasitic, and backward. The first article focused on Naples, depicted as a static and acquiescent city, which failed to be moved even by the miserable conditions of its children. Its passivity was underlined in the headline which read: "At the soup kitchen for poor children parents look on". Above the headline was a picture portraying two ragged and dirty children – a boy and a girl – staring towards the camera. The caption read: "Naples. Two *scugnizzi* (street kids) in the area of the port. Like many other Neapolitan children, these too live on alms. At mid-day they can benefit from the soup kitchen for poor children".

Besozzi's account started from an episode that occurred a few days earlier: a three-storeyed house had collapsed, causing the death of two women and a child. The evacuation of the whole road, decided upon by the authorities as a precautionary measure, and the difficulties in providing them with an alternative accommodation, had sparked "uproar" among the inhabitants.

What was even more striking – according to Besozzi – was that some of the families had not left the *bassi* in which they lived, as they had been ordered to do: "after having breached the wall, they got in crawling, passing through a court behind the alley, from where nobody could suspect they could have access".[126] The case epitomized in Besozzi's words the "tragedy of Naples". Tourists would still find the most renowned hotels – which had been rebuilt after the war following the "criteria of modernity" – the typical restaurants, and the *San Carlo* theatre. However, "behind the shield of shining buildings and of a pleasant life, the most squalid misery that one can ever imagine is hidden".

The city was described as populated by half-starved people: all productive activity – including the port and industries – had stopped; children could only eat the food provided by the soup kitchen while their mothers sold their bread on the black market; illnesses killed tens of people; houses collapsed. The Neapolitans, though, were passive. They "accepted their misery as a fatality which nobody could mitigate". Instead of joining left-wing parties or organizing demonstrations – Besozzi remarked – "everyone prefers to fend for himself and inventiveness never lets them down". Naples and its inhabitants thus were not providing any form of resistance to the misery and the squalor in which they were alleged to be completely immersed. They seemed to adapt to it as if it were their own natural condition. Likewise, they had benefited from the Allied occupation, as Besozzi recalled:

> "For a certain period, two years ago, money started to flow with fabulous abundance in these filthy alleys. In every house, every night, there was a party: hangings and lights; guitars and mandolins; the negroes sat in the *bassi* and got drunk singing 'O sole mio'; straw mattresses were stretched out on the sacks of sugars, on the boxes of preserves, on the stolen tyres; American lorries arrived empty at their destination; the cargo of entire ships disappeared. There was money for all the Neapolitans. Even the poorest would have been able to cover the walls of his burrow with the *amlire* and they would have some left over".

The sexual promiscuity with the black invader, here subtly suggested by the reference to the straw mattresses put just after the image of the drunken negro soldiers singing 'O sole mio', was meant to give readers the sense that the irremediable misery of Naples was not only material, but above all moral. It is worth remarking that up to a few years earlier, from the late 1930s, mixed-race relationships in the colonies had been forbidden on account of the degenerative effects that these unions and their offspring allegedly had on the Italian race. As Silvana Palma has pointed out, periodicals such as *La difesa della razza* had fuelled the dissemination in the motherland of the new "racial conscience", based on a strict separation between white and black subjects.[127] Fascist sexual segregationist policy and propaganda, though, had mostly targeted unions between white men and black women, since those between a "white woman and a black man [were] not even taken in consideration".[128] Male sexual domination indeed epitomized the possession of the feminized colonial territory. In the case of Naples during the Allied occupation, even the taboo preventing a white woman from having a sexual relationship with a black man had been broken, thereby representing the culmination of immorality and the reversal of a sacred value.[129]

The immoral promiscuity – between white men and women this time – had continued even after the end of the Allied occupation: once the "last negro [had] left [...] the alleys of Naples returned the reign of misery". People, however, did not seem to be surprised or appalled. On the contrary, they continued on their track to moral corruption without realizing the state of depravity into which they had sunk: "They adapted without rebellion. [...] As for the mixing between the sexes, it is something which disturbs only us, who are watching from outside".

The second article of the survey, published at the beginning of March, also focused on Naples and specifically on the evacuees in the caves of

Mergellina, whose houses had been damaged by bombings.[130] In this case too, the headline brought children to the attention of the readers and, at the same time, turned upside down the stereotype of Naples as the city of sun. It read: "Children of Naples do not eat sun"; the sub-headline continued: "they dream of the white bread of the *Pianura Padana* (Padan Plain)". The article was accompanied by five pictures in which only women and children were portrayed.

The first part of the article called for the intervention of the whole country to rescue the *Mezzogiorno*. It insisted that the aim of the survey was to provide Italians as a whole with knowledge and awareness about the conditions in the South in order to promote action: "the brothers of the *Mezzogiorno* are to be saved: the Italians have to know". At the same time, however, Besozzi prophesied that the "hopes" for the future of the Southern regions were "great" – so much so that "in a hundred years the map of Italian economy will be reversed [and] heavy industry will move to the South". The position of Naples in such a revived landscape would certainly have been of "great prominence". In striking contrast to the shameful situation he had sketched in his previous article, he stated this time: "Naples is a living city. It's a city of enormous resources. Today's misery is the result of a fact for which nobody will ever be able to hold the Neapolitans responsible: in no other centre of the Peninsula has the war left such deep wounds".

The initially optimistic view of a city moving towards a bright, though still distant, future was, however, immediately belied by the description of the life in the caves of Mergellina, defined as "troglodytic". People who had lost their homes during the war – Besozzi explained – had built their own shanties inside the caves. Those closest to the entrance were wider and often "had a small terrace with some flowerpots or basil; a wooden floor, some even have wallpaper". One of the pictures was meant to confirm this account: it portrayed a girl combing her hair before a basket in which a baby, with a dummy and wearing a cap, was crying; the girl is well-dressed and tidy; the wallpaper covers the wall, which is also adorned with pictures. The caption, however, warned that "this was the only [shanty] to have any wallpaper; the others are bare, water gets in through the walls, and the mattresses go mouldy on the floor". All the other dwellings – Besozzi went on – were incredibly damp with devastating effects on the bodies of the people inhabiting them: "these wretched people reduced to living in a cavern [...] lay on the floor crouched on the mattresses; [...] around them everything exudes humidity, smells of decomposed matter". Their living environment was bringing them back to an earlier stage of history: "there is an open hatred among those who founded the troglodytic village and those who followed; the former, laying claims of priority, would want to impose on the latter a rule which is little less than one of servitude".

Suddenly, Besozzi's plea was extended from the caves of Mergellina to the whole city, addressing specifically the problem of children: "there is, in all the alleys of Naples, the desolating spectacle of undernourished and ill children". He provided statistics demonstrating the extent of the tragedy and distinguished between two categories of children, without missing the opportunity of subtly recalling the dark recent past. Those older than four years of age were still the "*scugnizzi* they used to be. Naples is their home: they were born when poverty was less severe; they knew moments of affluence; they gained experience during the fabulous but not far distant days when the negroes knocked on the doors of the *bassi* with boxes of preserves". The new generation, on the other hand, was more dependent, able only to "wait for a crust of bread". Pale and swollen, these were "the children of the misery of Naples on whom the sun does not shine".

The survey was temporarily stopped in the following issue, though in an ambiguous way. The magazine ran an article by Besozzi which focused on Natuzza Evolo, a Calabrian peasant woman, living in the village of Paravati, who claimed to be able to talk to the dead, sweat blood, and even to imprint the silhouettes of angels and Madonnas or biblical sentences on any surface touching her bloody skin.[131] The piece was apparently not linked to the *reportage* on the condition of the *Mezzogiorno*. However, the two pictures accompanying the article and portraying the dreadful situation of the primary school of Africo, another Calabrian village, could mislead the reader. On the one hand, there was no connection between Natuzza Evolo and the condition of the Africo school; and for this reason – as will be discussed in more depth in the following chapter – the pictures seemed to stand even more than others as evidence of an objective and indisputable reality, not requiring further discussion. On the other hand, however, though in an extremely equivocal manner, their publication with the article on Natuzza, brought her story into the survey on the *Mezzogiorno*. This impression is confirmed by the fact that the survey in the following issue restarted exactly from Africo. The pictures thus served as a *trait d'union* and suggested that the woman's powers and particularly the blind faith the Calabrians placed in them were to be included among the several manifestations of Southern backwardness. The subheading of the article, for example, suggested the unbridgeable distance between the approach of the scientists towards Natuzza's case and what the local people believed: "For ten years science has been studying Natuzza of the Dead but for the Calabrians she is the woman of the miracle".

Scientific interpretations of the phenomenon were given great space and prominence. According to "the psychologists", the reasons for the woman's abilities lay in the existence of an "atavistic, ancestral conscience, in whose depths the experiences which mankind has overcome would be stratified". Natuzza was thus one of those "individuals [in whom] something moves that primordial base and thus memories, feelings, experiences of the human generation living millennia before us reappear". Others compared Natuzza to a fakir able to obtain a perfect control of his blood vessels. A further hypothesis was that she was a medium, as even the eminent scientist Nicola Pende was reported to have suggested. The "Calabrians", though, were not interested in scientific explanations: for them, Natuzza was only the "woman of the miracle".

The last part of Besozzi's enquiry focused on Africo, a village on the Aspromonte, in Calabria. Africo had already attracted the attention of the public in the past.[132] In 1928, the meridionalist Umberto Zanotti Bianco had visited the village. Zanotti Bianco – as will be discussed in Chapter 2 – was among the founders and leading figures of the *Associazione nazionale per gli interessi del Mezzogiorno d'Italia* (ANIMI, National Association for the Interests of Italy's South), largely concerned with educational issues. The diary of his experience in Africo was published in 1946, first by the periodical *Il Ponte* with the title – significant in itself – "Among the lost people" (*Tra la perduta gente*), borrowed from the opening of the third canto of Dante's *Inferno*.[133]

The article – whose headline and sub-headline read "Streets too narrow for an open umbrella. The most desperate village of Calabria" – was published together with a set of five pictures, taken by the photographer Tino Petrelli, once more portraying women and children only.[134] The captions leave no doubt about the meaning they were meant to convey. For example, above the headline was a picture of a woman, folding a sheet of pastry on a wooden tray supported on what seems only to be a chest; next to her is a crouching child, whose legs are bare; in front of them, another crouching barefoot child – older than the other – is apparently trying to light the fire under a big pot. The caption reads: "Africo (Reggio Calabria). The only room of the house of a shepherd. In this room there is no table. Africo is a village which has remained as it was two centuries ago". Another picture, at the bottom of the same page, portrayed instead a woman, knitting and seated next to a wooden plank, her bare feet protruding from her long skirt and placed on the floor covered with rubble; a pig – which could, however, be mistaken for a dog owing to its position and to the picture being in black and white – peeps out from under the plank. The caption reads "Africo (Reggio Calabria). A shepherd's wife in a corner of his house. In Africo beasts and man live in the same premises".

In one case, the caption did not even provide a description of what the reader should view: three children – a girl and two boys – are seated on a bed; the girl, in the middle, is looking towards one of them and smiling; one of the boys is barefoot and is playing the *ciaramedda*, an instrument similar to a bagpipe; the other has his back turned, but it seems that he is smiling; he wears a jacket torn on one side and shepherd's sandals; under the bed is a woodpile and in front of it, a goat. The caption reads: "Africo (Reggio Calabria). An interior. The main reason for the primitive state in which the '*africoti*' (inhabitants of Africo) live is, above all, the lack of roads of communication with nearby centres". Regardless of the explanation concerning the lack of roads – which has nothing to do with the content of the picture – the most important message to be conveyed was the primitiveness in which the people of Africo were supposed to live. This primitiveness was embodied by their children, even when they were playing and having fun as any other 'normal' child would do.

The article corroborated the representation offered by the pictures of a village excluded from the flow of history, in which people lived in dehumanized conditions:

> "In Africo [...] houses, with the exception of a few, have one room only in which people and beasts live together. [...] In Africo only three people own an umbrella [but] streets are too narrow to open it. Cows, in every season, roam free on the mountain and nobody looks after them, as they don't have milk. [...] Shepherds use flint and steel to light the fire. [...] They have no wine, or cheese, or oil, or vegetables. The land does not bear fruit. [...] The main reason for the misery of Africo is the lack of roads connecting it to the rest of the world. [...] the isolation [of] these people has ended up stifling their energy in a sort of resigned and lazy fatalism from which they will be rescued with difficulty"

In the past, Africo had not been so isolated – Besozzi added. At the beginning of the twentieth century, it had been visited by journalists following the case of the brigand Musolino. A monk sent by the Church to replace the local priest, who had killed his sister for reasons of honour, tried to "stir things up". The ANIMI "worked with less uproar, but in a more constructive way". The "great protector" of Africo had been, however, the "Count Zanotti Bianco". The shepherds used to talk about him as if he was the "character of a fairy tale". After that, nothing else had changed. Even the local priest's proposal of moving the whole village to Argentina had produced no reaction. It was thus necessary – Besozzi concluded – to build a road, to make "contacts with the civil world more frequent". It was time for "these shepherds annihilated by their misery to start to learn that there is another way of living, very different and better". When this happened, "they will certainly wake up".

1.3.2 The South of *Epoca*

Launched in the 1950s by the publishing house Mondadori, *Epoca* took its inspiration from the American magazine *Life*. The use of photographs in *Epoca* was probably more prominent than in other *rotocalchi*. As Forgacs and Gundle have noted "the ratio of pictures to text varied according to the feature but in special reports it was particularly high and in some cases the pictures were by internationally renowned photographers".[135] With its often coloured pictures and its glossy paper, *Epoca* "tended to present itself" – Ajello has argued – "as the weekly magazine of a country industrially developed, a 'European' country".[136] The combination of a popularizing approach concerning a vast array of themes and the wide employment of photographs made it appear a collectible "modern visual atlas" of Italy and the world.[137]

Between 1950 and 1951, the magazine ran two reports on the South by the journalist, writer and poet Alfonso Gatto and the photographer Paul M. Pietzsch.[138] The first, entitled "The miracle of the Gargano", was an account of Gatto's and Pietzsch's journey through the Apulian massif. The title probably referred to the shrine of Monte Sant'Angelo – one of the villages of the Gargano – where people used to leave voting offerings as a sign of gratitude for miracles they had received. Only two pages out of eight were devoted to the shrine and the *ex voto*, though. The main focus of the article was, instead, the Gargano, whose villages and inhabitants were represented as an enclosed microcosm and a virgin land detached from the rest of the world, where man and nature were one.

"The Gargano" – Gatto wrote – "[is] not only a mountain [...] but the idea of a world, an island maybe". The area was described as an almost inaccessible place: "it is unusual that one comes [here] to stay or to seek one's fortune". Communicating with the locals too had been difficult – Gatto suggested – for "those men and women were real 'indigenous' people whom one can rarely see [and] they did not offer anything to the curiosity of others". The only person with whom they had had the opportunity to establish a contact was a small inn hostess, who had barely answered their questions. That "lazy Venus", that "beautiful woman, with her indefinite smile" was to Gatto "the symbol of the Gargano, more remote and virgin than a Pacific Island, impregnable in spite of the curiosity and the excitement of the discoverers".

Gatto's brief and allusive text was accompanied by thirteen pictures – offering a visual itinerary of the Gargano – and by a notice providing further comments. The pictures and their captions were meant to evoke in the readers the image of a land, both beautiful and isolated at the same time, but also to provide them with first-hand knowledge about such a place.

This was the case, for example, of the view from the sea of Rodi, one of the villages on the Gargano. The houses lean one against each other and seem uninhabited; the beach is deserted and the heads of two boys, turning their backs, are barely visible in the corner of the picture. The caption read: "Rodi is the village of the Gargano whose fame has been revived in the last few years and made the symbol of a land unknown to most of the people and considered as remote as the moon. Rodi is indeed the frontispiece of the inimitable white and blue book leafed through by the sun and the wind of the sea up to Peschici, Vieste and Mattinata [other villages] between beaches and forests". The picture just below this was, instead, a view from above of a road running along the edge of a mountain. Two women walking together and, in the distance, some sacks – their carrier not visible – constitute the only signs of human presence. The caption read: "The roadway with its broad curves leads to Peschici: few cars and many donkeys pass through it. All the inhabitants use the stairs". Peschici had not yet been reached by the automobile civilization: donkeys were still the most common means of transport at least for those carrying loads; all the others used the stairs instead.

Other photographs portrayed the people of the Gargano. One showed a small crowd around a stall placed behind a two-storeyed house. Another on the same page depicted a group of girls and women looking at a man carrying a stick topped with flowers; stone buildings are in the background. The caption provided the context enabling people to 'read' the pictures: "The stall of a clothes peddler, the arrival of a stranger, or the seller of red and blue paper flowers crying out among the houses, are enough to make Peschici feel they have company. When there is nobody, the village stays by itself, white with its lime and blue with its sea, on the rock bathed in the sun". The "village", its houses and inhabitants forming a single entity, could thus temporarily be taken out of its natural isolation and be vivified only by the arrival of people from the exterior. Once the strangers went away, it returned to its position as a motionless part of the natural landscape.

The pictures were not supposed to serve only as a visual journey through the Gargano. The unsigned text accompanying them made explicit what the existence of such a place meant in the context of post-war Italy. "From Rodi to Peschici, to Vieste, passing through the pine forest of San Menaio" – it read – "one discovers an intact world which has not been corrupted yet". A reality of striking contrasts stood behind the beauty of nature and of the landscape and the peaceful loneliness of the people, though: "the miracles and the prayers, the debts and the privations [gripping local people] mean that where Italy is most beautiful it is sad, where it is whitest it is dirty, where it is brightest it is dark". Peschici, which "from a distance seems an absolute image of absolute happiness", was revealed as a place in which "it is impossible to live". A boy who had acted as a guide to Gatto and Pietzsch was reported to be aware of "living at the periphery of a panorama". He was willing to "come to Milan to work as a mechanic" and thus – the text concluded – to follow the "destiny of all Southern men [that is] turning themselves once more away from Paradise with their own hands".

The following report by Gatto and Pietzsch was dedicated to "Matera, the city of the *sassi*", as the title read.[139] Between the late 1940s and the early 1950s, Matera, a city in Basilicata, with its typical houses, the so-called *sassi*, attracted the attention of scholars and public opinion and became one of the icons of Southern backwardness.[140] In the previous article, local people had been represented as reluctant to communicate and as an element of the natural landscape. In the case of Matera, on the other hand, the declared aim of Gatto's article was to denounce the situation of those living in the *sassi* and to be their mouthpiece. The *sassi* – Gatto wrote – stood as an "incredible necropolis inhabited by men" and as "absurd primitive monuments of a primitive life". The condition of the people inhabiting them was not to be romantically idealized, he warned. On the contrary, it constituted a pressing and practical concern: "the indigenous people of the *sasso* do not live in a Bible of stone, even though they figure in it, and face immediate problems". A woman, named Maria Di Taranto, was reported to have said "we are like beasts, like donkeys [...] we've never seen the cinema". Another, Elisabetta Vizzola, showed the journalist her "house with animals" in which she lived with two children and "a donkey, chicks and hens". It was time – Gatto claimed – to "close the book of the Southern apocalypse", of which the *sassi* were a significant episode, and to find practical solutions to practical problems. That of the "thirst of all the cave-dwellers" was one of the more pressing. Five hundred people living in the neighbourhood of *Casalnuovo* lacked a fountain to provide them with water. Any "good reporter from Matera" could assume he had done his duty – he noted in conclusion – only when the fountain was made available for the people of the *sassi*. The rhetoric of civic journalism helping common people to make their voices heard by the great public masked the use of an anthropological vocabulary by means of which the people of the *sassi* were depicted as "cave-dwellers" and their houses a "necropolis".

The pictures, as had been the case of the Gargano, captured the attention of the readers much more than Gatto's text. They made more explicit the representation of the *sassi* as an archaeological find whose existence was disclosed to the readers. The image accompanying the title and occupying almost the whole page, for example, was a black and white view of the *sassi*: the deserted buildings and the rocks in the foreground looking like monoliths are the protagonists. The brief caption read: "These are the *sassi* of Matera, the troglodytic city living under the official city, that of offices, banks and schools". The picture thus provided evidence of the presence of a relic of the past under the modern city, which, however, was not given any visibility in the report. Matera was thus to be identified with the *sassi*. Other pictures showed instead the life within the *sassi*. One portrayed a woman sewing and seated on a chair in the middle of a room; close to her on the floor are three chicks while on the opposite side there is a bigger animal. The caption explained that the woman was named Elisabetta Vizzella: "she is darning close to her high bed, well kept and clean; beyond the arch there are the donkey and other animals". Furthermore, the caption added information which could not be obtained by simply looking at the picture but was evidently deemed essential to 'read' it: "no cleaning could ever remove the pigsty stench impregnating everything".

The report ended with a colour picture depicting the entrance of a house, adorned with flowers and surmounted by the rock; a woman, her back turned and her head covered, is going in. The caption read: "this is the typical façade of a house carved in the *sasso*; the colours express its dry and pathetic poverty; [...] the woman [...] is thriving considering that she lives in a tomb and assembles her loves, affections, children, and hopes in it. All the women of the *sassi* are very lovely; some are beautiful and proud. It's evident that they descend from an ancient race: they are no longer Lucanian and they are not Apulian yet; they have the liveliness and the passionate restlessness of border women". The picture was thus supposed to communicate to the readers the poverty and the desolation of life in the *sassi* as well as the liminal status of their inhabitants – especially of women – suspended between past and present, life and death.

1.3.3 *L'Espresso:* "Africa at home"

The representations of the South offered by *L'Europeo* and *Epoca* have some elements in common. The two magazines certainly adopted different approaches: the aim of the former was to raise awareness of the economic, social, and moral problem which the South was alleged to constitute; the latter, on the other hand, especially with regard to the Gargano, tended to depict the *Mezzogiorno* as a picturesque site and a lost paradise. Nonetheless, both magazines projected an image of that part of the country as substantially backward and excluded from history and civilization. Furthermore, women and children were given more prominence and, above all, in the pictures, stood as the embodiment of Southern backwardness. The survey published by *L'Espresso* in 1959 followed the same pattern.

L'Espresso was founded in 1955 and its first editor was Arrigo Benedetti. The magazine – Ajello has remarked – dealt with a vast array of topics, from politics to culture and even gossip in a characteristically trenchant style.[141] A few months after its first issue had been published, it attracted the attention of public opinion with an article on property speculation in Rome.[142]

On 26 April 1959, the front-page of *L'Espresso* announced the publication of a survey on the *Mezzogiorno*, entitled "Africa at home".[143] The survey consisted of several unsigned pieces. The names of the journalists who had conducted it – Nicola Caracciolo, Gianni Corbi, Manlio Del Bosco, Paolo Glorioso, Eugenio Scalfari, and Livio Zanetti – were reported in a box placed on the last page of each article. The pictures had been taken by different photographers, including Enrico Sarsini, Enzo Sellerio, Franco Pinna.

It is interesting to note that the subheading read: "why they escape toward the North". As was pointed out in the presentation of the survey: "some minimal democratic activity, the diffusion of newspapers and, above all, of magazines, cinema, radio and television have reached the areas of age-long misery and have spread among the inhabitants the image of a better Italy". This phenomenon was claimed to have brought about "a huge migration [...] of peasants and farmhands [...] moving toward the North in search of better conditions of life". Migrations from the South, though, remained in the background and were not investigated throughout the survey. The main focus was, instead, on the "condition of African misery subsisting in the *Mezzogiorno*" defined as "the Italy that does not change [...] prisoner of its own isolation". The declared aim of the survey was to launch "an appeal to public opinion" and in particular to shake the "well-off Italy, which is today a sort of Benelux and is composed of the triangle Turin-Venice-Rome".

The survey reproduced one of the most common and long-lasting representations of the South as Italy's internal Africa. Africa, especially in the nineteenth and the twentieth centuries, epitomized in European imagery the negation of progress and civilization. Europe was, on the contrary,

supposed to be the standard bearer of modern values and thereby entitled to bring them to the 'dark' continent. Before and after unification, the
Southern part of the Italian peninsula had often been depicted by foreign
travellers and observers as a liminal zone suspended between Europe and
Africa. As has been mentioned above, the image of the South as Africa
had also been deployed by Italian ruling and intellectual elites. Its main
function was to mark the distance between an Italy eager to join the club
of the civilized European nations and a portion of its territory alleged to
constitute an impediment to the fulfilment of this purpose.[144]

It was probably not coincidental that *L'Espresso* drew on this image just
when, in the late 1950s, Italy was regaining its position as a developed and
modern country. Regardless of the reason, though, what can certainly be
argued is that the equation between the South and Africa has as its purpose
to present the former as inherently 'other'. This aim is also evident in the
choice of some of the headlines of the instalments that made up the survey,
such as "the four casbahs of Palermo" and "the tribes of the Aspromonte".

Next to the title on the front-page was a picture of a child. The caption read "Nuoro. A child from Irgoli, a town of the Cedrino valley above
Orosei, on the eastern side of Sardinia". Beyond the fact that the child was
from Sardinia, no explanation was provided for using his picture to introduce a survey on thebackwardness of the South. The picture was probably
aimed at appealing to readers' emotions. At the same time, however, this
picture, as well as the many others portraying little boys and girls and
accompanying the survey, suggested a close identification between the economic, social, and moral problems of the South and its children.

The first instalment of the survey, published in the 26th April issue,
focused on Sicily. The journey through the region started from Tudia, a
farm not far from Caltanissetta, where people – the article read – lived in
"African tukuls", houses made of "straw and mud". People were reported
to have neither bed sheets nor pillows, neither crockery nor cutlery: "the
soup is poured into an enamelled iron basin from which the family members draw with a ladle passing from hand to hand; as for pasta, they do not
use the ladle and eat it with their fingers". This situation was not peculiar
to Tudia, but was described as common to the whole of Sicily and to the
rest of the *Mezzogiorno*. Even where people lived in "houses of lime and
bricks", their condition was claimed to be no better. In addition to material
poverty, ignorance was deemed to affect the population. The fact that a
woman from Palma di Montechiaro did not know the names of the Prime
Minister or of the Pope was produced as evidence.

In the second instalment, the situation of rural Sicily was compared to
that of Palermo, openly judged to be "hopeless".[145] In Palermo indeed –
the article explained – "misery becomes an economic system, acquires an
organization, is the basis of society [and its] immediate outcome [is] the corruption of the social body". Unlike modern industrial cities, where slums
were usually located on the outskirts, moral and material degradation were

alleged to be well rooted in the centre of Palermo owing to the legacy of Arab domination: "the four neighbourhoods of Alberghiera, Monte di Pietà, Kalza and Borgo have maintained their initial characteristics, remaining impenetrable to the progress of modern civilization". This backwardness was exemplified by the array of jobs which the Palermitans were reported to do and which were supposed not to "exist (with the only exception of Naples) in any other part of Italy and probably of the world". Among these jobs was that of *petrusinaro*, a greengrocer selling parsley, basil, and other herbs: "it seems impossible – the article argued – that in an economy like this there could be someone buying herbs". The mystery was soon revealed, however. Herbs were indeed used in the "cuisine of the Palermitan casbah" in a completely different manner from that of "bourgeois cuisine". It was not uncommon in Palermo to eat "pasta with parsley" and other "strange and even more repugnant food [such as] the *quarume*, a mixture of animals' entrails thrown away by butchers [or] the boiled heads of hens". Food, and culinary practices too thus served as tropes of Palermitans' abject 'otherness'. A large picture of a garlic seller offered readers the opportunity to see with their own eyes how far the food-selling habits of the Palermitans diverged from the bourgeois model. A man carrying on his shoulders several strings of garlic, his eyes covered by the visor of his cap and with his mouth open, stands in the centre of the picture; in the background are lines of washing hanging in a disorderly fashion from one side of the street to the other, an old car, basins and piled-up furnishings, a half-bent woman. The caption simply read "Palermo. A garlic seller at *Cortile Cascino* [one of the poorest neighbourhoods of Palermo]".

The uniqueness of certain professional figures – such as that of *aggiustatore* (fitter) – was also supposed to characterize Naples and particularly those neighbourhoods where people lived in the *bassi*. The account in this case clearly echoed the stereotype of Neapolitans' *arte di arrangiarsi* (art of getting by). The population of the "casbah of Naples" was depicted as irremediably trapped in their own condition to the extent that "if forced to move elsewhere, into better houses and a more developed social environment, they would probably not survive, being unable to set themselves in a modern productive system".[146] For this reason, "their misery" was defined as "not only serious, but eternal" and deemed not only material, but also moral. As had already been the case of *L'Europeo*'s 1948 survey, "promiscuity" was indicated as causing moral degradation among the populace of Naples. It was, indeed, alleged to lead to early pregnancy and to "more and more frequent cases of homosexuality". The reference to the "alleys in which one can see many homosexuals moving around [...] usually youngsters between 18 and 30 years of age who walk most often in groups [and are] perfectly assimilated to the rest of the community" suggested the image of a corrupted and compromised social fabric, unaware of the most common rules of public decency to the extent that homosexuals could walk undisturbed across the streets with no need to hide their deviance. The indifference of the Neapolitans towards violations of public decency and decorum was also expressed by a picture portraying a completely naked child crying in the street while clothed adults, only visible from the waist down, just passed him by. The caption – which read, "Naples. The Market of Via Tribunali" – implicitly highlighted, in its apparent neutrality, how common it was in Naples to see naked children walking in the streets amidst total indifference.

The survey also focused on Africo, the village of the Aspromonte already visited by Tommaso Besozzi.[147] Africo had in the meantime been destroyed by a flood and the whole population was reported to have been moved nearby; the construction of a new village "to be paid by all the Italian tax-payers" had been promised by the government. The promise had remained unfulfilled and the people of Africo were still "living on alms" and were isolated from the rest of the world, it was pointed out. Africo did not constitute an exceptional case, though. The whole Aspromonte was depicted as characterized by "complete isolation, lack of any kind of relation with nearby communities, and tribal organization". The living conditions of Roghudi were defined as "primitive": owing to the lack of roads, children were reported usually to "learn of the existence of the wheel from the only primary school teacher of the village".

The last instalment was dedicated to a particular aspect of Southern backwardness: "material poverty" was indeed claimed to be accompanied by a "not less deep and rooted spiritual and cultural poverty" which made of the South "a medieval and pre-Christian world" dominated by "witch-craft, spells, exorcisms, superstition".[148] Though the article focused on the province of Matera, the readers were warned that "it would be mistaken to think that this was an isolated case limited to a single region". On the contrary, "well rooted superstitions [were] in the whole *Mezzogiorno* the constant companions of poverty".

It is interesting to note that the article clearly drew – without properly acknowledging it – on Ernesto De Martino's book *Sud e Magia*, published in March 1959.[149] Furthermore, some of the information provided was wrong. For example, in the article, the magician "uncle Giuseppe" was reported to be from Valsinni, a village in the province of Matera, whereas he was from Albano, not far from Tricarico in the province of Potenza. Even more importantly, De Martino's articulated analysis of the magic practices he had observed in Lucania was not taken into account and, to a certain extent, was deliberately falsified. The cause of the persistence of these practices was indeed supposed to lie in the lack of "any contact" between the "enlightenment of the educated class of the Kingdom of the Two Sicilies and the primitive mentality of Southern peasants and sub-proletarians". De Martino in reality argued the exact opposite. In his view indeed, the participation of Neapolitan intellectuals in the Enlightenment had been meagre and their position with respect to the "alternative between magic and rationality from which modern civilization originated" had been ambiguous.[150] The only purpose of the article was thus to offer readers a collection of anecdotes and a gallery of characters aimed at proving once more how "primitive, mysterious, irrational and incompatible with modern civilization" was the culture of Southern peasants. People such as uncle Giuseppe or Antonio Mazzarese, a man from Matera who was reported to claim that the magician had cured him, were taken as symbols of a microcosm perpetually extraneous to modernity and progress.

1.4 Up to the North

As mentioned above, the survey of *L'Espresso* had taken its cue from South–North migration. In the late 1950s, when the survey was published, the phenomenon had already acquired prominence owing not only to its quantitative dimensions but also to its impact on the 'host' communities. The arrival of thousands of Southerners in the North-Western industrialized cities was generally perceived as a problem. Southern migrants were deemed 'different' and, for this reason, a threat to local culture and well-being. Before turning attention to this issue, though, it is important to look briefly at the wider context of internal population movement in which migrations from the South towards the industrial triangle took place.

1I.4.1 A country in movement

In the post-war period, Italy witnessed huge movements of population that went hand in hand with structural economic and social changes. Eugenio Sonnino has noted that, between 1955 and 1970, 24,800,000 people transferred their residency within the national territory. Of these, 15,000,000 moved from one place to another within the Centre-North; more than 5,000,000 moved within the South; more than 3,000,000 from the South headed to the Centre-North, while more than 1,000,000 took the opposite route.[151] According to the data reported by Ginsborg, in the period 1955–71, about 9,140,000 individuals moved from one region to another.[152] At the same time, many Italians were migrating abroad, mostly towards North-Western European countries.[153]

It is worth stressing that internal migrations were not peculiar to the post-war period only. In one of the very few pieces of research on pre-war internal migrations, Anna Treves warned against the risk of considering Fascist Italy a substantially immobile country.[154] On the contrary, Treves' study shows that huge population movements took place during Fascism, in spite of the anti-urban policy enacted by the regime. Since the aftermath of the First World War, indeed the rates of inter-regional migration had been high and the 1931 census revealed that the movement from the South to the North was notable. In the late 1920s, both in Milan and in Turin, the presence of Southern workers and especially of those coming from Apulia was considerable. In the Piedmontese capital, Southern building workers, for example, were not welcomed by the locals. Treves thus remarks that the post-war process of population redistribution and urban growth had already been set in motion under the dictatorship.

The anti-urbanism measures issued throughout the late 1920s and the 1930s as part of the demographic policy of Fascism had remained largely ineffective.[155] As a result, in 1939, a new and much more restrictive law was issued. It established that in order to move to communes with a population of more than 25,000 inhabitants, one had to find a job; at the same time, to be hired, one was compelled to exhibit the certificate of residence.[156] This legislation remained in force in the post-war period up to 1961, when it was eventually repealed. According to Amalia Signorelli, it served the purpose of "transforming a conspicuous part of the immigrants into outlaws, into illegal workers of sorts in their own country".[157] These circumstances made it easier for employers to exploit migrants' work. In Turin, for example, the so-called cooperatives recruited Southern migrants who were used as cheap labour by local companies. Workers paid a sum in order to be part of the cooperative, and they received their salary through the cooperative itself which kept part of it.[158] The condition of illegality prevented migrants from enjoying the rights of regular workers to which they were entitled, including health and safety, pension schemes, and trade unions.

As Anna Badino's research has showed, Southern women living in Turin were largely employed in "irregular or marginal work", which included all the jobs whose duration was less than a year, which were carried out at the worker's domicile and generally without proper contracts.[159] Many worked as maids and were hired by families, hotels, or companies. Unskilled women were also frequently employed as caregivers, not dissimilarly – Badino remarks – from the foreign women working today in Italy as *badanti*, as foreign elderly carers are now commonly referred to. In some cases, women had more than one job. Others, especially those who could not rely on family networks, had to leave regular jobs after having children and, once the latter had grown up, found irregular jobs which could more easily be combined with their domestic duties. Having a regular job meant having more rigid working hours, whereas irregular jobs allowed women to have more control over their time.

Housing was also a major issue for migrants. In his book on Milan, John Foot has pointed out that the majority of migrants were "forced to seek housing either on the extreme urban periphery or in the newly urbanized belt around the *Comune*".[160] It was also common for the newly arrived, however, to find accommodation, often just rooms or beds, in the "'historic' periphery that had developed around Milan's first industrial revolution at the turn of the century".[161] Foot has also provided a critical analysis to the phenomenon of the so-called *coree*, areas of Milan characterized by a high concentration of houses built by their occupants. The *coree* appeared for the first time in the early 1950s and owed their name to the Korean war which took place in the same period. The word *coree* "was used to refer to village-type zones, consisting of self-constructed houses built by immigrants who had purchased small amounts of land at the edge of the city of Milan".[162] It was commonly believed that the *coree* symbolized the degradation of migrants' living conditions. According to Foot, however, the phenomenon was a complicated one and the *coree* cannot be "pigeon-holed into the categories of marginality, poverty, exploitation and peripheralisation".[163] The *coree* were an attempt by the migrants to transform urban space according to their needs and to solve by themselves the problem of the housing shortage resulting from the lack of institutional initiatives. The *coree* were the subject of one of first research projects on migrations towards the industrial triangle. The investigation was carried out by a factory worker, Franco Alasia, and a sociologist, Danilo Montaldi, and resulted in the publication of a book by the then radical publisher Feltrinelli in 1960.[164] A few years later, in 1964, Feltrinelli published the result of the research on Southern migrants living in Turin conducted by Goffredo Fofi.[165]

Sociological works on internal migrations and particularly on migrations from the South towards the North-West flourished throughout the 1960s. The most hotly debated issue was that of the so-called integration of migrants within the 'host' society. The more the migrant was integrated, the better it was for him/her and the entire community where he/she was living. Integration was employed – according to John Foot – as an "*unproblematic* and *positive* (and undefined) term".[166] More than a category of analysis, integration was the point every migrant had to reach. The burden of integration was placed entirely on the shoulders of the migrants. The 'host' societies were instead portrayed "as static and passive recipients" of the migrants and as not undergoing any kind of transformation.[167]

1.4.2 Southern migrants in the Turinese press

'Host' societies were, on the contrary, deeply affected by the arrival of migrants. They were rapidly growing and changing. According to the data reported by the historian Fabio Levi, between 1929 and 1969, the population of Turin doubled. This growth is to be viewed with circumspection because of the Fascist legislation which inhibited people from registering their presence in the place of arrival. However, it is undeniable – in Levi's view – that the growing trend was never interrupted in the period considered.[168] Since the early 1950s, people from rural areas of Piedmont, Veneto, and Southern regions arrived in Turin. Migrants, however, were almost immediately identified with the Southerners.

In 1956, a newly founded political party, the *Movimento per l'autonomia regionale piemontese* (MARP, Movement for the Regional Autonomy of Piedmont) obtained 31.526 votes – 5% – at the council elections and formed an alliance with the Christian Democrats in support of the mayor Amedeo Peyron. The MARP was introduced to the voters by the local press as an anti-Southern party. Enrica Capussotti has offered a study of the activity of the MARP carried out through its official journal, *Piemonte nuovo*. The MARP was an autonomist party whose main aims were the institution of regions according to the Constitution, as well as opposition to central bureaucracy and taxes. Piedmont – MARP politicians maintained – was deprived of its resources by taxation, which was squandered by the central government in Rome or wasted by the *Cassa del Mezzogiorno*. The latter was one of the MARP's favourite targets as a result of its supposed impotence in stopping the alleged exodus of the Southerners towards Turin, indicated as a threat to the integrity of the city. The MARP was particularly concerned with the issue. Indeed it asked for the application of the anti-urbanism laws, and for governmental funds to help the local administration deal with the burden of poor families coming from the South.[169]

The MARP disappeared from the political scene in the early 1960s. Its political experience was thus short-lived. However, this should not lead us to underestimate the context that made its success possible. Capussotti has analysed the two most important Turinese newspapers of that time, the Fiat-owned *La Stampa* – renowned at a national level too – and the *Gazzetta del Popolo*. Both the newspapers contributed to reinforcing the "definition of a hierarchical difference between natives of Turin and of the Piedmont region on one side and *meridionali* on the other". As Capussotti has shown old images and representations of the South and its inhabitants – which, as has been previously discussed, were still vital in the post-war period – "provided a complex repertoire" through which the newcomers were made sense of.[170]

In the middle of the 1950s, when the MARP was founded, *La Stampa* started to publish unsigned articles informing its readers of the rise in the number of migrants arriving in Turin. The tone of the articles became increasingly alarmist. In early 1955, for example, the "arrival of strangers" was still presented as a means "to bring new life to our city" whose demo-graphic growth had stopped for many years.[171] The majority of those moving to Turin were from Piedmont and Veneto. As a result, "the common opinion that Turin is invaded by the 'Neapolitans' [...] a generic definition indicating all the immigrants arrived from the South" was shown as base-less. At the same time, however, *La Stampa* warned of the "risk for the Turinese of becoming a minority in their own city"[172] and of the possibility that those who arrived to seek jobs could be infiltrated by "those who seek their fortune on the edge of the law".[173] The newspaper thus applauded the initiative taken by the mayor and the head of police to "send all these undesirable elements back to their countries of origin with a warrant for compulsory repatriation (*foglio di via*)".[174]

The equation of "immigrants" with criminality was more and more explicit and supported by theoretical evidence. In addition, "immigrant" became synonymous with Southerner. Autumn and winter – it was reported – witnessed a rise of criminality owing to the growth of unemployment among migrants:

> "During the summer it is easier, especially for the Southern worker, to find a job, even though not a stable one, in construction sites, but during the winter the construction of houses is almost stopped and unemployment rises. We do not want to say things under the influence of prejudice or hostility, we are just talking about facts and figures showing the situation of Turin for what it is. Those who leave poorer towns to seek job opportunities in more developed and industrialized areas deserve our consideration. [...] Fatally among those people seeking honest earnings, there are some equivocal elements, who prefer living by their wits and can commit, as in the recent episodes, thefts and robberies".[175]

The request to prevent migrants from reaching Turin was expressed by readers in their letters to the newspaper and implicitly even by the mayor, the Christian Democrat Amedeo Peyron, who did not hesitate to declare that it was "unfair [that Turin] was burdened with the needs of so many Southern families".[176] Migrants were thus not only potential criminals but also an economic burden. Thousands of men, "humiliated by poverty" and attracted by the "mirage of easy money", were swelling the ranks of those living in "environments where life is unworthy of human beings".[177] According to the estimate of the city council, "the cost" for each migrant, including "public services, welfare, school, water, medicines, and public housing [was] one million and a hundred and forty thousand liras".[178]

Besides the costs for the assistance of migrants, *La Stampa* also denounced the way the small amount of funding assigned by the central government to Turin had to be employed for migrants rather than for its own needs:

> "The *Mezzogiorno* is to be helped; but, if enormous amounts of money are spent for the *Mezzogiorno*, it is also important to alleviate the great sacrifices made by the industrialized areas. To date the funding assigned to Piedmont and Turin has been used to solve the extremely serious problems created by immigration".[179]

The resentment towards the South and Southern migrants was strongly felt, to the extent that the situation of Turin, which, between 1951 and 1956, had welcomed more than 120,000 new people, was compared to that of Naples, which, though "benefiting from much capital and many initiatives", had not faced a significant increase in its population.[180]

The fears that the South and its problems could contaminate Turin were often expressed. The case of a man from Apulia who had killed his wife, for example, offered the opportunity to inform the readers that the "*bassi* did not take root only in Naples or in other zones of Southern Italy, but also in Turin: the *bassi* are in our city too".[181] Using a plural indicating that what was going to be said did not refer only to that specific situation, but was a generalized problem, the article continued:

> "We have been in places where men, women, elders and children slept, ate, and breathed in a few square metres, without light and air, and with dampness and dirt: places where the dignity of human beings is reduced to an unbelievable level".[182]

Southern migrants living in other areas of the North-West, such as Liguria, were also represented as members of a society inherently 'different' and following principles typical of the state of nature. The Calabrians, for example, were reported to be one of the most violent groups:

> "For a few years a numerous colony of Calabrians [living in Liguria] increased the work-load of magistrates and solicitors. [...] Unfortunately, many of the Calabrians who arrived here to seek jobs have brought with them, besides their few belongings, the burden of the worst local traditions: revenge, crimes of honour and even robberies. [...] They work hard, but they are still too hot-blooded. A trial taking place in Sanremo is revealing the living style of people still reluctant to abide by the discipline of law".[183]

Honour was defined as the "the iron rule regulating relationships among the Southerners" and its violent safeguard was attributed to the Southerners only.[184] Enrica Capussotti has pointed out that Turinese newspapers followed the same strategy when it came to crimes of honour: "the pages dedicated to local events were dominated by big titles underlining the Southern regional origin of the offender".[185] It is worth remembering that the gender relations in post-war Italy were anything but fair. Abortion and contraception were illegal and even the Constitution had established the prominence of the "essential familial role" of women.[186] The "*delitto d'onore*" – Capussotti argues – formed part of "legal and political cultures and interests dominated by aged elites, by a misogynistic and reactionary Catholic Church, and by a Communist Party which rarely disagreed with the Christian Democrats on issues regarding family and sexuality".[187] In spite of this complex interrelation of factors, it was one of the most powerful symbols of supposed Southern backwardness.

As was the case with the representation of the South in the early post-war period, children were used as signifiers of Southern migrants' poverty and naturalness. The attics of the city centre, where migrants used to settle soon after their arrival, were described as "hundreds of small rooms full of children with coal-black eyes and teeth like *maioliche*, undernourished children to whom nature gives absurd colours of health".[188] Southern children, typically belonging to overcrowded families, were depicted as different from the locals, toughened by a hard life to which they were accustomed:

> "They live all together in the same house and each family has five or six children. The children pop out from everywhere; they stay on the balcony, in the backyard; they fall in the canal and do not sink; they climb beds where too many poor people sleep".[189]

Unaware of technical progress, Southern children with their faces of "peasant angels [looked] with their intense and astonished eyes at the camera" of the journalists taking pictures of them and continued to make plastic flowers with their small hands and "sacrificing their childish bodies as they have been used to doing since they were born".[190] The stories of children living "alone in an attic in the cold, darkness and fear" were countless.[191] Southern children in Turin were – as a headline of *La Stampa* read – "at the gates of civilization".[192] They were not "loved or nourished [and] like their fathers, former *braccianti* or miners, they were marked by eternal poverty". They were "sub-children [...] living in the darkness" and excluded from any form of "scientific civilization and well-being".[193] They epitomized the state of primitive childhood of their mothers and fathers whose transition to a civilized adulthood was desired but depicted as impossible.

Notes

1 "Presentazione", *Meridiana*, I, 1, 1987, p. 10.
2 Gribaudi, G., "Images of the South. The *Mezzogiorno* as seen by Insiders and Outsiders", in Lumley, R., Morris, J., (eds), *The New History of the Italian South. The Mezzogiorno Revisited*, Exeter: University of Exeter Press, 1997, p. 83.
3 Idem, p. 84.
4 Nani, M., *Ai confini della nazione. Stampa e razzismo nell'Italia di fine Ottocento*, Rome: Carocci, 2006.
5 Moe, N., *The View from the Vesuvius. Italian Culture and the Southern Question*, Berkeley: University of California Press, 2002.
6 Petrusewicz, M., *Come il Meridione divenne una Questione*, Soveria Mannelli: Rubettino, 1998.
7 Idem, p. 136. Emphasis in the text.
8 Moe, N., cit., p. 181.
9 Dickie, J., *Darkest Italy. The Nation and Stereotypes of the Mezzogiorno, 1860-1900*, Basingstoke: Macmillan, 1999, p. 33.
10 Idem, p. 34
11 Idem, p. 35
12 Petraccone, C., *Le due civiltà. Settentrionali e meridionali nella storia d'Italia*, Rome: Laterza, 2000, p. 64.
13 For a critical analysis the use of the term *meridionalisti* see Lupo, S., "Storia del Mezzogiorno, questione meridionale, meridionalismo", in *Meridiana*, 32, 1998, pp. 17–52.

14 Dickie, J., *Darkest Italy*. cit.

15 See Gribaudi, G., cit.

16 Pick, D., *Faces of Degeneration. A European Disorder, c. 1848-c. 1918*, Cambridge: Cambridge University Press, 1999, p. 122. On Lombroso see at least Gibson, M., *Born to Crime. Cesare Lombroso and the Origins of Biological Criminology*, Westport: Praeger, 2002; Montaldo, S., Tappero, P., (eds), *Cesare Lombroso cento anni dopo*, Turin: UTET, 2009; Montaldo, S. (ed.), *Cesare Lombroso. Gli scienziati e la nuova Italia*, Bologna: Il Mulino, 2011.

17 See Gibson, M., cit.

18 For a wider discussion of Lombroso's concept of atavism which he revised several times, see the editors' Introduction in Lombroso, C., *Criminal Man*. Translated and with a New Introduction by Mary Gibson and Nicole Hahn Rafter, Durham: Duke University Press, 2006 pp. 1–36.

19 Pick, D., cit., p. 126.

20 Passione, R., "Il Sud di Cesare Lombroso tra scienza e politica", *Il Risorgimento*, LII, 1, 2000, pp. 133–54.

21 Idem, p. 145.

22 Gibson, M., cit., p. 109.

23 Petraccone, C., cit., p. 160.

24 Dickie, J., "Stereotypes of the Italian South 1860-1900", in Lumley, R., Morris, J., (eds), cit., pp. 118–19.

25 Wong, A. S., *Race and the Nation in Liberal Italy 1861-1911. Meridionalism, Empire and Diaspora*, Basingstoke: Palgrave, 2006, p. 65.

26 Moe, N., cit., p. 196.

27 Moe, N., cit., pp. 202–6.

28 Dickie, J., *Darkest Italy*, cit., p. 94.

29 Nani, M., cit., p. 111.

30 Nani, M., cit., p. 117.

31 Idem, p. 118.

32 Lombroso, P., "L'Italia barbara contemporanea", *Gazzetta del Popolo*, 22 May 1898 cited in Nani, M., cit., p. 140.

33 Idem, p. 143. On the debate between Niceforo and Colajanni, also involving Lombroso, Guglielmo Ferrero and others see also Petraccone, C., cit. and for an earlier account Salvadori, M. L., *Il mito del buongoverno. La questione meridionale da Cavour a Gramsci*, Turin: Einaudi, 1963.

34 Bollati, G., "Note su fotografia e storia", in Bollati, G., Bertelli, C., (eds), *Storia d'Italia, Annali 2, L'immagine fotografica 1845-1945*, Turin: Einaudi, 1979, p. 31.

35 Triulzi, A., "Napoli e l'immagine dell'Africa nella collezione fotografica della Società Africana d'Italia (ca. 1880–1940), in Casti, E., Turco, A. (eds), *Culture dell'alterità. Il territorio africano e le sue rappresentazioni*, Milan: Unicopli, 1998, p. 185. See also Id., "L'Africa come icona. Rappresentazioni dell'alterità nell'immaginario coloniale italiano di fine Ottocento", in Del Boca, A., (ed.), *Adua. Le ragioni di una sconfitta*, Rome: Laterza, 1997, pp. 255–81.

36 The *Società africana d'Italia* (SAI, African Society of Italy), the most "aggressive and expansionist of Italian geographical societies" had been founded in Naples in 1882. Idem, p. 187. For a review of the studies on photography and Italian colonial history carried out on the last decades see Rossetto, T., "Africa in fotografia. Un percorso multidisciplinare in ambito italiano", *Erreffe. La ricerca folklorica*, 54, 2006, pp. 39–56.

37 Triulzi, A., cit., p. 186.

38 Idem, p. 193.

39 Palma, S., "Fotografia di una colonia. L'Eritrea di Luigi Naretti (1885-1900)", *Quaderni Storici*, 109, 2002, p. 95.

40 Petraccone, C., *Le due civiltà*, cit. For example, Enrico Corradini, one of the greatest advocate of the occupation of Libya, underlined how "solving the question of the South and occupying the Tripolitania [were] not two separate actions". Corradini, E., *L'ora di Tripoli*, Milan: Treves, 1911, p. 231 cited in Del Boca, A., *Gli Italiani in Libia. Tripoli bel suol d'amore 1860-1922*, Rome: Laterza, 1986 [Milan: Mondadori, 1993, p. 54]. This view encountered the opposition of prominent intellectuals and politicians such as Gaetano Salvemini, but also of less renowned figures. The priest Giuseppe Cavadini, for example, warned that in certain Sardianian villages, people still lived in a primitive state. "These are the peoples under the rule of those Italians who, in the name of progress and civilization, are waging armed war against the savage Arabs of Tripolitania", was his bitter comment. Cavadini, G., *In Tripolitania o in Sardegna?*, Bergamo: Stab. Tip. Alessandro, 1912, pp. 5–11 cited in Del Boca, cit., [p. 62].

41 Tallarico, G., "L'uomo del Mezzogiorno e l'Impero d'Etiopia", *Il Mattino*, 21 July 1926 cited in Petraccone, C., *Le 'due Italie'. La questione meridionale tra realtà e rappresentazione*, Rome: Laterza, 2005, p. 193.

42 Faeta, F., "Rivolti verso il Mediterraneo. Immagini, questione meridionale e processi di 'orientalizzazione' interna", in Id., *Questioni italiane. Demologia, antropologia, critica culturale*, Turin: Bollati Boringhieri, 2005, p. 137.

43 Benigno, F., Lupo, S., "Mezzogiorno in idea: a mo' di introduzione", *Meridiana*, 47–48, 2003, pp. 10–11.

44 Idem, p. 11.

45 Ginsborg, P., *A History of Contemporary Italy. 1943-1980*, London: Penguin, 1990, p. 98.

46 Amendola, G., "Prime considerazioni sulle elezioni del Mezzogiorno", *Rinascita*, III, 5–6, 1946, cited in ibidem.

47 Chinaese, G., *Quando uscimmo dai rifugi. Il Mezzogiorno tra guerra e dopoguerra (1943-1946)*, Rome: Carocci, 2004, p. 221.

48 Idem, p. 224.

49 Chabod, F., *L'Italia contemporanea (1918-1948)*, Turin: Einaudi, 1961 [2002, p. 120].

50 Gribaudi, G., (ed.), *Terra bruciata. Le stragi naziste sul fronte meridionale*, Naples: L'Ancora del Mediterraneo, 2003; Id., *Guerra totale. Tra bombe alleate e violenze naziste. Napoli e il fronte meridionale 1940-44*, Turin: Bollati Boringhieri, 2005.

51 Idem, p. 18.

52 Semelin defines civil resistance as the "spontaneous process of resistance by civilian society using unarmed means, and mobilizing either its principal institutions or its people – or both at the same time" Semelin, J., *Unarmed against Hitler. Civilian Resistance in Europe, 1939-1943*, Westport: Praeger, 1993, p. 2. For a discussion of the concept of civil resistance in the framework of Italian history see also Bravo, A., "Armed and unarmed: struggles without weapons in Europe and Italy", *Journal of Modern Italian Studies*, X, 4, 2005, pp. 468–84.

53 Gribaudi, G., *Guerra totale*. cit., p. 303.

54 Bravo, A., Bruzzone, A. M., *In guerra senz'armi. Storie di donne. 1940-1945*, Rome: Laterza, 1995.

55 Gribaudi, G., *Guerra totale*. cit., p. 627. On the Allied occupation of Naples see also De Marco, P., "L'occupazione alleata a Napoli", in Gallerano, N. (ed.), *L'altro dopoguerra. Roma e il Sud 1943-1945*, Milan: Angeli, 1985, pp. 261–73.

56 Chianese, G., cit., p. 106.
57 Idem, p. 116. For a history of State-regulated prostitution between nineteenth and early twentieth century see Gibson, M., *Prostitution and the State in Italy, 1860-1915*, New Brunswick: Rutgers University Press, 1986. For the Fascist period see De Grazia, V., *How Fascism Ruled Women: Italy, 1922-1945*, Berkeley: University of California Press, 1992.
58 Chianese, G., "Ceti popolari e comportamenti quotidiani a Napoli", in Gallerano, N. (ed.), cit., p. 281.
59 Malaparte, C., *La pelle*, Rome: Aria d'Italia, 1949 [Milan: Adelphi, 2010].
60 Simonsen, E., "Children in danger: dangerous children", in Ericsson, K., Simonsen, E., *Children of World War Two: the Hidden Enemy Legacy*, Oxford: Berg, 2005, p. 281.
61 Unfortunately, only a handful of scholarly studies concerning this important aspect of the post-war social history of the country and addressing the issue from a critical perspective are available to date. See, for example, Bernini, S., *Family Life and Individual Welfare in Post-war Europe. Britain and Italy Compared*, Basingstoke: Palgrave, 2008; Ponzani, M., *Figli del nemico. Le relazioni d'amore in tempo di guerra, 1943-1948*, Rome: Laterza, 2015; Patriarca, S., *Race in Post-Fascist Italy 'War Children' and the Color of the Nation*, Cambridge: Cambridge University Press, 2022.
62 Gonella, G., *Salviamo il fanciullo. Discorso tenuto in Campidoglio per l'inaugurazione del Convegno Nazionale dell'Ente per la Protezione Morale del Fanciullo*, Rome: Istituto Poligrafico dello Stato, 1946, pp. 3–4.
63 Minella, A., Spano, A., Terranova, F., *Cari bambini, vi aspettiamo con gioia. Il movimento di solidarietà popolare per la salvezza dell'infanzia nel dopoguerra*, Milan: Teti, 1980.
64 Idem, p. 39.
65 Idem, p. 40.
66 Macchiaroli, G., *Un'esperienza popolare del dopoguerra per la salvezza dei bambini di Napoli*, Naples, 1979, pp. 2–3. On Altavilla and the Naples Federation of the ONMI see Arena, G., "L'ONMI a Napoli dalla battaglia demografica ai tentativi di modernizzazione negli anni Sessanta", in Minesso, M. (ed.) *Stato e infanzia nell'Italia contemporanea: origini, sviluppo e fine dell'ONMI, 1925-1975*, Bologna: Il Mulino, 2007, pp. 325–63. On the history of the ONMI see De Grazia, V., cit. and Quine, M. S., *Italy's Social Revolution: Charity and Welfare from Liberalism to Fascism*, London: Palgrave, 2002.
67 Minella, A., Spano, A., Terranova, F., *Cari bambini, vi aspettiamo con gioia*, cit.
68 Comitato per la salvezza dei bambini di Napoli, *Aiutiamo i bambini di Napoli*, Naples, 1946, p. 1. See also Maida, B., *I treni dell'accoglienza. Infanzia, povertà e solidarietà nell'Italia del dopoguerra, 1945-1948*, Turin: Einaudi, 2020.
69 Ibidem.
70 Idem, p. 2.
71 Idem, p. 3.
72 Idem, p. 4.
73 Idem, p. 5.
74 Idem, p. 8.
75 Ibidem.
76 Idem, p. 9.
77 Idem, p. 10. The *amlira* was the military currency issued by the Allies during the occupation of Italy.
78 Ibidem.

79 Idem, p. 11.
80 Idem, p. 17.
81 Idem, p. 21.
82 Pasquinelli, C., "Gli intellettuali di fronte all'irrompere nella storia del mondo popolare subalterno", in Id. (ed.), *Antropologia e questione meridionale. Ernesto De Martino e il dibattito sul mondo popolare subalterno negli anni 1948-1955*, Florence: La Nuova Italia, 1977 p. 1.
83 Chianese, G., *Quando uscimmo dai rifugi*, cit.
84 Idem, pp. 128–30.
85 Ginsborg, P., cit., pp. 60–1. For a more detailed analysis see Id., "The Communist Party and the agrarian question in Southern Italy, 1943-1948", *History Workshop Journal*, 17, 1984, pp. 81–101.
86 Ibidem.
87 Idem, p. 122.
88 Goretti, L., *I 'neri bianchi'. Mezzadri di Greve in Chianti tra lotte sindacali e fuga dalle campagne (1945-1950)*, Rome: Odradek, 2008.
89 Crainz, G., "I braccianti padani", in Chianese, G., Crainz, G., Da Vela, M., Gribaudi, G., (eds) *Italia 1945-1950. Conflitti e trasformazioni sociali*, Milan: Angeli, 1985, pp. 173–326.
90 Benigno, F., Lupo, S., cit.
91 Levi, C., *Christ Stopped at Eboli*, London: Penguin, 1982, pp. 11–12.
92 Giarrizzo, G., "Mezzogiorno e civiltà contadina", in Id., *Mezzogiorno senza meridionalismo. La Sicilia, lo sviluppo, il potere*, Venice: Marsilio, 1992, p. 203.
93 Levi, C., cit. p. 78.
94 Idem, p. 79.
95 Muscetta, C., *Letteratura militante*, Florence: Parenti, 1953 cited in Giarrizzo, G., cit., p. 205. See also McGauley, P., *Matera, 1945-1960. The History of a 'National Disgrace'*, Oxford, Peter Lang, 2019.
96 Meoni, M. L., "Sul 'Mondo popolare subalterno'", in Clemente, P., Meoni, M. L., Squillacciotti, M., (eds), *Il dibattito sul folklore in Italia*, Milan: Edizioni di Cultura Popolare, 1976, pp. 39–62.
97 De Martino, E., "Intorno a una storia del mondo popolare subalterno", *Società*, V, 3, 1949, pp. 411–35 now in Pasquinelli, C. cit., pp. 46–63.
98 Idem, p. 46.
99 See Gundle, S., "The Legacy of the Prison Notebooks: Gramsci, the PCI and Italian culture in the Cold War period", in Duggan, C., Wagstaff, C., (eds), *Italy in the Cold War: Politics, Culture and Society, 1948-1958*, Washington: Berg, 1995, pp. 131–47.
100 De Martino, E., "Intorno a una storia del mondo popolare subalterno", p. 46.
101 Idem, p. 48.
102 Idem, p. 55.
103 Idem, p. 57.
104 Idem, p. 56.
105 Idem, p. 58.
106 Saunders, R., "'Critical Ethnocentrism' and the Ethnology of Ernesto De Martino", *American Anthropologist*, VC, 4, 1993, p. 881.
107 Luporini, C., "Intorno alla storia del 'Mondo popolare subalterno'", *Società*, VI, 1, 1950, pp. 95–106 now in Pasquinelli, C., cit., p. 82.
108 Gundle, S., *Between Hollywood and Moscow. The Italian Communists and the Challenge of Mass Culture, 1943-1991*, Durham: Duke University Press, 2000, p. 60.
109 Clemente, P., "Il caso Scotellaro", in Clemente, P., Meoni, M. L., Squillacciotti, M., (eds), cit., pp. 145–61; Petraccone, C., *Le 'due Italie'* cit. The books published by Levi and Rossi Doria were respectively: Scotellaro, R., *È fatto*

giorno: 1940–1953, Milan: Mondadori, 1954 and Id., *Contadini del Sud*, Bari: Laterza, 1954.

110 Alicata, M., "Il meridionalismo non si può fermare a Eboli", *Cronache meridionali*, I, 9, 1954, pp. 585–603, now in Pasquinelli, C., (ed.). cit., p. 195.

111 Ibidem.

112 Idem, p. 198.

113 Petraccone, C., *Le 'due Italie'* cit.

114 Gribaudi, G., "Images of the South" cit., p. 105.

115 Faeta, F., cit., p. 144.

116 Forgacs, D., Gundle, S., *Mass Culture and Italian Society from Fascism to the Cold War*, Bloomington: Indiana University Press, 2007, p. 36.

117 Ajello, N., "Il settimanale di attualità", in Castronovo, V., Tranfaglia, N. (eds), *La stampa italiana del neocapitalismo*, Rome: Laterza, 1976, pp. 175–248.

118 Murialdi, P., *La stampa italiana dal dopoguerra ad oggi, 1943-1972*, Rome: Laterza, 1973. See also Ajello, N. cit.

119 For a broader discussion of the documentary function of photojournalism in the post-war period see Hamilton, P., "Representing the Social: France and Frenchness in ^Post-War Humanist Photography", in Hall, S., (ed.), *Representation. Cultural Representations and Signifying Practices*, London: Sage in association with the Open University, 1997, pp. 75–150.

120 Mazzacane, L., "Napoli in posa: luoghi e immagini di uno stereotipo", in Signorelli, A., (ed.), *Cultura popolare a Napoli e in Campania nel Novecento*, Naples: Edizioni del Millennio, 2002, pp. 25–43.

121 Ajello, N., cit.

122 Tranfaglia, N., *Mafia, politica e affari nell'Italia repubblicana, 1943-1991*, Rome: Laterza, 1992.

123 Besozzi, T., "Alla mensa dei bimbi poveri i genitori stanno a guardare", *L'Europeo*, IV, 8, 22 February 1948.

124 Lepre, A., *Storia della prima Repubblica: l'Italia dal 1943 al 1998*, Bologna: Il Mulino, 1999.

125 Soddu, P., *L'Italia del dopoguerra. 1947-1953: una democrazia precaria*, Rome: Editori Riuniti, 1998.

126 The word *bassi* indicates unhealthy street-level houses considered typical of Naples.

127 Palma, S., *L'Italia coloniale*, cit., p. 53. On Fascist sexual legislation in the colonies, see also Barrera, G., *Dangerous Liasons: Colonial Concubinage in Eritrea, 1890-1941*, PAS Working Papers No. 1, Program of African Studies, Northwestern University, 1996.

128 Ibidem.

129 Patriarca, S., cit.

130 Besozzi, T., "I bambini di Napoli non mangiano sole", *L'Europeo*, IV, 10, 7 March 1948.

131 Besozzi, T., "L'errore del vescovo di Mileto", *L'Europeo*, IV, 11, 14 March 1948.

132 Besozzi, T., "Troppo strette le strade per l'ombrello aperto", *L'Europeo*, IV, 12, 21 March 1948.

133 Zanotti Bianco, U., "Tra la perduta gente (Africo)", *Il Ponte*, II, 5, 1946, pp. 405–14; Id., "Tra la perduta gente (Africo)", *Il Ponte*, II, 6, 1946, pp. 509–19; Id., "Tra la perduta gente. Continuazione e fine", *Il Ponte*, II, 7–8, 1946, pp. 642–8.

134 Petrelli's name was not indicated in the article. The captions of all the pictures published with the survey only reported that they were owned by the photographic agency Publifoto. See Teti, V., *Il senso dei luoghi: memoria e storia dei paesi abbandonati*, Rome, Donzelli, 2004.

135 Forgacs, D., Gundle, S., cit., p. 110.

136 Ajello, cit., p. 205.
137 Idem, p. 206.
138 Gatto, A., Pietzsch, P. M., "Il miracolo del Garagno", *Epoca*, I, 11, 23 December 1950.
139 Gatto, A., Pietzsch, P. M., "Matera, la città dei sassi", *Epoca*, II, 15, 20 January 1951. On Matera see McGauley, P., cit.
140 In the early 1950s Matera had been chosen as a case study by the sociologist Friedrik Friedmann, who directed a team of scholars, sponsored by the UNRRA-CASAS programme, working on the living conditions of the inhabitants of the *sassi*. See Petraccone, C., *Le 'due Italie'* cit. On the post-war studies on the South conducted by foreign anthropologists and sociologists see Minicucci, M., "Antropologi e Mezzogiorno", *Meridiana*, 47–48, 2003, pp. 139–74.
141 Ajello, N., cit.
142 Murialdi, P., cit.
143 "L'Africa in casa", *L'Espresso*, V, 17, 26 April 1959.
144 For a broader discussion of these issues see Moe, N., cit.
145 "Le quattro casbah di Palermo", *L'Espresso*, V, 18, 3 May 1959.
146 "Il cielo non si mangia", *L'Espresso*, V, 19, 10 May 1959.
147 "Le tribù dell'Aspromonte", *L'Espresso*, V, 20, 17 May 1959.
148 "Gli stregoni di Valsinni", *L'Espresso*, V, 22, 31 May 1959.
149 De Martino, E., *Sud e magia*, Milan: Feltrinelli, 1959 [1966].
150 Idem, p. 137.
151 Sonnino, E., "La popolazione italiana dall'espansione al contenimento", in Barbagallo, F., (ed.), *Storia dell'Italia repubblicana*, I, 1, Turin: Einaudi, 1995.
152 Ginsborg, P., cit., p. 219.
153 Colucci, M., *Lavoro in movimento. L'emigrazione italiana in Europa 1945-57*, Rome: Donzelli, 2008 and Rinauro, S., *Il cammino della speranza. L'emigrazione clandestina degli italiani nel secondo dopoguerra*, Turin: Einaudi, 2009.
154 Treves, A., *Le migrazioni interne nell'Italia fascista*, Turin: Einaudi, 1976.
155 On Fascist demographic policy see also Ipsen, C., *Dictating Demography. The Problem of Population in Fascist Italy*, Cambridge: Cambridge University Press, 1996.
156 Treves, A., cit.
157 Signorelli, A., "Movimenti di popolazione e trasformazioni culturali", in *Storia dell'Italia repubblicana*, volume I, Turin: Einaudi, 1995, p. 624. On the abrogation of the Fascist anti-urbanism legislation see also Gallo, S., "Scontri istituzionali sulle anagrafi. L'ISTAT e l'abrogazione della legge contro l'urbanesimo (1947-61)", in Colucci, M., Gallo, S., (eds), *L'arte di spostarsi. Rapporto 2014 sulle migrazioni interne in Italia*, Rome: Donzelli, 2014, pp. 77–94.
158 The issue has been investigated by Fofi, G., *L'immigrazione meridionale a Torino*, Milan: Feltrinelli, 1964.
159 Badino, A., *Tutte a casa? Donne tra migrazione e lavoro nella Torino degli anni Sessanta*, Rome: Viella, 2008.
160 Foot, J., *Milan Since the Miracle. City, Culture and Identity*, Oxford: Berg, 2001, p. 53.
161 Ibidem.
162 Foot, J., "Revisiting the *Coree*. Self-Construction, Memory and Immigration on the Milanese Periphery, 1950-2000", in Lumley, R., Foot, J., (eds), *Italian Citiscapes. Culture and Urban Change in Contemporary Italy*, Exeter: University of Exeter Press, 2004, p. 47.
163 Idem, p. 50.

164 Alasia, F., Montaldi, D., *Milano, Corea. Inchiesta sugli immigrati*, Milan: Feltrinelli, 1960.
165 Fofi, G., *L'immigrazione meridionale a Torino*, Milan: Feltrinelli, 1964.
166 Foot, J., *Milan Since the Miracle*, cit., p. 41.
167 Idem, p. 42.
168 Levi., F., "L'immigrazione", in Tranfaglia, N., (ed.) *Storia di Torino. Gli anni della Repubblica*, Turin: Einaudi, 1999, pp. 156–87.
169 Capussotti, E., "'Arretrati per civiltà'. L'identità italiana alla prova delle migrazioni interne", *Zapruder*, 28, 2012, pp. 40–56.
170 Capussotti, E., "*Nordisti contro Sudisti*: Internal Migrations and Racism in Turin, Italy: 1950s and 1960s", *Italian Culture*, XVIII, 2, 2010, p. 123.
171 "In 24 anni la popolazione è aumentata solo per l'arrivo di immigrati", *La Stampa*, 2 March 1955.
172 Ibidem.
173 "Il foglio di via obbligatorio per gli immigrati irregolari", *La Stampa*, 23 October 1955.
174 Ibidem.
175 "In nove mesi sono giunti circa 40 mila immigrati", *La Stampa*, 23 October 1955.
176 "La corsa al Nord", *La Stampa*, 5 February 1956.
177 "In un anno 56 mila immigrati a Torino da ogni parte d'Italia", *La Stampa*, 13 June 1956.
178 Ibidem.
179 Cravero, R., "I problemi di Torino sono aggravati dal continuo flusso immigratorio", *La Stampa*, 11 October 1956.
180 Ibidem.
181 "Siamo un po' tutti responsabili", *La Stampa*, 1 February 1956.
182 Ibidem.
183 Ghirotti, G., "I calabresi della Riviera condannano il ratto solo perché eseguito con le armi", *La Stampa*, 18 November 1956.
184 "Un ambulante uccide con sei rivoltellate il compaesano che corteggia sua sorella", *La Stampa*, 19 July 1956.
185 Capussotti, E., "*Nordisti contro Sudisti*" cit., p. 132.
186 Article 37. On the topic see Rossi Doria, A., "Le donne sulla scena politica", in *Storia dell'Italia repubblicana. La costruzione della democrazia*, Turin: Einaudi, 1994, pp. 780–846.
187 Capussotti, E., "*Nordisti contro Sudisti*" cit., p. 132.
188 Perotti, C., "Alla conquista di una soffitta", *Gazzetta del Popolo*, 15 July 1962.
189 Perotti, C., "Mezza Corleone si è trasferita a Borgaro", *Gazzetta del Popolo*, 9 September, 1962. On the stigma attached to Southerners' supposedly backward reproductive habits see Schneider, J. C., Schneider, P. T., *Festival of the Poor. Fertility Decline and the Ideology of Class in Italy, 1860-1980*, Tucson: University of Arizona Press, 1996.
190 Ibidem.
191 Mussa, C., "Il piatto di minestra sotto l'albero di Natale", *Gazzetta del Popolo*, 21 December 1971.
192 Grifoni, C., "Infanzia alle porte della civiltà", *La Stampa*, 11 February 1969.
193 Ibidem.

2   Educational 'otherness'

The previous chapter analysed the persistence of an image of the South and its inhabitants as internal 'others' in the post-war period. In a country aspiring to be modern and developed, the *Mezzogiorno* constituted a static and residual entity and an impediment to progress. This stereotyped view also informed the representation of the thousands of Southerners who, between the 1950s and the 1960s, moved towards the North-Western cities. Southern migrants in Turin were commonly depicted as a backward and inherently 'different' out-group, posing a threat to local order and well-being. Children, in particular, became one of the most powerful symbols of the inferiority of the South and Southern migrant families, regarded as infantile and needing guidance towards adulthood.

The current chapter analyses how the discourse on the 'otherness' of the South was articulated in the educational realm. Throughout the 1950s and the 1960s, the presence of Southern pupils in Turin primary schools became a compelling problem. Not only were they reckoned to put pressure on building and classroom space, but they were widely felt to be below required standards in achievement and behaviour.

This issue needs to be set in the wider context of post-war educational institutions. Section "Post-war Italian education: a historical overview" therefore provides a general overview of the organization of post-war Italian education and particular attention is devoted to primary schools. The key issues will be shown to be insufficient reform, the lack of resources, and the selectiveness of the system.

Section "The educational Southern Question" analyses how the educational backwardness of the *Mezzogiorno* represented, in the post-war period as well as before, an important marker of its 'difference' from the rest of the country. High rates of illiteracy and the miserable condition of school buildings were indicated as both the cause and the expression of the protracted exclusion of the South from the flow of progress.

Finally, section "'Others' in the classroom" investigates how Southern migrant children in Turin were viewed by teachers' journals, local education authorities, and primary school teachers. The cases of two Turin primary

DOI: 10.4324/9781003100546-3

schools, the "Margherita di Savoia" and the "Gian Enrico Pestalozzi" are examined closely.

2.1 Post-war Italian education: a historical overview

Continuity is a recurrent theme within the historiographical debate on post-war Italy. Since Claudio Pavone's landmark essay on the "continuity of the state" between Fascism and the Republic first appeared in 1974,[1] many scholars dealing with different aspects of the country's history in the last 60 years have stressed the relevance of Fascist legacies in the life of democratic Italy. Pavone focused, above all, on the continuity involving the State "as apparatus and organization, a complex of offices, services, procedures, as bureaucracy",[2] specifying, however, that many other realms had been affected by "a high degree of continuity".[3]

Education is one of them. The education system, as it had been organized by Fascism, survived the transition to the Republic.[4] One of the pillars of the 1923 reform of education devised by the then Minister of Public Instruction, the philosopher Giovanni Gentile, had been the creation of a "strict, selective and aristocratic" school, whose symbol became the *liceo classico* (classical lyceum), a higher secondary school functioning as the "training ground of the future ruling class".[5] Social selection, however, characterized even primary education. As Anna Laura Fadiga Zanatta has noted, in the school year 1924–25 30.3% of primary school pupils had been failed.[6]

This situation remained substantially unchanged at least until the 1960s. Some modifications were then introduced – as will be further discussed in this section – but the aim of reorganizing education, from primary schools to universities, remained incomplete. Moreover, if the reform of lower secondary education was finally realized after more than a decade of debate at the end of 1962, that of upper secondary education, though announced several times, never took place.[7] Some *ad hoc* changes were introduced in 1969, as a result of the pressure of the student protest movement. The new state examination at the end of secondary schools, the extension to five years of vocational schools (*istituti professionali*) and the consequent liberalization of access to the university represented the government response, albeit limited, to demands for the democratization of higher education. It is worth noting, however, that the new state examination, which was meant to be a "biennial experiment", actually lasted until 1999. Such a prolonged duration was not on account of "a positive evaluation of the experiment, but of a sort of process of making chronic the provisional".[8] The measure had certainly been adopted to "ease the tension [...] and foreshadow a different organization of secondary education".[9] When the tension finally eased, in the absence of any high school reform project, the mere fact that the new norms on state examination were in force justified their existence.[10]

Such an approach was not reserved for education only but fitted into a long-term ruling strategy which has been defined as "governing at the margins".[11] Instead of trying to channel the "social forces liberated by the change", occurring both on the economic and social level between the 1950s and 1960s, post-war governments mostly aimed to perpetuate their mandate and their power.[12] The huge demand for reforms in vital sections of Italian society was destined not to be heard.[13]

2.1.1 Between Fascism and the Republic

A huge element of continuity from the Fascist regime was represented by education personnel, who, at different levels, were scarcely touched by the purge of Fascist collaborators. Many teachers, heads of school and civil servants of the Ministry of Public Instruction who had been strong Fascist supporters kept their positions in the post-war period. Not only in education but in most branches of the administration, the number of purged bureaucrats proved to be small and "on this terrain the continuity of the State celebrated one of its greatest successes".[14] However, as Guido Melis has remarked, amongst the Ministries, that of Public Instruction was the one where "the traces of the past were strongest"[15]: seven out of eight post-war General Directors had been appointed by Giuseppe Bottai, the last Fascist Minister of National Education, who after his return to Italy continued to be in close contact with many of them.[16]

A partial and half-hearted attempt at eradicating Fascism from Italian educational institutions came from the Allies during their occupation of the country between 1943 and 1945. In July 1943, Robert Gayre,[17] anthropologist and, at that time, Staff Officer for Education at Oxford University, was appointed Educational Adviser to the Allied Military Government "in view of [his] knowledge of continental Universities"[18]; and he was subsequently also nominated Director of the Education Sub-Committee of the Allied Control Commission. From the very first days of his arrival in Sicily, Gayre's activity was made slow and difficult, owing to the inefficient organization and the absence of directions from the Allied headquarters. It has been argued that Allied policy toward education was "nebulous" and emblematic of the "planned disorganization" characterizing their administration of the Italian freed territories.[19] For example, in spite of his role as Director, Gayre was not even informed that Lieutenant Colonel Charles Poletti, in his capacity as Chief Civil Affair Officer, had decided to repeal Bottai's "School Charter", issued in 1939, and he learned the news from the newspaper *Sicilia liberata*.[20] This was an episode which seemed to confirm the lack of communication between the Allied Officers and the small importance generally accorded to educational issues.

The most notable figure of the Education Sub-Commission was, however, the American pedagogue Carleton Washburne. A disciple of John Dewey and a progressive educator himself, he was sent to Milan as Director of the United States Information Service (USIS) after having left the Education Sub-Commission. As he himself described in 1970 in one of the main

Italian educational periodicals, he was asked by the U.S. army to "help t
re-establish the educational institutions of an enemy country, as soon as ıt
was conquered".[21] The task of the Sub-Commission was extremely difficult, not only because of the war – "we were often under the bombings or
under the artillery fire" he said – but also because of the condition of Italian
schools.[22] Besides the countless material impediments – such as the lack of
buildings, which in the vast majority of cases had been bombed or used for
military purposes or by the civilians whose houses had been damaged or
destroyed – it was the responsibility of the Sub-Commission to "verify that
no Fascists were occupying key posts and that school textbooks were no
longer an instrument of Fascist propaganda".[23]

The issue of the defascistization of school textbooks well exemplifies
the continuity into the Republic of the former regime. In this case too, a
series of practical obstacles ended up influencing the final result. First of
all, the schools had to be reopened as soon as possible and the need for
sufficient approved textbooks was urgent. In primary schools, where since
1929 the State Common Text (*Testo unico di Stato*) had been introduced,
the risk was that they would have been left with no texts if the purging
process was too slow or if, as an extreme measure, it was decided to abolish Fascist textbooks. For this reason, especially in the first phases, the
purge consisted only of the elimination of overt Fascist propaganda.[24]
However, even when, in the immediate aftermath of war, new textbooks
were published, they did not seem to be inspired by the founding values
of the Republic; and, more generally, they were divorced from reality. Any
reference to the social, political, and economic situation of the country
was banned.

Gianni Rodari, the renowned children's author, in 1947 underlined in the
columns of the Milan edition of the communist newspaper *L'Unità* how,
looking through the pages of post-war primary school textbooks, it seemed
that Italian pupils were forbidden to know that the Italian Republic had by
then reached its first year of life. Those books seemed to Rodari intended
for children wearing sailor suits forty years earlier, rather than for those
who had just experienced the bombings and seen with their own eyes the
national insurrection, the executions of partisans and Mussolini strung up
in Piazzale Loreto.[25] Instead of representing a window on the real world,
textbooks offered a reassuring portrait of "families so 'normal' as to look
unreal, workers so satisfied as not to want anything else from life, children
good enough to spend their time on never-ending good manners contests or
collecting vows under the wing of saints, Madonnas, Baby Jesuses, guard-
ian angels and above all mothers".[26]

The mother represented a pivotal figure within textbooks' pedagogic discourse, which centred on the family as the only form of social organization,
to the exclusion of others. Such an attitude was certainly influenced and
encouraged by the Church, which exerted a predominant control over education for a long time.

2.1.2 *The influence of the Catholic Church*

Since the Allied landing in 1943, the Church had successfully tried to re-assert its power over educational institutions, and it was the main force of resistance to change throughout the whole post-war period. The episode regarding the "Advice for the Modernization of Primary Schools" (*Consigli per la modernizzazione della scuola elementare*), formulated in 1943 by the eminent pedagogue, Gino Ferretti, is a significant example of this. Professor of pedagogy at the University of Palermo, Ferretti was a convinced and passionate supporter of democratic and secular education.[27] The declared aim of the Advice was to "orientate teaching towards a more modern sense of culture, closer to the new world democratic movements".[28] He recommended enhancing "children's disposition to play" and did not consider religion a compulsory subject, but as a matter to be dealt with by those teachers who felt "morally disposed" to do it.[29]

As a result of a protest by the Archbishop of Palermo, Cardinal Lavit-rano, Ferretti's Advice was withdrawn and destroyed by the Allies a few days after its publication. Arriving in Naples in October 1943, Washburne appointed a Monsignor to form part of the commission in charge of the revision of textbooks and of the curriculum.[30] Contrary to what Ferretti had proposed, the new curriculum adopted in October 1945 "revealed the precise purpose of a moral, civil, religious, professional restoration".[31] In conformity with Italian convention, the section devoted to religion was at the beginning of the text, where the means by which the "religious norm" was to be instilled through the "spontaneous adhesion of the spirit to the principles of the Gospels and [through] the evidence of the links between these principles and the moral and civil law" was outlined.[32]

The influence of the Church was, furthermore, very evident, especially with regard to the leading role assigned to the family in the education of children. In the section devoted to nursery schools, it was stated that "the first natural child's educator is the mother. The nursery school cannot replace the family and the mother".[33] As Gaetano Bonetta has pointed out, "this maternal-familistic education" was the result of the "conquest of the State by political Catholicism and by Christian Democracy, supported by Pope Pius XII and the indefatigable militia of the ecclesiastical army as never before".[34]

The Christian Democrats' view of education was outlined by Guido Gonella, soon to become Minister of Public Instruction, during the first national conference of the party in 1946: both the State and the school were considered simply as "auxiliaries" of the family which had the "natural" duty to educate its children and the right to "choose freely the school correspond-ing to its educational ideal"; the Church, too, had the right to teach religion and other disciplines, since "instruction and education fall into its aims".[35] The content of the Italian family's "educational ideal" was unequivocally specified when it was stated that "the Italian family is Christian, and it demands religion to be the foundation and crown of any kind of education".[36]

Their programme did not seem to include any desire to renew the education system except for those measures favouring confessional teaching and the interests of private schools.[37] The class-based ideology characterizing the organization of education was not to be challenged, since the "high humanistic tradition of our literary and artistic culture [were] confirmed and strengthened", while technical and vocational education was only meant to "confer more dignity to work".[38] Furthermore, the pre-eminence of the family over the State as an educational agency revealed the intention to perpetuate social inequalities, instead of tackling them through a redistribution of opportunities and resources, as only the State could guarantee.

According to Remo Fornaca, the programme of Christian Democracy aimed both to preserve and to extend the undeniable privileges that the Church had acquired during Fascism, in spite of the contrasts with the regime.[39] The introduction of the state examination, called for by the Catholics for many years and sanctioned by the Gentile Reform in 1923, was the first in a series of unprecedented concessions. The larger role assigned to private education had consolidated the monopoly of the Catholics in this field, while the presence of religion in State education had grown progressively. Gentile imposed it as a compulsory subject in primary schools and one of his successors, Pietro Fedele, was especially "inclined to favour the educational initiative of the Church, as well as to make the State school more and more Catholic".[40] The Concordat between State and Church finally guaranteed the right of students attending Catholic schools to take the State examination and declared "the teaching of Christian doctrine, according to the form handed down by Catholic tradition, [to be] the foundation and crown of public education".[41] For this reason, religious teaching was to be extended to middle and high schools and teachers' recruitment was to be approved by the ecclesiastical authority.[42]

The Catholics could claim another victory in the inclusion of Lateran Pacts in the Constitution.[43] The debates of the Constituent Assembly were marked by discussions focusing almost exclusively on issues such as the laity and the freedom of teaching, State, and private education, following an agenda dictated by the Christian Democrats. All these questions were undeniably important, but others regarding the education system, though not less significant, were not addressed.[44] The Gentile Reform and its elitism were not challenged by any political force thereby making the path to the true democratization of Italian school much longer and tortuous.[45]

The appointment of Guido Gonella as Minister of Public Instruction in the second De Gasperi government marked the beginning of an era of abuse and of "clerical restoration".[46] The "infeudation" of the Ministry by the Christian Democrats and their complete control over the bureaucracy assisted the ideological penetration of State education.[47] The supervision of university professors, local officers, and schoolteachers took on the form of repression, especially in the aftermath of the 1948 general elections and as a result of the exacerbation of the Cold War.[48] In order to safeguard lay education and stem the tide of State funding to private schools, a group of intellectuals set up in 1946 the *Associazione per la difesa della scuola nazionale* (ADSN, Association for the Defence of the National School) which could count on the support of figures like Benedetto Croce, Aldo Capitini, Guido De Ruggiero, Pietro Calamandrei, Ernesto Codignola, and Concetto Marchesi.[49] In February 1947, the ADSN appealed to the President of the Republic to denounce the boycott of State education by the Christian Democracy party and ask for the appointment of a non-Catholic as Minister. The plea was ignored and Gonella was not only reconfirmed in the third De Gasperi government but retained his office until 1951.[50]

2.1.3 *A selective system of education*

Gonella's policy was also directed towards the preservation of the rigid selective structure of education and the defence of corporatist interests' groups, such as primary schoolteachers. The reform project submitted to Parliament in 1951 and originating from the works of the "National Commission of Enquiry for School Reform" (*Commissione nazionale d'inchiesta per la riforma della scuola*), established in 1947, was intended to serve these purposes.[51] As far as lower secondary education was concerned, the plan provided for the creation of three different kinds of school: the *secondaria classica* (classical secondary school), characterized by the compulsory teaching of Latin and allowing access to every upper secondary school; the *secondaria tecnica* (technical secondary school), whose students could choose between technical and vocational schools; and the *secondaria normale* (normal secondary school), also referred to as post-elementary school, a dead-end school opening the doors to vocational institutes only and employing primary schoolteachers.[52] These were among the most affected by post-war intellectual unemployment and the majority of them were members of the *Associazione italiana maestri cattolici* (AIMC, Italian Association of Catholic Teachers), the most powerful post-war teachers' organization.[53]

The AIMC, not only represented three quarters of the primary schoolteachers and was able to control their votes, but from 1953, the Association had its own candidates in the lists of Christian Democracy: its influence over the party was thus not in doubt.[54] Gonella himself had declared in a 1946 radio speech that about eighty thousand primary schoolteachers were jobless and that, in order to tackle the issue, the State had the duty to support the establishment of the *scuola popolare* (people's school) and of a "solid post-elementary school, welcoming the sons of the people".[55] The *scuola popolare* was set up in 1947 and its main objective – at least according to the text of the law – was to reduce adult illiteracy. It was indeed intended for people over 12 years of age and the classes were taught by primary schoolteachers.[56] The way in which the measure was put into effect was strongly criticized, as it revealed that the principal concern of the government was not tackling illiteracy but teachers' unemployment.[57]

As Gonnella himself pointed out in his January 1948 radio speech to announce the establishment of the *scuola popolare*, this kind of school was also meant to be "a contribution to solving the great problem of teachers' unemployment".[58] The effectiveness of the struggle against illiteracy had thus been subordinated to this interest and it was no coincidence that the organization of part of the courses was assigned to the AIMC.[59]

The priority of the AIMC was, however, to favour the inclusion of primary schoolteachers into lower secondary education, through the creation of the post-elementary school. The purpose of creating a dead-end school giving access only to vocational institutes was the result of its reactionary ideology. Already in 1949, its founder, president, future MP, and Vice-Minister of Public Instruction, Maria Badaloni, had written that:

> "the equality of human beings and their rights does not make them a single set, a single stamp. On the contrary, each has a body and a soul, similar but not identical, to those of his brothers, differentially endowed: each has his own spiritual physiognomy and his own vocation, namely his place, or rather his task assigned to him by the divine will within the marvellous framework of providence which transcends time and space and the individual mind just as the Creator transcends the creature".[60]

The 1951 bill sank without even being discussed by Parliament, but the project of the post-elementary school was not abandoned. In 1955, the Minister Giuseppe Ermini promulgated the new primary school curriculum which included a section on post-elementary school. Such a move sounded like an implicit acknowledgement of this kind of school.[61] The measure also introduced a new examination to be undertaken after the first two years of primary school, thus reinforcing the selective system.[62] A proof of its enduring effectiveness was the high number of failing pupils, even at the elementary level. According to the data provided by the *Istituto Nazionale di Statistica* (ISTAT, Italian National Institute of Statistics) and referring to the school year 1953/54, only 51.2% of pupils were in a grade corresponding to their age, 17.2% had been failed, and 65.9% of the enrolled did not reach the last grade of primary school.[63]

2.1.4 The *scuola media unica*

The institution of the so-called *scuola media unica* (unified middle school) at the end of 1962 was meant to inflict a blow on this mechanism of selection. Divided into two separated channels – *scuola media* (middle school) and *avviamento professionale* (lower vocational school) – the organization of lower secondary education was one of the symbols of the social stratification of the Italian schools. The *avviamento* was indeed a dead-end school and only those attending the *scuola media* could continue their studies.

The reform came as a result of the new political climate accompanying the birth of the centre-left.[64] The first to present a bill to the Senate, in 1959, had been the Communists, who, since 1955, had paid greater attention than before to educational issues and strongly supported mass schooling.[65] Even if the draft was never discussed by Parliament, it drew the government's attention to the issue.

After three years of intense debate, the law was eventually approved: a unified middle school was established. Latin – which had previously marked the difference between the *scuola media* and the *avviamento* – became an optional subject to be taught in the third grade only. However, for those students who wanted to attend the *liceo classico* , the teaching of Latin continued to be compulsory and was a State examination subject.[66]

Notwithstanding the undoubted changes, a certain degree of continuity with the past remained. Moreover, the effects of some innovations proved to be controversial. The creation of *classi di aggiornamento* (catching-up classes) for pupils needing "particular care in order to attend with profit the first grade" or for those who had failed in the third grade and of the *classi differenziali*, intended for "educationally maladjusted pupils" favoured the exclusion from mainstream education of an increasing number of students.[67] At the same time, although the provision concerned middle school, its extension to primary school was implicitly legitimized. As will be discussed in Chapter 3, special education grew enormously between the 1960s and the 1970s. In the industrialized cities of the North-West, hugely affected by internal migrations, special education contributed to "institutionalising the presumed 'diversity' and the so-called maladjustment of the migrants.[68]

Although the reform was far from radical, it nevertheless aroused sharp opposition. For instance, even the progressive educational journal, *Scuola e città*, warned of the risk that the new schools could simply "adapt" themselves to the new pupils who had previously been excluded from the *scuola media*.[69] Their presence was a perplexing problem. Not only was the gap between their culture and that of the school huge, but their social class background negatively influenced their intelligence, as the results of the IQ tests demonstrated. This was partly on account of their "innate potential", but above all because of their living environment and life experiences.[70] A simple modification of middle school structure was considered useless and counterproductive without a substantial change in educational practice. The school had to open itself to the community in order to offer the students an alternative to their native "subculture" and "enlighten" parents about the opportunity given to their children.[71]

Middle school teachers saw unified middle school as an attack on the seriousness and prestige of the educational system as a whole. This attitude was a source of inspiration for the renowned study of middle school teachers conducted between 1965 and 1969 by Marcello Dei and Marzio Barbagli. As the authors pointed out, a "silent and very violent opposition of the great majority of [the teaching staff] to the innovations introduced by the reform law" characterized the years after 1962.[72] "The first year I thought I had arrived into an asylum, into a menagerie", a teacher said.[73] "To say that my attitude was negative is to say little. [...] I was for selective school [...] I was considered a very severe teacher [...] now it is no longer possible", another declared.[74] What they feared most was the unification of the two channels, which had caused – in their view – culture to be "levelled down" and "declassed".[75] It was the students wishing to pursue their studies who paid the price: "[those] who continue to study, who want to attend the high school, always are the victims". On the contrary, "children from needy families, coming into contact with the kids of rich people, can learn something".[76]The 1962 reform was destined to remain an isolated achievement. An enormous amount of money was indiscriminately lavished on schools throughout the 1960s, while the extent of the fundamental changes required of the education system was not recognized. According to the *Piano di sviluppo della scuola nel decennio 1959–1969* (Plan for the Development of the School in the Decade 1959–1969) – brought before the Senate in 1958 – more than 2,000 billion liras were to be spent on education.[77] The Plan was, however, strongly criticized. As one of its more ardent opponents – the socialist Tristano Codignola – pointed out, it not only entailed a "substantial acceptance of the school structure" but was meant as a "restraint on the great structural and democratic reform that the school needed".[78] Subsequently withdrawn, it was replaced by a *stralcio*, known as *Piano per lo sviluppo della scuola nel triennio dal 1962 al 1965* (Plan for the Development of the School in the Triennium 1962–1965).[79] The results of a special commission of enquiry, instituted to set the direction for education in relation to the economic, social, and cultural development of the country, were substantially inadequate and disappointing.[80]

At the end of the centre-left experience, in 1968, the only significant element of novelty, apart from the middle school reform, was the law for State nursery schools. The transformation of the Italian family owing to women's extra-domestic work had made it a compelling need. Though representing a step forward, the marks of the Catholic "ideological totalitarianism" that had characterized the previous decade had not disappeared completely.[81] Men were excluded from the teaching staff and the role of the family was still considered pre-eminent.[82] Resistance to change was thus still strong, at least at an institutional level. From below, however, the need to call everything into question was growing dramatically.

2.2 The educational Southern Question

In spite of the insufficient reform, a high level of attention was devoted by the media and public opinion to the issue of education throughout the 1950s and 1960s. In a country witnessing a huge but extremely unbalanced transformation, schools were considered unfit to meet the needs and the standards of a modern society. It was firmly believed, even at a governmental level, that in order "to recover the time lost, to reach the level of the most advanced European countries, and to guarantee adequate working forces to our required economic development, it is necessary to make all the sacrifices and provide the Italian nation with the school it urgently needs".[83] The inadequacy of educational institutions as well as the persistence of high rates of illiteracy were considered to be both the cause and the evidence of the difficulties Italy had to face before achieving full modernization. They thus constituted a powerful metaphor for the contradictions of a country still suspended between tradition and modernity. The South, more than other areas, was deemed particularly affected by these problems. Widespread illiteracy and the state of its school premises were used as signifiers of its educational 'difference' and backwardness. The following pages will offer an insight into the origin and the main themes of what can be referred to as the educational Southern Question.

2.2.1 From unification to Fascism

The identification of education and literacy with progress was certainly not a novelty. In the course of the nineteenth century, Western European and Anglo-American governments had promoted the creation of systems of mass State-sponsored education as an instrument of control and social stability. It was not only skills, but moral values that schools were intended to transmit through the vehicle of literacy. The latter, closely associated with the habits and precepts inculcated in the masses by school education, represented "the source of cohesion and order, and the defence of progress, in a developing and modernizing capitalist society".[84] Its functional meaning was thus obscured by its symbolic and ideological connotation. Formal schooling and instruction in literacy became synonymous with individual and societal development, whereas illiteracy was regarded as both symptom and cause of moral, economic, and cultural backwardness.

Moreover, literacy was considered peculiar to Western civilization as opposed to non-European barbarian and savage societies.[85] During the colonial period, sub-Saharan Africa, for example, was imagined and represented as out of history because of its inhabitants' lack of writing skills. It was as if the continent was locked into an eternal present and unable to progress without the intervention of the white colonizers.[86] Up to the 1950s, the dominant ideology – even among scholars – was that expressed by the British historian Arthur Percival Newton in 1923: "[Sub-Saharan] Africa possesses practically no history before the coming of Europeans [because] history only begins when men take to writing".[87]

In Italy, illiteracy had constituted one of the main concerns of post-unification governments. The discovery that three quarters of the population over the age of five was illiterate – as the 1861 census data had revealed – generated frustration and bewilderment among the ruling class, whose attitude was, however, influenced by two opposite forces.[88] Alongside those viewing favourably the spread of popular education – which could also have helped the integration of the lower classes into the nation-state – others considered it a potential source of social disorder. Fears regarding the potentially subversive outcome of education surfaced especially in the aftermath of the Paris Commune. In 1874, in the course of the Parliamentary debate on the bill for compulsory primary education, the deputy Paolo Lioy accused teachers of being "the apostles of those subversive notions by means of which the corrupt members of society hope to overthrow the civil association".[89] By contrast, Benedetto Castiglia identified the papers – which "the children of misery" would have been able to read if the bill passed – as the source of that "kind of knowledge that leads to socialism".[90]

Such alarm was also echoed in Pasquale Villari's 1872 essay on *La scuola e la questione sociale in Italia*. Convinced that education was useless in a context of moral and material misery, he expressed the belief that "if one day you succeeded in teaching that multitude to read and write, leaving it in the conditions in which it is now, you would prepare one of the most tremendous social revolutions".[91] Only if accompanied by economic and social rebuilding, could the alphabet open the souls of the Neapolitan plebs to "that moral world which still seems closed to them"; they could then be turned into "soldiers, if not more valiant, certainly more numerous, more robust, and more clever", as he had written a few years earlier in his *Di chi è la colpa?*[92] Villari was referring to the troublesome condition of the South, deemed – more than any other area of the country – almost completely immersed in the darkness of ignorance.

In the immediate aftermath of unification, ignorance had also been indicated as one of the main causes of brigandage. According to the report of the parliamentary commission of enquiry read by Giuseppe Massari to the Chamber of Deputies in May 1863, "the unhappy social condition" and poverty of the Neapolitan provinces would not be so harmful had they not been reinforced by "ignorance [...] superstition [...] and absolute lack of trust in law and justice".[93] Illiteracy and lack of education were looked upon as important aspects of the social problems and moral backwardness plaguing the *Mezzogiorno* and its inhabitants, who thus constituted a heavy burden on the new-born country.

At the beginning of the twentieth century, elementary instruction still constituted an unresolved issue. Illiteracy rates continued to be high and school attendance poor.[94] Moreover, the need to create a more effective school apparatus which could sustain the incipient industrialization of the country and disseminate its fundamental moral and cultural values was also becoming urgent. As the Minister of Public Instruction, Eduardo Daneo, pointed out in his speech to Parliament supporting the bill to take primary schools away from municipalities and assign their administration and financing to the State, "the clever factory worker, the wise man working in the fields, cannot conceive of themselves today as illiterate".[95]

The condition of education in the South continued to appear particularly problematic in many respects and to attract the attention of a widening circle of intellectuals and politicians who decided to take action. In 1910, for instance, prominent figures like Giustino Fortunato, Giuseppe Lombardo Radice, Gaetano Salvemini, Umberto Zanotti Bianco, and others set up the *Associazione per gli interessi del Mezzogiorno d'Italia* (ANIMI, Association for the interests of Italy's South). The decision to create the Association came in the wake of the 1908 earthquake, which had almost completely destroyed the cities of Reggio Calabria and Messina. The catastrophe indeed represented for many a sudden revelation of the inner essence of the South, its history and its problems, and triggered a wave of voluntarism.[96] In the first years of activity, the Association was mainly concerned with the creation of nursery schools and popular libraries.[97] Nursery schoolteachers usually belonged to wealthy Northern families, whose habits of hygiene – it was hoped – could be spread among the still uncivilized Southern populations.[98] Their attitude towards the latter reflected the most common perception of the South as an internal and inferior 'other': children were often defined as "coarse, violent and dirty" and one of them, writing in 1921, expressed her sense of estrangement at being among people unable to "appreciate anything more than the animal materiality of life".[99]

The ANIMI also aimed to continue the long-standing tradition of studies and inquiry characterizing Meridionalism. Between August and September 1909, Giovanni Malvezzi and Zanotti Bianco, visited thirty-six communes of the *Aspromonte occidentale*, investigating their economic, social, religious, and educational situation.[100] Their main goal was to shake and stir that "Italy [which was] not barbarous…but abandoned".[101] As far as education was concerned, the task was extremely difficult: it was a case of "scattering seeds of life on a stagnating dead sadness".[102] Though referring to Calabria only, the authors made it clear that such a situation was common to almost the whole *Mezzogiorno*, which was held responsible for the fact that Italy's rates of illiteracy were the highest in Europe, with the exception of the Iberian Peninsula and the Balkans. And high illiteracy was obviously associated with lack of progress. Its causes supposedly lay in the psychology of the Southern people, who were seen as particularly excitable, superficial, and lacking powers of concentration. Alongside other economic and social factors, this "illness of the will" generated a considerable level of "indifference towards any cultural renaissance" and hence ignorance.[103] These were not, however, the only characteristics attributed to the Calabrians: they also had an "incomplete conception" of state and government, "from which everything is to be expected"; they were indifferent; their mistrust hindered any form of initiative; they did not cultivate any hope for the future.[104] The remedy proposed for this state of "abandon" – made even worse by "undernourishment, which causes a series of organic degenerations" – was the intervention of those who could morally and intellectually influence the people, such as the clergy, the judiciary, and the upper classes.[105] Under their tutelage, the Calabrians and more generally the Southern populace would finally see the light of instruction and progress.

Partially different, though no less imbued with the progressive rhetoric about the enlightening power of schooling, was the approach of a survey on the condition of Reggio Calabria schools conducted by Gaetano Salvemini, Giovanni Cena, Sibilla Aleramo, and Giuseppina Lemaire, which had been a source of inspiration for Malvezzi and Zanotti Bianco. The study, published in March 1910 in the distinguished periodical *Nuova Antologia*, revealed that the vast majority of the classrooms of the province had been destroyed by the earthquake.[106] This was not to be considered as a great loss, however – in the authors' opinion – since many of them were "filthy rat holes" where "children were tortured as if they were in prison", crowded into small desks or seated on the floor.[107]

A novelty was represented by a "deep psychological transformation" occurring among the rural population whose demand for instruction had grown considerably. According to the data provided by the local *Provveditorato agli Studi* (the provincial office of the Ministry of Public Instruction), 61% of children of compulsory school age (6–12 years, then) were officially enrolled in local primary schools. Considering all the obstacles that many of them had to confront every day to reach their schools – those from Grotteria had to wade through a river, for instance – this figure appeared as a "desire for light, a moral effort of the multitudes".[108] Peasants' demand for instruction was so deeply felt that a number of families resorted to private instruction, considered more efficient than that provided by the state, whose rigid organization was not suited to the needs of the population. Local ruling classes, however, were not eager to promote popular instruction, considering the ability to read and write a "disgrace"; teachers, on the other hand, were blamed for having taken advantage of the earthquake to fall into idleness.[109] Administrative and financial reforms were not considered sufficient to change the situation. The real requirement was a "new national educational spirit", which was already growing in Northern and Central Italy but was completely lacking in the *Mezzogiorno*. Though aware of the importance of schools, the populace was not able to induce the local elites to create them. This aim had to be pursued instead by "private associations of other Italian regions", who could at least partially replace the inept local elites, gather the morally and intellectually good but isolated elements and support virtuous initiatives.[110]

After the First World War, the Association contributed greatly to the campaign against illiteracy initiated by the Minister Orso Mario Corbino in Calabria, Lucania, Sicily and Sardinia.[111] The action of "penetration and conquest" by the "alphabet missionaries" – it was believed – would defeat the illiteracy and ignorance of "the man of savage nature, [who], still dominated by nature, felt and feels so distant and inferior with respect to the «other man» who dominates nature".[112] The path to the intellectual and moral redemption of the Southern populace was, however, beset with obstacles. The conditions of school buildings, the indifference or, sometimes, the open hostility of local authorities, and the ignorance of the population obstructed teachers' educating mission, evoking colonial analogies among the observers. Southern schools even occupied a lower point on a scale of educational progress than those of countries still in need of European domination and guidance. To Zanotti Bianco, they indeed appeared even worse than those of Sumatra, as he stated in the introduction to one of his most famous books, *Il martirio della scuola in Calabria* (The martyrdom of the school in Calabria):

> "My dear Lombardo Radice, I was reading the other day a book of an Italian traveller who organized scientific expeditions to Malaya: 'In Benculen the school with numerous pupils excels in order and neatness'. Benculen!...the school excels...order...neatness! My thoughts turned – with a feeling of envy and bitterness – to the schools of our poor Mezzogiorno: (yet how can the civilization of our country be compared to that of the remote island of Sumatra?) and I mentally asked myself this question: 'What town of our countryside would merit the honour of such praise?'".[113]

In his view, owing to the defective state of the infrastructure of Calabrian schools and the shocking barbarity of living conditions, "teachers' innovative spirit" could not fulfil its regenerative function. Entering the houses, one had the disturbing perception of "sinking into the impure": children, "with an intelligent physiognomy often altered by an incipient illness, naked, or with dirty shirts which barely cover their bellies", were crouched among scraps and animals; sick people with a "resigned gaze" were looked after by dogs and lay in bed surrounded by flies.[114] No words or pictures could describe the "cruel impression of that decaying life, as if in a vacuous abyss, without any thought or hope of a remote dawn [...] that life [which] has the sense of a dark useless sinking into shadow".[115] Several teachers, overwhelmed by the squalor and loneliness of their lives, lost the "sense of their mission". This was true of a young lady from Sicily who viewed the small Calabrian village where she was teaching as "the annihilation of education, the negation of the school and civilization" and decided to resign. Others – the teacher was reported to have written to the local *Provveditore* – especially women "who cannot stand abandonment", had even lost their minds.[116]

During Fascism, the struggle against illiteracy became a matter of national pride.[117] The regime declared in due course that it had solved the problem: in 1928, the Minister Pietro Fedele announced that the plague had been "virtually eradicated", though, at the same time, he commissioned an inquiry into the "special causes" of its persistence in the South.[118] In 1936, the question about literacy was even removed from the census, in order to eliminate the risk that the data could damage the prestige of the new-born Empire.[119]

2.2.2 The post-war period

In the post-war period, the issue came to the surface again and was closely linked to the task of reconstructing the country on renewed bases. At the same time, the question of schools and education more generally formed an important part of the moral panic about the immorality of children and youth as a result of the war.[120] In his inaugural speech as Minister of Public Instruction in 1946 – significantly entitled "L'Italia rinascerà dalla scuola" (Italy will be reborn from school) – Guido Gonella pointed out that school needed fresh life blood in order to "save youth from illiteracy and corruption" and to ensure that democracy would cease to be simply a word but could instead "find its most solid base: the education and the elevation of the people".[121] This process of "social redemption", along with the promotion of "knowledge aristocracy", would restore Italy's "intellectual primacy in the world".[122] Beyond children and youth, however, the attention of politicians and public opinion also addressed adult literacy, which the creation of the *scuola popolare* in 1947 was intended to tackle.[123]

The ANIMI decided to focus on sectors other than education, but its past commitment to the cause of Southerners' education was widely celebrated. Not only did post-war organizations and activists constantly refer to and praise its activity, but some of its leading members continued to influence the debate. This was the case of Zanotti Bianco, who was named Life Senator and regarded as one of the most authoritative experts on Southern schools' issues.[124] The work of the Association, especially its inquiries, constituted a source of inspiration for post-war activists and scholars. Rocco Scotellaro's survey on Basilicata schools, conducted in 1949 and posthumously published in *Nord e Sud*, was directly linked – according to the periodical – to Zanotti Bianco's and ANIMI's tradition of studies.

Scotellaro considered illiteracy to encapsulate "all the aspects of a population's way of life" and to be characteristic of "Southern society". Basilicata's "civil and economic inferiority" was to be ascribed to it.[125] There were, however, interesting new elements in his approach, which were in line with the new role assigned to schools as social service institutions. Especially in Basilicata, Scotellaro suggested that schools had to provide a wide range of services and, in certain respects, had to give pupils that support which in other zones of the country they received from their families. It was up to schools – in his view – to offer children suitable places for doing their homework in the afternoon – their houses being overcrowded – and to provide a balanced diet, enabling them to make the intellectual effort required. Moreover, schools had to become monitoring centres for children's health, while particular attention was to be devoted to the mentally defective – who were more numerous than it would seem owing to the precarious living conditions.

The ANIMI's previous efforts over education were also praised by educational periodicals, such as the prominent *Scuola e città*, which defined them as "heroic".[126] In 1947, its legacy was taken up by the *Unione nazionale per la lotta all'analfabetismo* (UNLA, National Union Against Illiteracy), which – though its name did not seem to indicate any geographically limited range of activity – operated exclusively and significantly in the South. In line with the new democratic course of Italian political and social life, UNLA's founders declared that they were not interested in replicating the model of an Association run by "a good and noble intellectual bourgeoisie" and guided by the aim of rescuing an "abandoned population"; they intended instead to promote popular participation through the creation of communal committees, among whose members were "representatives elected by the population (such as the mayor and representatives of workers) and all those persons, from the parish priest and the doctor to the leaders of local associations, interested in the problem".[127]

The evolutionary and deterministic approach to literacy, schooling, and education as strictly interrelated and symbolizing progress and hope had not changed, however. And the consequent division and hierarchization between those enlightened by writing and knowledge and those still buried in ignorance and brutishness – identified with Southern lower classes – persisted. Illiteracy continued to connote exclusion from the flow of history and its persistence, if only in limited areas, could send Italy back to the backward situation of the past.

As Anna Lorenzetto – a leading figure of the UNLA – pointed out in her 1962 book on post-war literacy campaigns, "a civil country in which wide areas of illiteracy still exist today absurdly appears as a country of the past, a country fallen back in time, where human rights are still ignored, the conquests of thought, the democratic and civil achievements are still to come".[128] Illiteracy had not ceased to be considered a moral issue and its defeat to be regarded as an indispensable prerequisite for economic and civil progress. The main difficulties in carrying out the post-war agrarian reform originated, in Lorenzetto's view, from the *braccianti*'s lack of education: "with their mind and soul confused, they have suffered changes as much as they had earlier suffered poverty and immobility".[129] Southern populations were described as "largely illiterate, unable to obtain any job qualification, spiritually and morally unprepared to deal with the forms of economy, of cooperation, of civic collaboration".[130]

At the same time, illiteracy raised concerns about its presumed links with criminality, especially in areas considered particularly isolated. This was the case with Sardinia, where in the first half of the 1950s, the issue of banditry attracted the attention of public opinion at both a local and national level. Both illiteracy and banditry could be considered – according to the lawyer and Sardinian Action Party member, Gonario Pinna – as the result of the economic and social 'backwardness' of the island. Though not establishing a strict causal relationship between the two phenomena, he expressed the conviction that "the knowledge of the alphabet, by breaking the nocturnal circle of that isolation which is produced by absolute ignorance, modifies the primitive man's view of life and can contribute to reducing the intensity of certain crimes: those originating from primitiveness".[131]

The view of an immobile South was shared by various groups of intellectuals irrespective of their political affiliation. Southern peasants were denied the status of active subjects and conceived of only as potential recipients of external pedagogical action. The Communist Giuseppe Petronio, for instance, in 1948, emphasized the invigorating force of "the teacher and the book", that if brought to the "dusty villages" of Calabria, Puglia, and Lucania would have "shaken all that world from its secular inertia".[132]

The discourse on the backwardness of Southern schools and their educational provision was also echoed in newspapers, magazines, and educational periodicals. Photographs – as has already been described in the previous chapter – proved to be an extremely powerful means to convey the stereotype of the persistent inferiority of the South. Those 'documenting' and denouncing the conditions of Southern schools not only formed an integral part of this system of representation but reveal how crucial educational issues were to the construction of a certain image of the *Mezzogiorno* and how the most common *topoi* on its schools' backwardness continued to be reproduced.

As mentioned in the previous chapter, one of the articles published in 1948 in *L'Europeo* as part of the survey on the *Mezzogiorno* was accompanied by two photographs of Africo's mixed-sex primary school, both taken by the photographer Tino Petrelli.[133] Interestingly enough, the pictures did not accompany the *reportage* from Africo – as would seem logical – but (as mentioned earlier) that on Natuzza Evolo, better known as Natuzza dei Morti. The smallest picture portrays two children seated at the same school desk. They are turned sideways and are deeply engaged in reading, under the gaze of their teacher, who seems to be semi-bent towards them, but whose face is not visible. The picture evokes an immediate sense of squalor: the children are visibly dirty and ragged; the foot of the child in the foreground is bare and sticks out of the desk, thus focusing the viewer's attention on the dirty floor covered with rubble; next to the foot there is a brazier, while at the other extreme of the desk are the teacher's large and dirty hands. The caption reads: "Africo (Reggio Calabria). In the mixed-sex school classroom. Windows are lacking, the heating is provided by the pupils themselves who put some embers into an old bowl. The problem of the *Mezzogiorno* has various aspects, but that of schools combines them together. It was not solved by the Fascist dictatorship, it will not be solved by any other dictatorship, but by the country's concern".

Two girls are portrayed in the largest photograph: they are seated at an antiquated wooden desk, too big for them, while reading their schoolbooks, following the line with their fingers; the wall behind their backs is clearly not plastered; the feet of the child in the forefront are bare, almost touching a brazier; her head is covered by a shawl which makes her seem a small-scale version of the stereotypical Southern woman. The caption reads: "Africo (Reggio Calabria). The mixed-sex school. Now on the eve of the poll, even the Calabrian population's poverty risks becoming an electoral issue. The propagandists come up from the plain trying to awaken men and women dazed by need".

Both the pictures are completely out of context. There is no evident linkage between the condition of Africo schools and the story of Natuzza Evolo. It thus appears that what is displayed by the pictures does not need any further explication, being an objective reality. The purpose is evidently to shock the viewer, without even attempting an analysis of the phenomenon, the terms of which are presented as self-evident. Even the captions do not provide any description or information other than the name of the village and the fact that the school was mixed-sex, something which was not perceived as positive in the immediate post-war period and could perhaps evoke a sense of moral as well as material dirtiness. At the same time, the caption of the smallest picture stresses the relevance of the issue of schools, which is defined as the sum of all those problems concerning the *Mezzogiorno*. The abject condition of school is thus not only an indisputable matter of fact, but also an emblem of the evils plaguing the South. Such a heavy problem can only be solved – the caption seems to indicate – through the intervention of the "country", without specifying if and how local populations should be involved.

The impact, particularly of the smallest picture, was huge: as Vito Teti has pointed out, the smallest picture attracted worldwide attention.[134] Moreover, it is still circulating today. The original version of the shot – depicting a total of six girls, all in the same pose in front of a backdrop of a partially torn map of Calabria – is indeed available on Gian Antonio Stella's popular website devoted to the promotion of his best-selling book *L'orda. Quando gli albanesi eravamo noi*.[135] In this case, it has been entitled "Third World Schools" and included in the website section "Italy as it was". The caption reports where and when it was taken, the photographer's name, and a series of statistical data on Italy's "historical delay" in dealing with its "appalling" rates of illiteracy, far higher than those of Northern European countries such as Germany, Austria, Switzerland, Sweden, Norway, Denmark, Holland, Belgium, and England. The data are thus meant to provide a 'scientific' explanation of the situation depicted in the picture, regardless of the fact that the children have been captured just in the act of reading. Illiteracy is, therefore, once again not referred to as the mere lack of certain skills, but as a moral issue and associated with deprivation and poverty. Moreover, the fact that the picture has been selected for publication on such a popular website, which is part of a larger investment by a leading Italian publisher, confirms its great and long-standing influence on collective imagery.

The extreme poverty and inadequacy of classroom furniture as well as its consequences on children's bodies constitute two of the main features of the photographic representation of Southern schools' 'otherness'. They characterized not only Tino Petrelli's pictures, but also those taken by the well-known photo-journalist Federico Patellani and published in *Epoca* in 1952. This time, the photographs accompanied an article focusing on the issue and significantly entitled "The impossible schools", whose author was Patellani himself.[136] As he pointed out, however, "the pictures presented here comment better than any words on those incredible scenarios".[137] More than his covert implication that Southern teachers and school personnel should be blamed for their presumed laziness and the subtle comparison between persons and animals, schools and stables or pigsties, it is the pictures that captivate the readers' attention.[138] The one next to the title and covering almost two pages is certainly the most striking. A row of three enormous, old-fashioned school desks and a big chair whose straw bottom is visibly holed are the real subjects; a child, with a shaved head and wearing an oversized tailored jacket, dirty trousers and clogs, is precariously balanced between his too-high desk and the chair; his left elbow partially covers his face, leaving only the eyes visible; his desk-mate does not even have a chair, while the frightened gaze of another child pops out from the row behind; a beret and a schoolbag lying on the floor further contribute to an impression of messiness and lack of order. The caption reads "Giant desks, bottomless straw chairs and the squalid poverty of a Jotta classroom. Many Southern schools are unfortunately in this almost incredible state of neglect". Unsuitable buildings and classrooms, dilapidated and obsolete school furniture and implements epitomized the backwardness of Southern schools. The twisted positions which children's bodies had to assume was the tangible proof that the South represented the negation of all the models of modern schooling, which established precise hygienic rules regarding desks, chairs, and, more generally, equipment. The inferiority of Southern schools' provision with respect to that of the rest of the country was furthermore underlined and transferred to children in the text of the article: the author mentioned Ghiandaro school, in the province of Cosenza, where the desks for second-grade pupils, aged between ten and twelve years, came from Northern nursery schools.

At the beginning of the 1960s, as a result of the various transformations occurring throughout the country and the expectations attached to the centre-left governments, schooling and education acquired new prominence. In March 1962, when it was announced that the failed ten-year government plan was going to be replaced by a three-year one and that 1,350 billion liras would be invested in education, the Turinese FIAT-owned newspaper *La Stampa* devoted a huge survey to the topic.[139] In presenting the series of articles – all written by Alberto Ronchey – to its readers, the paper described schooling as a "vital problem" for the present and, above all, for the future of the country. The issue of instruction for children aged between 6 and 14 years had to be addressed as a matter of urgency, since "in today's world, the prosperity and security of a State" depended on it.[140]

Ronchey's considerations are particularly indicative of the extent to which the discourse on education was strictly linked to that on modernization as well as of the enduring reproduction of a certain rhetoric. On one hand, the education system was not attuned to the needs of an industrialized society: Italy was reported to be the last country "in the modern world" where Latin was a compulsory subject and the demand for "technicians and skilled manpower" was still to be met.[141] On the other, though, important steps forward had been taken since the end of the war. "A still unknown 'Italian miracle'" had been made possible by greater financial investment in education and by an army of unemployed primary school teachers – "twenty thousand missionaries of the speller" – who, in order to get a stipend, had taken charge of gathering classes of illiterate adults wishing to attend school.[142] They were referred to as *maestri magri* (thin teachers) and, "without their poverty", the struggle against illiteracy would have never been so great.[143] Their task had been particularly arduous: "in today's world, adorned with posters, signs, papers, leaflets and books, the illiterate is alienated from his time and from material objects: he can hear [...] but he cannot decipher". Moreover, he "suffers because of his impairment, but is more ashamed of confessing it by attending school". It was thus extremely difficult to convince them to attend classes, since though "psychically normal" they were "obsessed with shame". The journalist emphatically announced, however, that illiterates' last reserve had been overcome by television. Its use as a didactic instrument had indeed offered them the "moral alibi" of being spectators instead of pupils.[144]

The centrality of education to the economic and social development of the country was clearly underlined by Ronchey's call for an immediate reform of middle school. The overwhelming changes Italy was witnessing had taken on the contours of a "social earthquake", whose epicentre was symbolically represented by school.[145] The increasing demand for schooling by the masses and the new "aspiration of the worker ranks" required the creation of a unified middle school, purged of the "classist discrimination" of the old one. The abolition of Latin and the inclusion in the curriculum of subjects like biology, physics, and chemistry – following the example of the United States and the Soviet Union – would help the training of future industrial personnel.

The obstacles to change came not only from the most conservative sectors of Italian society, but also from particularly backward areas exemplified by the case of Naples, to which one of the articles was devoted.[146] Represented as suspended between its picturesque image and a reality of economic, social, and moral depression, its condition testified that there could be no progress without schooling. Parents' unwillingness to send children to school, forcing them to work as errand boys or apprentices in small artisan shops, constituted the "calamity of Naples, the spiral that causes poverty". Lack of industry was almost completely due to the lack of skilled workers. Aware of the situation, teachers were desperately trying to break this vicious circle and to forge the local "miracle generation", but the desperate state of school buildings rendered their efforts useless: school had to rely on its "prestige" in order to change the "morality of the *bassi*".[147]

Neapolitans were not the only ones to be considered in need of pedagogical action in order to be directed towards development and progress. This was also the case of Southern migrants in Northern Italy. In Turin, as the title of the last of Ronchey's articles emphasized, the "anguishing problems of the South" were affecting schools. A "wave" of thousands of "new pupils", certainly "clever, but often undernourished and coming from primitive families" was undermining the stability of the "old and severe Piedmontese school", the sub-headline read.[148]

The arrival of Southerners was deemed responsible for the sudden rise in illiteracy rates in an area where the phenomenon had completely disappeared. Statistical data confirmed the accounts of teachers, depicted as the last bastion of the traditional rigour of local schools. Described as hungry, unable to read and write even though attending the fifth grade, slower and less prepared than their Turinese classmates, Southern children were clearly portrayed as a burden.

Both teachers and the journalist pointed their finger at families, whose characterization further contributed to the construction of the Southern pupil as disruptive and underachieving. A headmaster was reported to have denounced the case of parents forcing their children to beg, while in the *Casermette* (barracks) of *Borgo San Paolo*, where migrants were – in Ronchey's words – "living as if in a Calabrian-Lucanian village or in Naples alleys": the stereotypical image of "clothes hanging from one end to another of the parade ground" was combined with the reference to "straw mattresses, promiscuity and even some unexpected luxuries (some TV sets, motorbikes and even cars got from who knows what trading source)", suggesting that these people were constantly on the verge of deviance. Southerners had thus brought with them their living and moral habits and were deemed unable to meet Northern educational standards. They were hence putting Turin and its schools' proverbial order and leading role at risk. Although teachers' awareness that "the sub-proletarian world" was not to be held responsible for "its state", it was, however, imperative for the school "not to come down to the level of the slums, but [to] destroy them in the only possible way".[149] To destroy and rebuild the slums and their inhabitants in its own image, and to instil its superior values into them: this was what the school had the duty to accomplish.

2.3 'Others' in the classroom

Ronchey's view was not isolated and formed part of a wider discourse on Southern children attending Turin or, more generally Northern primary schools, during the years of post-war migrations. Teachers' periodicals also dealt with the issue, contributing to the dissemination among teachers themselves of an image of Southern pupils as unprepared, without proper familial guidance and needing particular care. This discourse, in which old and new *topoi* coalesced, influenced the attitude of primary school administrative and teaching personnel towards Southern pupils. However, in order to understand how these complex dynamics were operating, especially at a classroom level, it will be important to take power relations within primary schools into due account.

2.3.1 Teachers' journals

A year after its publication, the prominent teachers' journal *I diritti della scuola* drew on Rochey's article as a main source of information about the effects of Southern migrations on Turin primary schools. Large excerpts were quoted, including the definition of Southern families as "primitive", favouring the circulation of a negative image and the stereotypes they conveyed. Children's undernourishment, the "backwardness" of their level of preparation, the prevalent use of dialect and their exploitation by their parents were specifically brought to the attention of primary school teachers, who formed the target readership.[150] Journals were widely used by both pre- and post-war teachers who relied on them for their professional refreshment and for day-to-day didactic activities.[151]

I diritti della scuola was among the most popular. Founded in 1899, its main feature was the support it gave to the cause of laicism in education. It had also contributed at the beginning of the twentieth century to the foundation of the first Italian Teachers' Association *Unione magistrale nazionale* (UMN), of which it was the unofficial organ.[152] In the post-war period, notwithstanding the greater prominence of Catholic organizations among teachers and the disappearance of the UNM – dissolved by Fascism – it did not lose its readership and continued to be one of the "pillars of the teaching profession".[153] For this reason, its role in mirroring and shaping (and strengthening) teachers' collective views of Southern children should not be underestimated.

The piece published by *I diritti* and reporting the extracts from Ronchey's article was included in a survey, *Scuola e urbanesimo*, which, in spite of the use of generic and comprehensive terms, such as urbanization or internal migrations, was exclusively focused on migrations from the South towards the industrialized cities of the North and particularly the Piedmontese capital. The phenomenon – it was pointed out – was dramatically affecting local primary schools. Besides the lack of classrooms, ascribed to the increase in the school population, the sudden passage from the "old and traditional customs of a poor land [...] to the convulsive rhythm of an industrial city" was indicated as the main cause of "immeasurable problems".[154] If the former issue was slowly being remedied through the construction of new buildings, the main one still to be addressed was "the social integration of pupils".[155] Compelled to live in overcrowded and unhealthy houses,

Southern children could not even count on the help of their parents, who were affected by an "intellectual poverty due to scarcity of education and to the isolation from the surrounding social environment they live in".[156] Many children, having been forced to work in the fields with their parents, had "contributed to creating [a] mass of semi-illiterate and unprepared" pupils arriving in Turin.[157] Teachers were thus invited to go on "a short journey among the *'terroni'*, those Italians less lucky than many others", in order to "discover the youngster, the buds of that human tree that will produce its fruit with the help of the school".[158]

Edifying examples of the aid these children could be provided with by school were furnished by the pictures attached to the survey. One, for instance, portrayed a group of Southern children going to school, together with a dog, in Locana, a small town in Turin province. Their neat aprons and schoolbags demonstrated – the caption read – "the first beneficial effects" of the assistance provided by the local *patronato scolastico*.[159] In another one, instead, "a class of children from the South" was shown attending an "orthoepy lesson".[160]

The normalizing role of school and its effectiveness in changing Southern children's living habits was underlined by the contrast between these two pictures and a third depicting how the "children of emigrants from the South lived in the 'bidonvilles' on the outskirts of Turin".[161] A shack, with rubble and mud surrounding it, and two children stroking a dog tied to an old cart, symbolized the degradation in which they were immersed and from which school would rescue them.

The survey on school and urbanization was not, however, the first on the topic to be published by the periodical. In November 1962, an article by Fernando Rotondo, had already addressed the question of "childhood and internal migrations", offering the readers several examples of trite commonplaces and misguided assumptions. The author asserted that the South being "traditionally and notoriously prolific", a "large part" of the migrants were children. This statement was clearly unfounded, since the first to move usually were young males. However, it corroborated the image of a primary school almost overwhelmed by the "impressiveness of the phenomenon".[162]

Moreover, migrants were described as "the most dispossessed" among Southern families, to the extent that children were a "dead weight" to Northern schools. Their "integration" was supposedly hindered by several factors, above all, the family: "parents cannot give any spiritual help to their children, for whom the lack of an intellectually evolved and morally advanced familial tradition prevents any collaboration with the school". Teachers, on the other hand, did not understand the "particular psychology" of these children and did not take into due consideration their condition as "poor relics tossed from a remote rural world into mechanical civilization".

The proposed solution was to transform the school and its role completely, in order that it could restore "that cultural, moral and social unity which has crumbled". It also would help to remedy the harm caused by the "pseudo-racial pride" of many Northern youngsters, who habitually called their classmates from the South "*terroni*", considered all Southerners as 'scabs' and said that they ate soap. Racism was thus reduced by Rotondo to its external expression, while its supporting ideology which he helped to reproduce seemed not to be part of the problem. Rotondo's denigrating view of Southern children and their families indeed entailed and legitimized the existence of a hierarchy between Northern and Southern Italians. The use of an evolutionary vocabulary stressed the inferiority of the latter on the scale of progress.

The case of a Southern child had also been the subject of the column "Episodes of child psychology". Gianni, the eldest of three siblings, was attending the fifth grade. He had moved with his family from Monteburicchio – supposed to be a "Southern village" though the name was probably invented – to a Northern city.[163] In his town of birth "on the spurs of Sila", where he knew everybody, he was happy to go to school and eager to learn. Now, "in that city" – Turin – everything was different: he "used to feel at ease among expansive and perhaps rather noisy acquaintances", but he was not comfortable with "more reserved people who, above all, spoke a language he barely understood". Gianni spoke dialect and his teacher often reproved him. The cold and foggy environment of the city made him feel more and more lonely and sad. After a harsh reprimand, he decided to leave the school. One day – Gianni's father, a man with a "typically Southern figure" – approached the teacher who, after a quick conversation with him, entered the classroom and passionately explained to his pupils how sad their classmate was since he had nobody to help him. The children understood, and when the following day Gianni came back, both teacher and classmates were kind to him. Everything changed and, at the end of the school year, Gianni passed the final examinations. The text of the article was accompanied by the photograph of a ragged and sulky child, clearly representing a generic Gianni. Moreover, that picture was in sharp contrast with others – published on the same pages but referring to different sections – of children wearing clean aprons and intent on activities, such as painting, who represented the model of advanced and successful pupils to which children like Gianni had to conform.

Behind the mask of paternalistic benevolence, *I diritti* depicted Southern children attending Northern primary schools as problematic 'others'. This approach was consistent with the image offered by the general press, whose articles – as was the case of Alberto Rochey's piece – were often relied upon as if they offered an objective and neutral reproduction of reality.

2.3.2 *The local educational authorities*

Before focusing on the attitude of Turin primary school teachers towards their Southern pupils, it is worth analysing how the issue was regarded by the highest ranks in the local authorities. In Turin, city and province, since the second half of the 1950s, the arrival of migrants from the South – but also from different areas, such as the Veneto – engendered a sense of discomfort among primary school inspectors and heads of school. "Immigration" was continuously identified with deviations from the norm and was reported to cause a considerable increase in failure and truancy among pupils. The latter – along with their families – were commonly viewed as threatening the order of local schools and jeopardizing their renowned tradition.

In the school year 1958–59, the rates of failure – which for the first and fourth grades was, by order, adopted only as an exceptional measure – had been so high that the then *Provveditore agli studi* (the provincial representative of the Ministry of Public Instruction), Ernesto Lama, demanded an explanation from the heads of school.[164] One from Rivoli – a town of the province and among the most affected by migration both from the Veneto and the South – was adamant that the majority of pupils failing in the first grade were children of "families coming from Southern Italy or from the Western provinces of Northern Italy". The main reasons for failure were: "undernourishment", which had presumably caused "severe mental deficiencies"; lack of "school assistance" by parents; and an absence of "clothes and shoes suited to our climate", which prevented children from attending classes regularly. Neither new nor traditional teaching methods had proved of use for these children. Moreover, many of them were "really abnormal" and had been referred to "Turin mental health services".[165]

A year later, in 1960, a school inspector – presenting his job plan for the district he was in charge of to the *Provveditore* – underlined the "particular condition" Turin was experiencing, owing to the presence of Southerners. The new incoming pupils were indeed "unprepared to face school and social life in a big Northern city". And, in spite of the "eminent" and enduring educational importance of local schools at a national level, the difficulties in dealing with this question were "neither few nor light". He thus suggested that the "socio-educational action" had to be aimed not only at children but also at "immigrant families".[166] The "moral disorder of [immigrant] families more than their poor economic condition" was the main reason for truancy – according to one of his colleagues too.[167]

These opinions were expressed not only in bureaucratic reports or exclusively by the middle ranks of officialdom. In 1966, Lama himself participated – as the *Provveditore*, but also as president of an association named *Unione immigrati e meridionali* (Immigrants and Southerners Union) – in a TV debate, devoted to migrations from the South and chaired by the well-known journalist, Ugo Zatterin.[168] In his view, "the moral problem, the spiritual problem, the problem of a contrast between cultures" lay at the heart of the issue of both Southern children and adults.[169] Southerners were moving into a "higher civilization, where they [were] looking for a job and for better and more elevated living conditions [and] in which they have to integrate themselves". What he wished for, and – as he declared – "all the regional and provincial associations" were aiming at, was a "fusion, [which] we hope to be better and better". Moreover, he attributed the introduction of the widely deplored two or three shift system (*doppi o tripli turni*) to the "sudden and massive presence of immigrants bringing here enormous number of new children".[170]

The *Provveditore* should have been aware, however, that the problem was pre-existing. During the Fascist regime, overcrowding in Turin primary schools constituted a source of concern for local education authorities. In November 1938, the then *Provveditore* complained to the Ministry of National Education about the growth of the primary school population and the consequent lack of teachers, which was forcing them to adopt an 'alternate schedule' (*orario alternato*).[171] Some teachers were thus in charge of two classes, to be taught for three hours each. In spite of the fact that each class could not comprise more than forthy pupils, at the beginning of the school year 1938–39, 511 classes out of 1,045 did not respect this limit. In some schools, third- and fourth-grade students were taught in classes of eighty each. Demographic increase and the "immigration of the working family" to areas such as *Barriera di Milano*, *Borgata Monterosa* and *Borgo San Paolo* – working-class neighbourhoods where war-time and civil factories were located – were reported to have triggered this undesirable situation.[172]

After the war, the problem was still unresolved as a result of the damage caused by bombings of school buildings, many of which were also used as temporary houses for evacuees. One of the effects was the scarcity of classrooms and the overcrowding in classes. In 1948, some of them consisted of more than seventy children.[173] Only in 1955, when internal migration was already affecting Turin, was the programme of reconstruction of the old buildings in fact completed.[174] Yet, in the following years, buildings fell short of the needs of a growing population. Indeed in 1961, the two-shift system was in force for 375 classes, indicating that at least 500 more classrooms were still to be built.[175]

2.3.3 Teachers' attitudes

The existence of a huge gap dividing Southerners from all other children and making them almost irremediably 'different' was strongly felt by teachers too. Even in schools located in peripheral neighbourhoods, whose social landscape was extremely varied, children from the South and their families were often regarded as a problem more serious than any other.

This was the case of the primary school "Margherita di Savoia". It was situated in the working-class suburb of *Lucento*, which, since the aftermath of the Second World War, had witnessed the coming of several groups of people, such as refugees from the Eastern border or those repatriated from the former colonies.[176] Remarkable also was the number of those arriving from the *Veneto*, especially in the first half of the 1950s. However, migrations from the South were more substantial and frequent and their effects were more strongly felt. Throughout the 1960s, the number of children born in the *Mezzogiorno* and attending the "Margherita di Savoia" was remarkable in comparison with the previous decade, as an examination of the class registers reveals.

Already in the second-half of the 1950s, however, these pupils were associated with problems of various kinds. In March 1956, for instance, a first-grade teacher, A.T., complained about the "confusion" they brought with them, especially if they arrived when the school year had already started: "[they are] in a pitiful condition, lacking everything".[177] It is interesting to note that this comment was meant by the teacher to justify the "faults" and the "lacunae" found by the head of school during one of his periodical inspections of the class. Heads of school were in charge of evaluating teachers' performance and behaviour – both inside and outside the school – at the end of every school year, giving them a mark called *nota di qualifica*. For this reason, they used to "visit" the class – as teachers euphemistically reported in their registers – and test pupils. Teachers were thus assessed through the performance of their pupils. The "Margherita di Savoia" head of school was adamant that their "intense daily work must shine through pupils' mental and disciplinary preparation and through all their [pupils'] scripts".[178] The *nota di qualifica* played a significant role in teachers' careers. A high mark, confirmed for more than one year, could improve their chances of being transferred to a preferred school or site. Yet the criteria followed by the heads of school were frequently arbitrary: many were not willing to award a high mark to the youngest simply on account of their lack of experience, and irrespective of their ability and conduct.[179]

The *qualifica* was not the only burden the teaching staff had to endure. They were also obliged, for example, to reside where the school was situated. Moreover, even their personal lives and habits were under strict control. At the *"Margherita di Savoia"*, teachers had a long list of duties: they had to be punctual and provide an "example of morality"; they could not smoke; they could not receive calls from strangers; they had to avoid "all those things which could distract [them] from [their] work"; they had to collaborate with the head of school; they had to communicate with the secretaries with "speed and efficiency", keep pupils' families informed of the behaviour of their children and make them sign the exercise books; they had to write the register clearly and "without erasures and abrasions", note down the names of the absentees day by day, and give to the register's reader "a wide and precise idea of school life, of all the pupils in their physical, psychical and moral aspect without hiding the difficulties encountered while carrying out [their] educational task".[180]

This system of authoritarian surveillance, as well as the enormous load of responsibilities, were among the heaviest legacies of Fascist educational policies: in the post-war period, the teacher still was the "'inferior' to be entrusted to the watchful care of the superiors", as had been the case during Fascism.[181] These 'superiors', particularly heads of school, were both feared and adulated. Women teachers, more than men, did not miss an opportunity to praise the usually male headmaster for his "precious advice" dispensed during the inspection, for his "cordial and lively language, awakening the sympathy of the schoolchildren".[182] Some of them even openly stressed their agreement and support for his instructions, conscious that he would read their comments as part of his periodical examination of the register:

"Through an internal circular, the *signor Direttore* reminds us of the importance of religious teaching, justly considered by the current curriculum the foundation and crown of educational activity. I perfectly agree and I shall do my best to ensure that the whole educational action is permeated by a true and sincere religious spirit".[183]

The rituals of Catholicism permeated and, in some cases, obsessively marked school time. The initiative taken by the head of school of transmitting "sacred music every day through the loudspeaker" was welcomed as "excellent" by a teacher. Along with her pupils – all girls – she prayed and listened to the music in order to "offer God the school day".[184]

This submissive attitude was the legacy of the subaltern role to which women – both as students and teachers – had been relegated in the years of the regime. As Victoria De Grazia has tellingly pointed out in her study of women under the dictatorship, the Gentile Reform was "avowedly anti-feminist".[185] The number of *Istituti Magistrali* (Teacher Training Schools) – mostly attended by women – was drastically reduced from 153 to 87[186]. Furthermore, the *Liceo Femminile* (Female Lyceum) was created. It gave no access to university and was intended to provide the daughters of the bourgeoisie with the basic notions "fit for the intellectual and moral needs of the young ladies".[187] Its underlying aim was to relieve the *Liceo Classico* – the pinnacle of the selective and elitist secondary school system of Gentile – of the growing number of girls attending it.

At a professional level, in 1926 women were no longer allowed to teach Italian language and literature, Latin, Greek, history, and philosophy at the *licei* or Italian and history at the Technical Institutes. In 1928, they were forbidden to become principals of middle schools.[188] As primary school teachers, they were under rigid discipline both inside and outside the school. In 1934, the Minister of National Education, De Vecchi, ordered them not to put on make-up, to wear dark clothes, to be "morally austere" and of "genteel demeanour", and to "sacrifice every vanity happily and proudly" in accordance with their "superior maternal ideal".[189]

It is difficult to evaluate whether and to what extent they offered any resistance to this situation. According to Ester de Fort, even the most "independent and emancipated [...] were instrumental in an ideology extolling traditional feminine qualities (passivity, subordination)".[190] It can thus be hypothesized that those who had received their training or started their career in the course of the *Ventennio* were particularly likely to consider obedience and obsequious deference to male superiors as a duty. They probably experienced greater pressure than their male colleagues.

Such an unequal distribution of power within primary schools between teachers and the head of school, which – it can be supposed – was likely to affect women especially, is important for the understanding of teachers' attitudes towards Southern children. It is also worth underlining that the register itself was an instrument of control in the hands of the head of school. The comments of both women and male teachers on their pupils were thus certainly influenced by the function the register exerted and were meant above all to induce a positive assessment of their performance. As a result, teachers frequently relied on Southern schoolchildren's presumed 'deprivation' and underachievement – commonly assumed to be indisputable matters of fact – as an extenuating circumstance for their alleged shortcomings. On the other hand, however, it can be argued that their perception was consistent with the public discourse on Southern boys and girls, not dissimilar from those analysed in the previous section of this chapter.

Dirty

The above-mentioned teacher, A. T. reported a significant episode in her register:

"This morning the mother of a boy came here, looking very sad, and said that a 'big thing' had happened. Frightened, I ask the reason for her pain and I learn that she has seen two lice on the kid's head. I shuddered. In these days, among boys! I thank her for having informed me and I take measures. There is an immigrant from the South next to him: I examine him well and I write on his exercise book the warning to come back only when free from all that filth".[191]

This teacher was not the only one to suggest a link between Southerners and dirt. Another one, too, regretted that the apron of a seven-year-old boy from Sardinia, G. U., whose father was unemployed – as she had already mentioned when describing his "disordered movements" – was filthy. She declared herself sympathetic to him, however, since he could not be blamed for "living in a pigsty". He felt so "mortified for being so dirty" – she continued – "that he washes himself at school. His parents will be happy: they save soap (if they have it)".[192] The reference to the uncleanness of these two children was not a neutral observation, lacking any underlying value judgement. As the anthropologist Mary Douglas noted, the notion of dirt is rooted in a symbolic system and its cultural meaning is that of "matter out of place".[193] Dirt is a breach of the established order, it is "essentially disorder".[194] Remarking that people are dirty implies that they are not conforming to the standards of the society in which they live and from which they are separated by the boundary of cleanliness. These standards are based on the criterion of 'civilization'. As a teacher underlined in her register: "the civilized child shows himself to be clean".[195] The filthy bodies of the two Southern boys symbolized a deviation from the hygienic norms, which lay at the foundations of school – and more generally societal – organization and in respect of which the teacher had to pass judgement.

Moreover, since the end of the nineteenth century, an equivalence was drawn between soap and civilization. Soap figured in Victorian advertising campaigns as an allegory of the British civilizing mission in the colonies.[196] In Italy, the Fascist postcards picturing Italians, adults and children, bringing personal cleaning practices to unaware and sometimes reluctant Africans were widely circulating during the war against Ethiopia.[197] The suspicion that the Sardinian boy's parents did not possess soap alludes to their primitiveness.

Underachieving, maladjusted, less clever

The school performance of Southern children was also generally considered poor. Not only at the "Margherita di Savoia", but also at another school, the "Giovanni Enrico Pestalozzi", teachers often emphasized their underachievement.

Like the "Margherita di Savoia", this school was located in a working-class neighbourhood named "Barriera di Milano". Since the turn of the century, the area had been characterized by the installation of industrial plants and the settlement of people coming from outside Turin and working in the nearby factories. Particularly during the 1920s, the opening of the *Fiat Grandi Motori* attracted an unprecedented number of people.[198] The school was built between 1904 and 1906 in the *borgata Monte Bianco* and throughout the years, the number of children attending it grew in proportion to the expansion of the neighbourhood, to the extent that in 1939, it counted 1576 enrolled pupils.[199]

After the war, the school – and the neighbourhood, as well – was again affected by migration. The number of schoolchildren was high: in the school year 1962/63, there were 1001 for the main site, located in via Banfo, while the smaller branch, in via Ceresole, was attended by 607.[200] A huge proportion of these were of Southern origin, as the class registers show. Here too, particularly throughout the 1960s and 1970s, they raised concerns and were viewed as objects of particular attention. In April 1962, for example, a "didactic conference" on the "maladjustment of the immigrant pupil" was co-organized by the "Pestalozzi" and another primary school, the "Giuseppe Parini", and was attended by all the teaching staff.[201] One of them, E.T., a male, underlined how interesting it had been, owing to the "great number of the «maladjusted» populating our classes because of the remarkable immigration to our city". The "problem" – he went on – was "serious and not easy to solve"; it was "afflicting" Turin schools and its "human aspects [were] striking the inner chords of the souls of the educators of the people".[202]

This was not the only case of schools holding such conferences. In the same school year, Don Luciano Allais was invited by an inspector to give a talk on Southern children hosted by the primary school "Antonino Parato".[203] Don Allais had founded in 1961 the *Centro assistenza immigrati* (CAI, Centre for the Assistance of Immigrants) and had already promoted charitable activities for the migrants in a parish of the *Barriera di Milano*. The CAI was funded with contributions from the public, ecclesiastical organizations, and private donors, such as FIAT, banks, and the association of local industrialists. In the first-half of the 1960s, it offered religious and economic support for the new arrivals. Both Southern and Piedmontese priests were responsible for visiting migrant families and collecting information regarding their living conditions and their religious and moral habits. As Don Allais pointed out, Southern priests "talked the same dialect and have in their souls the same feelings and the same mentality [as the families]".[204] The priests teamed up with social workers, trained in Catholic schools, of the social service run by the *Opera nazionale assistenza religiosa e morale degli operai* (ONARMO, National Organization for Workers' Religious and Moral Assistance).[205] The main aim of the CAI was to bring the migrants closer to the local Catholic community, whose religious traditions and practices they did not share: as Don Vincenzo Serra – a leading figure of the CAI – put it, "the religious life of the Southerners bears the psychological characteristics of their temperament: lively sentiments, intense emotions, difficulty with perseverance".[206] At the same time, in the view of another priest – Don Antonio Denisi, from Reggio Calabria – the morality of the Southerners was influenced by the "regime of constraint, sometimes even of slavery, that unfortunately rested on the peoples of those regions for many centuries and that psychologically still is a remarkable burden on their social life".[207] They therefore needed to be instructed and educated in order to prevent moral disorientation in both themselves and their children.

Don Allais had thus probably been asked to give a talk to the teachers of the "Antonino Parato" as one of the most prominent persons dealing with the migrants and particularly with those from the South. During the meeting, he focused on the troubles that Southern children had to face in their new living environment, advising teachers on ways to help "these maladjusted".[208]

The use of the term maladjusted to refer to migrant children – above all those from the South – was not uncommon in Turin and, more generally, in the whole industrial triangle during those years. Borrowed from psychiatric and psychological discourse, the concept of maladjustment broadly indicated a condition of non-adaptation to the surrounding environment, which, in the case of children, could lead to school failure, behavioural disruptiveness, or even juvenile delinquency. Numerous psychiatrists, psychologists, social workers, and criminologists suggested that Southern migrant children – and also adults – found it extremely difficult to adjust to the new and more developed North-Western environment, owing to the deprivation and inherent inferiority of their culture. These issues will be discussed in detail in the next chapter. It is, however, worth highlighting here that the ease with which teachers employed the label maladjusted is an indication of the popularization of the concept itself especially in reference to migrants.

Maladjustment was only one of the several problems supposedly affecting migrant children. The teacher E.T. was also convinced that their poor performance was principally due to their insufficient intelligence. In the school year 1962/63, his fourth-grade all-male class consisted of thirty-four boys, of whom twenty were born in Turin, seven in the South, two in the Veneto, one in the province of Rome, and the rest in other areas of Piedmont.[209] From the first school day, he complained about his pupils, whom he had already taught during the previous year. Fifteen of them had passed only because of his "notable indulgence". However, too many continued to underachieve. Language skills were inadequate: the dictations were filled with mistakes, as a result of lexical ignorance. "Here it is not a matter of teaching methods" – he explained – "but of limits imposed by scarce natural gifts; and our classes, every year more crowded because of immigration, are even more burdened by these insufficiently gifted elements".[210]

Underachievement was also attributed to the fact that the preparation provided by Southern schools was not as good as that ensured by Northern or Turin schools. The male fourth-grade teacher E. G., reporting the "remarkable lack of preparation" of two of his pupils, commented that they had "attended the third grade in Southern towns [and that] the gap is clear, and is most unlikely to be made up".[211] One of them moved after a few days to another school, while the other, at the end of the school year, was failed.

In some cases, especially those who had just arrived in Turin, children were put one or more grades back: the ten years old T., who arrived in December 1960 from Brindisi, in Apulia, was considered by her new teacher "absolutely unable to attend the fifth grade" and – in agreement with her parents – was sent back to the previous grade.[212]

Poor and neglectful families

Great importance was given to families for children's education at the "Margherita di Savoia" and the "Pestalozzi" as well as at other schools. Their collaboration was deemed indispensable for children's school success. Some teachers praised them for the help and support they provided "with patience and constancy" and singled out mothers for their "fervour".[213]

Not all the families, however, satisfied what were believed to be the requirements of effective cooperation. This disregard was usually seen as linked to their economic condition and was supposed to influence not only their performance, but also the acquisition of certain behavioural and hygienic norms. Many of the thirty-seven first-grade girls taught by G.A. at the "Pestalozzi" belonged to families "in needy condition, [all living] in a very poor and distressing environment".[214] Their poverty – according to the teacher – prevented them from being clean and tidy, since "girls bring with them the values of their homes and express them in the smallest things".[215] Their hair lice too were "the result of their familial untidiness caused by cohabitation in small houses and by the absolute lack of the most elementary hygienic norms".[216] Their untidiness must certainly have appeared far less tolerable than that of their male peers. The attribution of responsibility

for children's messiness was also gendered and called into question the capacity of needy mothers to look after their sons and daughters: a woman
teacher proposed that "some mothers who do not have the slightest idea of
tidiness and cleanness" should be given a "special education". By contrast,
she praised mothers belonging to well-off families for bringing clothes and
shoes to be distributed among those lacking them.[217]

Poor migrant families were presumed to be less concerned about the education of their children than poor locals. There were some exceptions –
though these were regarded as an unexpected anomaly. The teacher V. C.,
introducing his all-males third-grade class, specified that "almost all the
pupils are children of factory workers who have migrated from various
parts of Italy, and as a result they are not wealthy". "*Nevertheless*", he
added "none is neglected by his parents": they were well clothed; they got
the school equipment, and the parents were supportive.[218]

Indigent families were entitled to receive assistance from the *patronato
scolastico*, a charitable organization whose aim was to provide hard-up pupils with free meals, books, stationery, shoes, and clothes and to organize
after-school activities (*doposcuola*). Established initially at the end of the
nineteenth century, the institution of the *patronato* was made compulsory
for communes in 1911 by the Daneo Credaro Law. Its members usually were
local notables – who might fund it – together with school officials, headmas-
ters, and teachers.[219] During the Fascist regime, the *patronati* were absorbed
into the *Opera nazionale Balilla* (ONB, National Balilla Organization), but
in the post-war period they were reinstated.[220] Besides giving material assistance, they were meant to make it possible for the school to "recover for
society" those children whose "familial assistance" was deficient. The president of the National Association of the *patronati scolastici* declared in 1955:
"the poor child must find in the school what the family refuses him [...],
he must find those institutions [...] that not only keep him away from the
street but direct him toward a sound social life".[221] Moreover, they had to
neutralize social conflict and exert a key educational role. According to the
Turin *Provveditore agli Studi*, Ernesto Lama, their main role was to make
it possible for the pupils, rich and poor, to "consider themselves as equals"
and help in the creation of "ties of friendship that will continue during adulthood".[222] The school meal, in particular, especially if it could be provided to
all the schoolchildren – regardless of family income – was envisaged as promoting "concord among social classes", the ministerial inspector Carmelo
Cottone pointed out.[223] However, if it was given solely to needy children,
it was important to ensure that the latter were not "morally humiliated",
that the school-meal service was delivered in a "humane and decent" way,
and that to the "nourishment of the body was added that of the spirit".[224] In
reality, schoolchildren aided by *patronato* were likely to be stigmatized as
poor. Their condition of poverty was not only made public by the fact that
they were given the school meal and stayed at school in the afternoon for the
doposcuola, while all the other children went back home. They were also

involved in a series of ceremonies that emphasized their subordinate position within the class and the school community as a whole. For example, the distribution of shoes took place in front of their classmates, and the beneficiaries – as a teacher made clear – were "bound to wear them during the school days and *compelled* (and I say compelled) to write a letter of thanks".[225] Moreover, they were expected to express their gratitude continuously by preserving what they had been granted: "the bad state to which some pupils have reduced the shoes of the *patronato* is striking and demonstrates the carelessness of the pupils, but perhaps above all of their families".[226]

The percentage of Southern children among those receiving assistance was high. There was a widespread belief that their parents' "only interest is not the school but the free school meal".[227] Southern mothers and fathers were thus conceived of as unable to understand the importance of schooling and, above all, as acting only under the impulse of need and hunger. Instinct and nature prevailed in them over intellect and morality, making them closer to animals than to model mothers and fathers well aware of the value of education to their children. At the same time, the idea that Southerners viewed school exclusively as a means to get a lunch for free contributed to the dissemination of the stereotype of the parasitic migrant from the *Mezzogiorno,* irresponsibly depleting local resources. Both these notions – that of animalized families and that of the parasites of the community – were widely aired by the press. Besides informing its readers of the high percentage of Southern children helped by the *patronato*, the local newspaper *La Stampa* reported stories like that of a girl from Calabria who had "never seen the dishes on the table" since in her family, the habit was to "eat all together from the cauldron" without using forks and napkins.[228]

Dialect speakers

Another marker of Southern children's 'otherness' was dialect. Its use was claimed by teachers to be an almost insurmountable impediment to Southern pupils' learning of the Italian language. While for those coming from the Veneto, it was more generally assumed only to have a negative effect on orthography, Southern dialects – often referred to as a single entity – were thought to be the source of major and more comprehensive problems of expression. The possibility of speaking both Italian and dialect was dismissed from the outset: a girl from Palermo was described as "struggling between Italian and Sicilian" and reported to be "surprised when [her teacher] employs words less elementary than usual".[229] According to some teachers, pupils would require an indefinite amount of time in order to remedy the mistakes engendered by the Southern dialect: "a month or a year in our school will not be enough, and perhaps the whole course of primary school as well", one of them warned.[230]

These attitudes towards dialect were certainly not a novelty. Since unification, school had been a major instrument for the dissemination of Italian as a national language to replace the cluster of local dialects which characterized the linguistic landscape of the country. The effort to eradicate the dialects formed part of the nation-building project, following a path not dissimilar from that of other European nation-states.[231] The debate on the *questione della lingua* (language question) influenced education policies and revolved around the arguments between the advocates of the adoption of Florentine as a common idiom to the detriment of the others and those opposed to the disappearance of dialects.[232] Overall, it was the first stance the adption of Florentine that prevailed. However, the results of the 1864 Matteucci inquiry – responsible for investigating the condition of the education system in post-unification Italy – raised alarm about the widespread use of dialects even by primary school teachers, who were unable themselves to talk and write properly in Italian.[233] The 1867 new curriculum issued by Minister Michele Coppino prescribed that teachers should employ the *"lingua patria"* and correct constantly the "imperfections deriving from the dialect of the province".[234] The following curricula – particularly that of 1905 – contained an increasingly pronounced *dialettofobia* (dialect-phobia), even though anti-dialect measures turned out to be rather ineffective, as the bureaucrats of the Ministry of Education continued to lament.

The Gentile Reform marked a turning-point, owing to the introduction by Giuseppe Lombardo Radice – General Director of the Ministerial Department for Primary Education – of the "from dialect to language" method. Exercises in translation from the regional dialect into Italian were among the most important innovations.[235] The ultimate aim of this approach, though, was the acquisition of Italian, and dialect continued to play a "subordinate role", since it was still considered to engender orthographic and grammatical mistakes.[236] Moreover, teachers did not seem particularly keen to adopt the new guidelines, and ideas about the inferiority of dialect and the "prejudice that [it] was something to be avoided before the majesty of language" persisted.[237] This opening-up towards dialect was not destined to last long. Fascist linguistic nationalism resulted in the elimination of any reference to dialect from the 1934 curriculum, while great prominence was attached to Italian grammar, thereby emphasizing the normative aspects of language teaching.[238]

In the post-war period, the 1955 curriculum – replaced by a new one only in 1985 – continued to prescribe the eradication of the *malerba dialettale* (dialect weeds): teachers were explicitly forbidden to talk in dialect to their pupils and were encouraged, especially for the last three grades, not to miss "any opportunity to wean them from idiotic mistakes and solecisms".[239] Only from the 1970s did traditional anti-dialect policies and practices start to be opposed. The content of the primary school curriculum revealed once again the deep divide between the educational institutions and the cultural and social background of the majority of Italian pupils. In 1951, dialect was indeed the "usual idiom to be used in any circumstance" for two-thirds of the population.[240] However, internal migrations and urbanization were among the factors that, throughout the 1950s and the 1960s, changed the linguistic situation of the country and encouraged the abandonment of dialects in favour of Italian.[241] Great importance was also attached by the curriculum to orthoepy, despite the fact that – according to the linguists – Italian being predominantly a written language, a standard and uniform pronunciation did not exist.[242] This characteristic of the national idiom favoured the affirmation of what has been defined as "school Italian" (*italiano scolastico*). As Arturo Tosi has noted, "this special language tended to replace everyday lexis with conventional 'proper' expressions". Tosi also reports some examples: *arrabbiarsi* (to get angry) became *adirarsi* (to lose one's temper); *mi stanco a fare* (I get tired doing) became *mi stanco nel fare* (I get tired in the doing).[243] Michele Cortelazzo has underlined how the "distinctive character of this variety [of Italian] is its autonomy with respect to any other variety, also written, of Italian" and that it was particularly widespread in Italian schools between the 1930s and the 1970s.[244]

In this context of stigmatization of dialects – which characterized not only the school environment but more generally post-war Italian society – the social prestige of those spoken in the South was even lower than that of the others. Research carried out since the second-half of the 1970s sheds light on the negative attitude towards Southern dialects and accents. Nora Galli de' Paratesi's survey conducted in three different cities – Milan, Florence, and Rome – showed the "indisputable discrimination" against Southern pronunciation defined as "foreign", "Arab", "disgusting", and "bad Italian".[245] This derogatory view was not uncommon even among the Southerners themselves and became more accentuated if the dialect-speaker was a woman.[246] It can thus be hypothesized that similar dynamics influenced teachers' judgements. I.R., for instance, imputed the difficulties with expression and the orthographic mistakes of the third-grade girls she was teaching to the "Ostrogothic dialects spoken by their families" and to "Southern wrong pronunciation".[247] The use of dialect seemed to be peculiar to Southern children only, in spite of the high rates of pupils coming from Turin province and the countryside where local dialects were still largely employed. It thus became further evidence of Southern children's distance from the norm and of their 'otherness'.

Notes

1   Pavone C., "La continuità dello Stato. Istituzioni e uomini", in Piscitelli, E., (ed.), *Italia 1945–48. Le origini della Repubblica*, Turin, 1974, pp. 139–289. Now in Pavone, C., *Alle origini della Repubblica. Scritti su Fascismo, antifascismo e continuità dello Stato*, Turin: Bollati Boringhieri, 1995, pp. 70–159.

2   Idem, p. 72.

3   Idem, p. 73.

4   For an overview of the history of Italian education in the post-war period, see Sani, R., Pazzaglia, L., (eds), *Scuola e società nell'Italia unita. Dalla legge Casati al centro-sinistra*, Brescia: La Scuola, 2001, particularly section II.

5   Ricuperati, G., "La scuola nell'Italia unita", *in Storia d'Italia*, Vol. V, *I documenti*, Turin: Einaudi, 1973 p. 1714.

6 Fadiga Zanatta, A.L., *Il sistema scolastico italiano*, Bologna: Il Mulino, 1971, p. 60.
7 Dei, M., "Cambiamento senza riforma: la scuola secondaria superiore negli ultimi trent'anni", in Soldani, S., Turi, G., (eds), *Fare gli italiani. Scuola e cultura nell'Italia contemporanea*, Vol. II, Bologna: Il Mulino, 1993, pp. 87–127.
8 Idem, p. 112.
9 Idem, p. 113.
10 Ibidem.
11 De Palma, G., "Risposte parlamentari alla crisi del regime: un problema di istituzionalizzazione", in Graziano, L., Tarrow, S., *La crisi italiana*, vol. II , *Sistema politico e istituzioni*, Turin: Einaudi, 1979, p. 378. See also Id., *Surviving without Governing. The Italian Parties in the Parliament*, Berkeley: University of California Press, 1977.
12 De Palma, G., *Suriving Without Governing*, cit., p. 121.
13 The issue of the "great transformation" of post-war Italy and of the failure by the political parties, both the majority and the opposition, in ruling it is the main theme of Guido Crainz's study on the period between the economic miracle and the 1980s. See Crainz, G., *Il paese mancato. Dal miracolo economico agli anni Ottanta*, Rome: Donzelli, 2003.
14 Pavone, C., cit., p. 140.
15 Melis, G., "Apparati di stato e democrazia repubblicana", *Quale Stato*, 4, 2006, p. 397.
16 Idem, p. 398.
17 Disciple of Hans F. K. Gunther, one of the most popular Nazi racial theorists, in the midst of the war, Gayre managed to publish one of his major works, *Teuton and Slav on the Polish Frontier*, in which he indicated the lack of "racial homogeneity" of nations as the main problem in Europe and "proposed that Germany's eastern border be redrawn to make [...] 'the Germans [...] considerably more Nordic'". See Tucker, W.H., *The Funding of Scientific Racism: Wickliffe Draper and the Pioneer Fund*, Urbana: University of Illinois Press, 2002, p. 91. See also Gayre, R., *Teuton and Slav on the Polish Frontier*, London: Eyre and Spottiswoode, 1944. After the war, Gayre founded and edited for many years the journal *The Mankind Quarterly* and was a member of the Executive Committee of the International Association for the Advancement of Ethnology and Eugenics (IAAEE). The main aims of both the journal and the IAAEE were to provide 'scientific' support to the campaign against the desegregation of American education and to oppose UNESCO's anti-racist stance. See Tucker, *cit.*, and Jackson, J.P., *Science for Segregation: Race, Law and the Case against Brown v Board of Education*, New York: New York University Press, 2005.
18 Gayre, G.R., *Italy in Transition*, London: Faber and Faber, 1946, p. 17.
19 Hearst, J.A., *The Evolution of Allied Military Government Policy in Italy*, PhD dissertation, Columbia University, 1960, p. 261 quoted in Sarracino, V., Piazza, R., *La ripresa: scuola e cultura in Italia (1943–1946)*, Lecce: Pensa Multimedia, 1998, p. 21.
20 Idem, pp. 81–2.
21 Washburne, C., "La riorganizzazione dell'istruzione in Italia", in *Scuola e città*, n. 6–7, 1970, pp. 273–7, quoted in Fornaca, R., *I problemi della scuola italiana dal 1943 alla Costituente*, Rome: Armando, 1972, p. 60.
22 Ibidem.
23 Idem, p. 61.
24 Allied Control Commission – Education Sub-commission, *La politica e la legislazione scolastica in Italia dal 1922 al 1943. Con cenni introdutivi sui*

periodi precedenti e una parte conclusiva sul post-fascismo, Milan: Garzanti, 1947, pp. 388–9 cited in Ascenzi, A., "L'educazione alla democrazia nei libri di testo: il caso dei manuali di storia", in Sani, R., Corsi, M., (eds) *L'educazione alla democrazia tra passato e presente*, Milan: V&P strumenti, 2004, p. 66.

25 Rodari, G., "Ragazzi nuovi e libri vecchi", *L'Unità* (Milan edition), 30 October 1947, cited in Ascenzi, *cit.*, p. 68.

26 Bacigalupi, M., Fossati, P., *Da plebe a popolo. L'educazione popolare nei libri di scuola dall'Unità alla Repubblica*, Florence: La Nuova Italia, 1986, p. 254.

27 Tomasi, T., *La scuola italiana dalla dittatura alla Repubblica 1943–1948*, Milan: ER, 1976, p. 17. On Ferretti see also D'Alessandro V., *Gino Ferretti e il rinnovamento della pedagogia*, Florence: La Nuova Italia, 1959; Patanè, L., (ed.), *Gino Ferretti*, Catania: Trincale, 1983.

28 *Programmi di studio e indicazioni didattiche per le scuole elementari per l'anno scolastico 1943–44. Parte seconda. Consigli per la modernizzazione della scuola elementare*, Printed and Distributed by the Allied Military Government, Palermo: Ires, 1943 cited in Sarracino, V., Piazza, R., *La ripresa. Scuola e cultura in Italia (1943–1946)*, Lecce: Pensa Multimedia, 1998, p. 49.

29 Idem, p. 52.

30 See Sarracino, V., Piazza, R., *cit.*, pp. 45–73.

31 Fornaca, R., *I problemi della scuola italiana dal 1943 alla Costituente*, Rome: Armando, 1972, p. 70.

32 *Programma, istruzioni e modelli per le scuole elementari e materne* (D.M. 9 febbraio 1945) quoted in Sarracino, *cit.*, p. 94.

33 *Programma, istruzioni e modelli*, *cit.*, quoted in Sarracino, V., *cit.*, p. 88.

34 Bonetta, G., "La scuola dell'infanzia", in Cives, G., (ed.), *La scuola italiana dall'Unità ai giorni nostri*, Florence: La Nuova Italia, 1990, p. 36.

35 Damilano, A., (ed.), *Atti e documenti della Democrazia Cristiana*, I, Rome, Cinque Lune, 1968, pp. 236–8 quoted in Canestri, G., Ricuperati, G., *La scuola in Italia dalla legge Casati ad oggi*, Torino, Loescher, 1976, pp. 227–8.

36 Ibidem.

37 Ambrosoli, L., *La scuola in Italia dal dopoguerra ad oggi*, Bologna: Il Mulino, 1982, p. 22

38 Damilano, A., (ed.), *cit.*, p. 228.

39 Fornaca, R., *cit.*, p. 83.

40 Galfré, M., *Una riforma alla prova. La scuola media di Gentile e il Fascismo*, Milan: Angeli, 2000, pp. 115–16. Fedele supported the teaching of both Church and Christian history in high schools and his 1925 curricula warned teachers that anything disturbing the "religious and moral conscience" of the pupils had to be avoided. See Idem, pp. 246–49.

41 All the documents are now available on the official website of the Vatican http://www.vatican.va/roman_curia/secretariat_state/archivio/documents/ rc_seg-st_19290211_patti-lateranensi_it.html#CONCORDATO_FRA_LA_ SANTA_SEDE_E_LITALIA [last time accessed 20/9/2021]

42 Religion had, however, already invaded Italian schools before the signing of the Concordat. In 1922, for example, the under-secretary Dario Lupi decided that the crucifix had to be displayed in classrooms. Parish priests and religious authorities were invited to attend and actively participate in school ceremonies. Teachers' morality was often considered as strictly related to their observance of Catholicism. See Galfré, M., *cit.*, pp. 116–17.

43 On the debate about the article 7 of the Constitution see Gambino, A., *Storia del dopoguerra. Dalla Liberazione al potere DC*, Rome: Laterza, 1975.

44 See Fornaca, *cit.* and Tomasi, *cit.*

45 Galfré, M., *Tutti a scuola! L'istruzione nell'Italia del Novecento*, Rome: Carocci, 2017.
46 Ambrosoli, L., cit., p. 43.
47 Semeraro, A., *Il mito della riforma. La parabola laica nella storia educativa della Repubblica*, Florence: La Nuova Italia, 1993, p. 61.
48 Semeraro, cit.
49 Ambrosoli, cit., p. 44.
50 Ibidem.
51 The Commission, whose works lasted until the end of April 1949, analyzed the results of a questionnaire regarding several aspects of school life. Thousands of teachers, principals, and bureaucrats took part in the survey, which excluded, however, students, parents, and trade unions. It also published its own periodical, *La riforma della scuola*. See Ambrosoli, cit., pp. 47–8.
52 Barbagli, M., *Educating for Unemployment. Politics, Labor Markets, and the School System. Italy, 1859–1973*, New York: Columbia University Press, 1982. Moreover, the bill provided that "religious teaching" was not a subject as any other, but the "source, the highest and most authoritative, for the whole educational work in its principles and supreme ends". Quoted in Ambrosoli, cit., p. 59.
53 See Dei, M., "Travaglio e apoteosi del movimento cattolico magistrale: 1924–1948", *Rivista di storia contemporanea*, XVI, 1, 1987, p. 85–115. See also Id., "Le elezioni magistrali dal 1909 al 1924: un approccio sociologico", *Rivista di storia contemporanea*, XIV, 4, 1985, p. 554–86. The unprecedented success of Catholic organizations was probably the result , according to Dei, of the increasing presence of the Church in the field of teachers' private training schools (*istituti magistrali*) during Fascism and after the Second World War. On the history of teachers' associations, see also De Fort, E., "L'associazionismo degli insegnanti elementari dall'età giolittiana al fascismo", *Movimento operaio e socialista*, IV, 4, 1981, pp. 375–404.
54 Barbagli, M., cit.
55 "Una campagna contro la disoccupazione degli intellettuali", in Gonella, G., *Cinque anni al Ministero della Pubblica Istruzione. Vol. 2: Libertà della scuola e nuovi ordinamenti scolastici*, Milan: Giuffrè, 1981, p. 83. It is also interesting to note that Gonella considered primary school teachers' and, more generally, intellectual unemployment not only as a social and economic problem but, above all, as a threat to the established order: "the social order" – he pointed out – "can be shattered not only by the unrest of the masses, but also by the slow deterioration and the consequent fall of those forces of the moral resistance, which are exactly the intellectual classes". Ibidem.
56 D.L. 17 Dicembre 1947, no. 1599.
57 See Lorenzetto, A., "La lotta contro l'analfabetismo e l'educazione degli adulti", *Il Ponte*, VI, 5, 1950, pp. 455–70.
58 "L'istituzione della scuola popolare. Un piano di lotta contro l'analfabetismo", in Gonella, G. *Cinque anni al Ministero della Pubblica Istruzione. Vol. 2*, cit., pp. 204–6.
59 Barbagli, M. cit.
60 Badaloni, M., "Scuola dei poveri?", *Il maestro*, 11, 1949 quoted in Barbagli, cit., p. 293
61 Barbagli, M., cit.
62 Ambrosoli, L., cit.
63 "L'insuccesso dell'alunno nella scuola primaria", *Scuola di base. Bollettino bimestrale del Centro didattico nazionale per la scuola elementare e il completamento dell'obbligo scolastico*, 1958, p. 2.

64 On the centre-left governments, see Ginsborg, P., *A History of Contemporary Italy: Society and Politics, 1943–1988*, London: Penguin, 1990; Crainz, G., *Il paese mancato. Dal miracolo economico agli anni Ottanta*, Roma: Donzelli, 2005.

65 Ambrosoli, L., cit.

66 On the complex and prolonged parliamentary debate leading to the passage of the bill, see Ambrosoli, cit, particularly Chapter five.

67 L. 31 December 1962, no. 1859.

68 Ambrosoli, cit., p. 71.

69 Tornatore, L., "Scuola media per tutti", *Scuola e città*, XV, 1, 1964 p. 8.

70 Idem, p. 11. The author wondered if the "contents and the mental processes" involved in IQ tests were "more familiar in a certain socio-cultural context" and if both the IQ tests and the school "unjustly favoured a certain type of youngster". These questions remained in the background, however, and did not prevent her from treating the "inferiority" of lower-class students as a matter of fact. See p. 11–12.

71 Idem, p. 13.

72 Dei, M., Barbagli, M., *Le vestali della classe media. Ricerca sociologica sugli insegnanti*, Bologna: Il Mulino, 1969, p. 8.

73 Idem, p. 81.

74 Ibidem.

75 Idem, p. 92.

76 Idem, p. 95.

77 Ambrosoli, p. 85. See also Ricuperati, G., "La politica scolastica", in Barbagallo, F., (ed.), *Storia dell'Italia repubblicana*, II, 2, Turin: Einaudi, 1995, pp. 707–78.

78 Codignola, T., *Nascita e morte di un piano. Tre anni di battaglia per la scuola pubblica*, Florence: La Nuova Italia, 1962, p. 4.

79 This Plan – as well as the previous – was based on the research provided by the SVIMEZ on the growth of the Italian economy, the changes in the job market and the ways in which education could meet the requirement for more skilled professional figures. The forecasts turned out to be totally wrong. See SVIMEZ, *Mutamenti nella struttura professionale e ruolo della scuola. Previsioni per il prossimo quindicennio*, Rome: Giuffrè, 1961; Id., *Trasformazioni sociali e culturali in Italia e loro riflessi sulla scuola*, Rome: Giuffrè, 1962.

80 The commission was made up of 31 members, including those of the opposition, and its works lasted between October 1962 and July 1963. The results are in Ministero della Pubblica Istruzione, *Relazione della commissione d'indagine sullo stato e sullo sviluppo della pubblica istruzione in Italia*, 2 voll., Rome, 1963. See Ambrosoli, cit. For a more positive judgement, see Ricuperati, cit.

81 See Bonetta, cit., p. 38.

82 See articles 1 and 7 of the law 18 March 1969, no. 444 "Ordinamento della scuola materna statale". It was no coincidence that the school was defined as *maternal*.

83 Medici, G., *Introduzione al piano di sviluppo della scuola*, Rome: Istituto Poligrafico dello Stato, 1959, p. 9.

84 Graff, H.J., *The Literacy Myth. Literacy and Social Structure in the Nineteenth Century*, New York: Academic Press, 1979, p. 36. For an overview of the different approaches to literacy, see Street, B.V., *Literacy in Theory and Practise*, Cambridge: Cambridge University Press, 1984.

85 Aschcroft, B., *On Post-colonial Futures: Transformations of Colonial Culture*, London: Continuum, 2001.

86 See Spurr, D., *The Rhetoric of the Empire: Colonial Discourse in Journalism, Travel Writing and Imperial Administration*, Durham: Duke University Press, 1993.

87 Newton, A.P., "Africa and Historical Research", XXII, 88, 1923, p. 267 quoted in Bernardi, B., Poni, C., Triulzi, A., (eds), *Fonti orali: antropologia e storia*, Milan, Angeli, 1978, p. 118.

88 Vigo, G., "Gli Italiani alla conquista dell'alfabeto", in Soldani, S., Turi, G., (eds), cit., pp. 37–66. Santoni Rugiu, A., *Storia sociale dell'educazione*, Milan: Principato, 1987.

89 *Atti Parlamentari, Camera*, Session of 20 January 1874, p. 770 and 784 quoted in Chabod, F., *Italian Foreign Policy*, Princeton: Princeton University Press, p. 226.

90 Ibidem.

91 Villari, P., "La scuola e la questione sociale in Italia", *Nuova Antologia*, 1 November 1872 now in *Le lettere meridionali e altri scritti sulla questione sociale in Italia*, Naples: Guida, 1979, p. 158.

92 Villari, P., "Di chi è la colpa? O sia la pace e la guerra", *Il Politecnico*, September 1866 now in *Le lettere meridionali*, cit., p. 136. For Villari's contribution to the construction of the Southern Question see Dickie, J., *Darkest Italy*. cit. See also Moe, N., *The View from Vesuvius*.cit.

93 Massari, G., *Il brigantaggio nelle province napoletane. Relazione dei deputati Massari e Catsagnola colla legge sul brigantaggio*, Milan: Ferrario, 1863, p. 24 quoted in Broccoli, A., *Educazione e politica nel Mezzogiorno d'Italia, 1767–1860*, Florence: La Nuova Italia, 1968, p. 212.

94 For an analysis of the statistical data throughout the twentieth century and for interesting considerations on their effective reliability, see De Fort, E., *Scuola e analfabetismo nell'Italia del Novecento*, Bologna: Il Mulino, 1995.

95 Relazione del ministro della Pubblica istruzione E. Daneo sul progetto di legge *Provvedimenti per l'istruzione elementare e popolare* quoted in Bonetta, G. *Scuola e socializzazione in Italia fra '800 e '900*, Milan: Angeli, 1989, p. 81.

96 See Dickie, J., *Una catastrofe patriottica. 1908: Il terremoto di Messina*, Rome: Laterza, 2008. Dickie underlines how particularly for Zanotti Bianco, the earthquake represented an "existential turning point". p. 130.

97 Isnardi, G., "L'attività educativa-scolastica dell'Associazione", in *L'Associazione nazionale per gli interessi del Mezzogiorno d'Italia nei suoi primi cinquant'anni di vita*, Rome: Collezione Meridionale, 1960, pp. 195–207.

98 Fusco, M., "L'Associazione nazionale per gli interessi del Mezzogiorno nella lotta contro l'analfabetismo (1910–1928)", Estratto da *Archivio Storico per le Province Napoletane*, XX, 1981, p. 25.

99 Idem, p. 27.

100 Malvezzi, G., Zanotti Bianco, U., *L'Aspromonte occidentale*, Milan: Libreria Editrice Milanese, 1910. On Zanotti Bianco and his work on education in the South see Misiani, S., "Educazione e tutela del paesaggio nell'azione meridionalista di Umberto Zanotti Bianco", *Meridiana*, 46, 2003, pp. 213–40.

101 Malvezzi, G., Zanotti Bianco, U., cit., p. 3.

102 Idem, p. 74.

103 Idem, p. 80.

104 Ibidem.

105 Idem, p. 81.

106 Salvemini, G, "La scuola popolare in provincia di Reggio Calabria", *Nuova Antologia*, 1 February 1910, now in Borghi, L., Finocchiaro, B., (eds) *Opere di Gaetano Salvemini. Scritti sulla scuola*, Milan: Feltrinelli, 1966, pp. 977–1000.

107 Idem, p. 978.

108 Idem, p. 984.

109 Idem, pp. 992–5.

110 Idem, p. 1000.

111 The so-called *Opera contro l'analfabetismo* was established in 1921. The creation in scarcely populated areas of schools for illiterate adults and of primary schools for children of compulsory education age was delegated by the state to private associations such as the ANIMI, the *Ente scuole per i contadini dell'Agro Romano*, the *Società umanitaria*, the *Consorzio nazionale dell'emigrazione e lavoro*. In 1923, it was transformed into the *Comitato contro l'analfabetismo*, but in the following years, the administration of the schools was progressively transferred from the delegated agencies to the *Opera nazionale Balilla*. See De Fort, E., *La scuola elementare dall'Unità alla caduta del Fascismo*, Bologna: Il Mulino, 1996. On the participation of the ANIMI and its renounce to the delegation in 1928 see Isnardi, G., cit.

112 *L'opera contro l'analfabetismo nella Sicilia orientale (1921–1922)*, Rome, ANIMI, 1923, pp. 50–64 quoted in De Fort, E., *Scuola e analfabetismo nell'Italia del Novecento*, cit. pp. 173–4.

113 Zanotti Bianco, U., *Il martirio della scuola in Calabria*, Florence: Vallecchi, 1925 (second edition), p. 7. In the introduction, written in the form of a letter to Giuseppe Lombardo Radice – who was then serving as Director-General of Primary Education – and dated March 1923, the author expressed his hope that the Gentile Reform did not follow, as it had already been the case in the past, "a uniform criterion for the whole Nation" (p. 8).

114 Idem, p. 71.

115 Ibidem.

116 Idem, pp. 72–3.

117 Klein, G., *La politica linguistica del Fascismo*, Bologna: Il Mulino, 1986, p. 30.

118 De Fort, E., *Scuola e analfabetismo nell'Italia del Novecento*, cit., pp. 247–8.

119 Marchesini, D., "Città e campagna nello specchio dell'analfabetismo", in Soldani, S., Turi, G., *Fare gli italiani*, cit., Vol. 2, p. 16.

120 See Chapter 1.

121 "L'Italia rinascerà dalla scuola", in Gonella, G., *Cinque anni al Ministero della Pubblica Istruzione*. Vol. 2, cit.,p. 117.

122 Idem, p. 118.

123 See Section "Post-war Italian education: a historical overview" in this chapter.

124 See for instance, his article on Calabrian schools published in *Il Ponte* or his contribution to the conference *Processo alla scuola* organized by the association *Amici del Mondo* and held in Rome in February 1956. Zanotti Bianco, U., "Il problema della scuola", *Il Ponte*, VI, 9–10, 1950, pp. 1149–54; Battaglia, A., (ed.), *Dibattito sulla scuola*, Bari: Laterza, 1956. He also addressed the Senate particularly on school buildings. See Misiani, S., "Educazione e tutela del paesaggio nell'azione meridionalista di Umberto Zanotti Bianco", cit., p. 238.

125 Scotellaro, R., "Scuole di Basilicata –I", *Nord e Sud*, I, 1, 1954, pp. 74–5. The survey was published in two parts. In the second part, Scotellaro underlined that "as a psychological and social fact, in its more typical expressions, illiteracy is linked beyond the economic conditions to a certain form of civilization. The lack of associated life and passive participation to State matters cause illiteracy". Scotellaro, R., "Scuole di Basilicata – II", *Nord e Sud*, II, 2, 1955, p. 87.

126 Tomasi, T., "Mezzo secolo di attività dell'Associazione per gli Interessi del Mezzogiorno d'Italia", *Scuola e città*, XII, 6, 1961, p. 227. The article was a review of a book on the history of the association published by the ANIMI itself in 1960. In Tomasi's view, Italian teachers almost completely ignored the real conditions of the areas where they were operating and the fact that their role as educators in a modern society was not limited to the mere teaching of notions and abilities. On the contrary, she thought that they should have co-operated with doctors, social workers, psychologists, and economists.

127 From the report *Un anno di lavoro dell'Unione nazionale per la lotta all'anal-fabetismo* quoted in Lorenzetto, A., "La lotta contro l'analfabetismo e il problema dell'educazione degli adulti", *Il Ponte*, VI, 5, 1950, p. 462.

128 Lorenzetto, A., *Alfabeto e analfabetismo*, Rome: Armando, 1962, p. 18.

129 Idem, p. 23.

130 Idem, p. 26.

131 Pinna, G., *Due problemi della Sardegna. Analfabetismo e delinquenza*, Sassari: Gallizzi, 1955, pp. 5–6. Pinna was criticized by Antonio Pigliaru, who argued that the rate of crimes was lower in areas with a higher percentage of illiteracy, such as the province of Cagliari. See Pigliaru, A., "Scuola e banditismo in Sardegna", *I problemi della pedagogia*, 1, 4, 1955, pp. 80–111.

132 Quoted in Semeraro, A., "Educazione e sviluppo nel Mezzogiorno. Momenti di un dibattito del dopoguerra", *Studi Storici*, 31, 4, 1990, p. 904.

133 Besozzi, T., "L'errore del vescovo di Mileto", *L'Europeo*, 14 March 1948.

134 Teti, V., *Il senso dei luoghi: memoria e storia dei paesi abbandonati*, Roma: Donzelli, 2004.

135 Stella, G.A., *L'orda. Quando gli Albanesi eravamo noi*, Milano: Rizzoli, 2002; http://www.speakers-corner.it/rizzoli/stella/immagini/foto/popup/italia-scuole.htm [last time accessed: 26/10/2022].

136 Patellani, F., "Le scuole impossibili", *Epoca*, 28 giugno 1952, pp. 44–8.

137 Idem, p. 45.

138 Patellani not only stressed that Southern school buildings often were former stables but added that in many cases "the teacher's words [were] continuously commented upon by cows' moos and pigs' grunts" coming from nearby sheds. Moreover, he reported having seen a calf in a Calabrian classroom and that neither the animal nor its foul-smelling breath seemed to cause any problem to either the teacher or the pupils.

139 The first article was: Ronchey, A., "C'è un milione di analfabeti adulti che si possono recuperare con trenta miliardi", *La Stampa*, 4 March 1962.

140 Ibidem.

141 Ibidem.

142 Ibidem.

143 This almost completely forgotten aspect of Italy's post-war illiteracy campaign has inspired Gian Antonio Stella's novel, *Il maestro magro*, Milan: Rizzoli, 2005.

144 Ibidem.

145 Ronchey, A., "La scuola media unica è una necessità urgente e chiara nell'Italia 'del miracolo'", *La Stampa*, 14 March 1962.

146 Ronchey, A., "Il sole di Napoli non giunge nelle aule ricavate da rifugi di fortuna", *La Stampa*, 23 March 1962.

147 Ibidem.

148 Ronchey, A., "Sulla scuola della cintura di Torino si ripercuotono gli angosciosi problemi del Sud", *La Stampa*, 31 March 1962.

149 Ibidem.
150 Tannozzini, F., "Scuola e urbanesimo. Inchiesta sull'emigrazione dal Sud al Nord", *I diritti della scuola*, LXIII, 14, 1 May 1963, p. 11–12.
151 According to the 1980s survey conducted by Marcello Dei on a sample of about 1500 former teachers, born not beyond 1910, 88% of men and 95% of women regularly used journals to prepare their classes. The author underlines how journals were an important part of their "professional equipment". See Dei, M., *Colletto bianco, grembiule nero. Gli insegnanti elementari italiani dall'inizio del secolo al secondo dopoguerra*, Bologna: Il Mulino, 1994, p. 162.
152 On the foundation of the *Unione magistrale nazionale* see De Fort, "L'associazionismo degli insegnanti elementari dall'età giolittiana al Fascismo", cit.
153 Dei., M., *Colletto bianco*, cit., p. 160.
154 Tannozzini, F., "Scuola e urbanesimo. Inchiesta sull'emigrazione dal Sud al Nord", *I diritti della scuola*, LXIII, 13, 15 April 1963, p. 11.
155 Idem, p. 12.
156 Tannozzini, "Scuola e urbanesimo. Inchiesta sull'emigrazione dal Sud al Nord. Cfr. n. 13", *I diritti della scuola*, LXIII, 14, 1 May 1963, p. 11.
157 Id., "Scuola e urbanesimo. Inchiesta sull'emigrazione dal Sud al Nord. Cfr. n. 13", *I diritti della scuola*, a. LXIII, 15, 15 May 1963, p. 18.
158 Ibidem. *Terrone* is a slur used by Northern Italians to refer to Southern Italians.
159 Tannozzini, F., cit., 15 April 1963, p. 12. The *patronato scolastico* was a charitable organization in charge of providing assistance for poor pupils. See section "Teachers' attitudes".
160 Ibidem.
161 Idem, p. 11.
162 Rotondo, F., "Infanzia e migrazioni interne", *I diritti della scuola*, LXIII, 4, 15 November 1962, p. 12.
163 Parente, G., "Un fanciullo e l'ambiente", *I diritti della scuola*, LXII, 16, 1 June 1962, pp. 24–5.
164 Turin State Archive (TSA), Provveditorato agli Studi, Folder 608.
165 Ibidem.
166 TSA, Provveditorato agli Studi, Folder 596, *Ispettorato scolastico. I Circoscrizione. Piano di lavoro annuale, 8 October 1960*.
167 Ibidem.
168 Bisiach, G., "I dibattiti televisivi: i meridionali al Nord", *Vie Assistenziali*, X, October 1966, pp. 44–48. The debate was broadcasted on national television on 18 May 1966.
169 Idem, p. 45.
170 Idem, p. 47.
171 TSA, Provveditorato agli studi, Folder 596, *Lettera del Regio Provveditorato agli Studi al Ministero dell'Educazione Nazionale, 16 November 1938*.
172 Id., *Relazione sulla situazione numerica delle classi e sui posti da insegnanti del Regio Ispettorato-I Circoscrizione, 29 October 1938*.
173 Id., *Ispettorato-I Circoscrizione al Provveditore agli Studi, 30 November 1948*.
174 Moraglio, M., "Amministrazioni locali e infrastrutture a Torino: 1945–1967", in Levi, F., Maida, B., (eds), *La città e lo sviluppo. Crescita e disordine a Torino, 1945–1970*, Milan: Angeli, 2002, pp. 395–433.
175 Cereja, F., "La crisi della scuola tradizionale e l'avvento della scuola di massa", in Tranfaglia, N., (ed.), *Storia di Torino. IX. Gli anni della Repubblica*, Turin: Einaudi, 1999, p. 773.

176 On the post-war refugees from Istria in Turin and particularly in *Lucento* see Miletto, E., *Con il mare negli occhi. Storia, luoghi e memorie dell'esodo istriano a Torino*, Milan: Angeli, 2005.

177 Archive of the Primary School "Margherita di Savoia", Registrer by A.T., Main Site, I grade male, 1955–56.

178 Archive of the Primary School "Margherita di Savoia", Circular found in the Register by M.O., Main Site, I grade, female, 1958/59.

179 On these points see Dei, M., *Colletto bianco, grembiule nero*, cit.

180 Archive of the Primary School "Margherita di Savoia", Register by I.R., Main Site, III grade male, 1960/61.

181 De Fort, E., "I maestri elementari italiani dai primi del Novecento alla caduta del Fascismo", *Nuova Rivista Storica*, 68, 1984, p. 537. A rigorously hierarchical structure – whose emblem became the figure of the "principal – *duce*" was also imposed by the Gentile Reform over high schools. See Galfré, M., *Una riforma alla prova*. cit. The definition of "principal-*duce*" has been coined by Antonio Santoni Rugiu, *Il professore nella scuola italiana*, Florence: La Nuova Italia, 1968. The rigid control over middle and high school teachers persisted in the post-war period. See Barbagli, M., Dei, M., cit. On the figure of the primary school teacher from the unification to the Republic see also Ulivieri, S., "I maestri", in Tomasi, T., (ed.), *L'istruzione di base in Italia. 1859–1977*, Florence: Vallecchi, 1978.

182 Archive of the primary school "Margherita di Savoia", Register by I.R., Main Site, I grade male, 1962/63.

183 Archive of the primary school "Margherita di Savoia", Register by M.T.F., Main Site, II grade female, 1962/63.

184 Archive of the primary school Margherita di Savoia", Register by L.M., Main Site, I grade female, 1964/65.

185 De Grazia, V., *How Fascism ruled women: Italy, 1922–1945*, Berkeley: University of California Press, 1992, p. 147. It is important to note, however, that the hostility towards women's education was already widespread before Fascism's rise to power. Carmela Covato has noted that, even though the Casati Law did not contain any explicit norm preventing women's access to secondary education, the prejudice against co-education and against the possibility for women to widen their culture was rather common at least since the unification. Until the first years of the nineteenth century, thus, "women's presence in upper secondary education was [...] an absolutely marginal phenomenon from the quantitative and social point of view". The high percentage of women attending primary school teachers training institutes (*scuole normali*) – far higher than that of men – was a consequence of their willingness to accept worse-paid and uncomfortable jobs. Moreover, it was generally believed that a "woman's natural destiny was to be a housewife or an educator". See Covato, C., "Educata a educare: ruolo materno e itinerari formativi", in Soldani, S., (ed.), *L'educazione delle donne: scuole e modelli di vita femminile nell'Italia dell'Ottocento*, Milan: Angeli, 1989, pp. 131–45.

186 Tonini, C., "Le maestre a scuola negli anni Trenta", in Gagliani, D., Salvati, M., *La sfera pubblica femminile. Percorsi di storia delle donne in età contemporanea*, Bologna: Clueb, 1992, pp. 155–62.

187 Gentile, G., *La riforma della scuola. Discorso tenuto il 15 Novembre 1923 al Consiglio Superiore della Pubblica Istruzione*, Bari: Laterza, 1294, p. 17 quoted in Barbagli, M., cit. p. 132. The creation of the *liceo femminile* was strongly criticized by feminists and subsequently even by women of proven Fascist faith. Having been almost deserted by girls, whose families considered it of no use, it was dismantled in 1928 See De Grazia, V., cit.

188 De Grazia, V., cit.

189 Tonini, C., cit., pp. 159–60.

190 De Fort E., "I maestri elementari italiani dai primi del Novecento alla caduta del Fascismo", cit., p. 576.

191 Archive of the Primary School "Margherita di Savoia", Register by A.T., Main Site, I grade male, 1955–56.

192 Archive of the Primary School "Margherita di Savoia", Register by V.F., Main Site, I grade mixed-sex, 1957/58.

193 Douglas, M., *Purity and Danger. An Analysis of the Concepts of Pollution and Taboo*, London: Routledge, 1966, [1991] p. 36.

194 Idem, p. 2.

195 Archive of the Primary School "Margherita di Savoia", Register by I.R., I grade, males, 1962/63.

196 McClintock, A., *Imperial Leather: Race, Gender and Sexuality in the Colonial Context*, London: Routledge, 1995.

197 Some examples can be found in Centro Furio Jesi (ed.), *La menzogna della razza. Documenti e immagini del razzismo e dell'anti-semitismo fascista*, Bologna: Grafis, 1994.

198 Castrovilli, A., Seminara, C., *Storia della Barriera di Milano,* Torino: Associazione culturale Officina della memoria, 2004.

199 Idem, pp. 162–5.

200 Archive of Turin City Council (ATCC),Ufficio Igiene e Sanità,cat. IX, cl. 2, fasc. 1, 1962, *Situazione scolastica 1962-1963.*

201 Archive of the Primary School "Gian Enrico Pestalozzi", register by E.C., I grade males, via Ceresole branch, 1962/63.

202 Archive of the Primary School "Gian Enrico Pestalozzi, register by E.T., IV grade, males, Main Site, 1962/63.

203 Archive of the Primary School "Antonino Parato", Register by S.A., III grade, mixed sex, "Balbis Garrone" branch, 1962/63.

204 Allais, L., "L'opera dei cattolici torinesi per l'integrazione degli immigrati nella nuova comunità. Una recente iniziativa nelle parrocchie cittadine: il Centro assistenza immigrati", *Atti del Convegno sui problemi assistenziali religiosi e morali relativi agli immigrati in Torino* quoted in Margotti, M., "La Chiesa cattolica di Torino di fronte ai processi di modernizzazione: il caso dell'immigrazione (1945–1965)", in Levi, F., Maida, B., (eds), cit., p. 87.

205 The ONARMO had been set up during the 1930s by monsignor Ferdinando Baldelli. The organization was closely tied to the Fascist regime and the industrialists. On its activities in Turin, particularly in the years of the Second World War, see Reineri, M., *Cattolici e Fascismo a Torino. 1925–1943,* Milan: Feltrinelli, 1978.

206 Quoted in Margotti, cit. p. 93.

207 Quoted in Margotti, cit. p. 94.

208 Archive of the Primary School "Antonino Parato", Register by S.A., cit.

209 It is unfortunately impossible to identify children born in Turin to Southern parents.

210 Archive of the Primary School "Gian Enrico Pestalozzi", Register by E.T. cit.

211 Archive of the Primary School "Margherita di Savoia", Register by E.S., Main Site, IV grade, males, 1959/60.

212 Archive of the Primary School "Margherita di Savoia", Register by M.D., Main Site, V grade, females, 1960/61.

213 Archive of the Primary School "Gian Enrico Pestalozzi", Register by A.S., I grade, female class, Main Site, 1962/63.

214 Archive of the Primary School "Gian Enrico Pestalozzi", Register by G.A., I grade, female class, Main Site, 1961/62.

215 Ibidem.

216 Ibidem.

217 Archive of the Primary School "Gian Enrico Pestalozzi", Register by G.G., II grade, male class, Main Site, 1961/62.

218 Archive of the Primary school "Margherita di Savoia", Register by V.C., III grade, male class, Main Site, 1959/60. Emphasis is mine.

219 See Inzerillo, G., *Storia della politica scolastica in Italia: da Casati a Gentile*, Rome: Editori Riuniti, 1974.

220 The *Opera nazionale Balilla* was a Fascist youth organization set up in 1926. Its male members were commonly called *Balilla*.

221 Stagnoli, G., "Aspetti educativi dell'assistenza scolastica", *Notiziario dell'Ufficio provinciale Attività assistenziali italiane e internazionali di Roma. Atti incontro di studio sull'assistenza scolastica organizzato dall'Attività assistenziali italiane e internazionali e dalla Associazione dei Patronati scolastici. Lido di Roma, 24–25 Aprile 1955*, 29 July 1955, pp. 39–40.

222 TSA, Provveditorato agli Studi, cartella 581, *Circolare del Provveditore agli Studi agli Ispettori scolastici di Torino e Provincia, 21 Ottobre 1958*.

223 Cottone, C., "Cosa sono e cosa potrebbero essere i centri di assistenza scolastica e di ricreazione", in *Atti del primo convegno dei centri educativi ricreativi*, Excerpt from *Assistenza d'oggi*, VII, 4, August 1956, p. 9.

224 Ibidem.

225 Archive of the Primary School "Margherita di Savoia", Register by M.D., V grade, female class, Main Site, 1960/61. Emphasis in the text.

226 Archive of the Primary School "Margherita di Savoia", Register by A.P., II grade, mixed-sex, Main Site, 1959/60.

227 Archive of the Primary School "Aristide Gabelli", Register by M.P., II grade, female class, Main Site, 1960/61.

228 "Un allievo su sei alle elementari appartiene a famiglie bisognose", *La Stampa*, 7 February 1958.

229 Archive of the Primary School "Margherita di Savoia", Register by V.F., I Grade, Mixed Sex Class, Main Site, 1957/58.

230 Archive of the Primary School "Aristide Gabelli", Register by I.B., II Grade, Male Class, Main Site, 1960/61.

231 On the links between nation-building and language in historical perspective see Hobsbawm, E., *Nations and Nationalism since 1870. Programme, Myth and Reality*, Cambridge: Cambridge University Press, 1992.

232 The bibliography on the *questione della lingua* is huge. Groundbreaking has been De Mauro, T., *Storia linguistica dell'Italia unita*, Rome: Laterza, 1963 [1984]. See also Steinberg, J., "The historian and the *Questione della lingua*", in Burke, P., Porter, R., (eds), *The Social History of Language*, Cambridge: Cambridge University Press, 1987, pp. 198–209.

233 Coveri, L., "Dialetto e scuola nell'Italia unita", *Rivista Italiana di Dialettologia*, 5–6, 1981–82, pp. 77–97.

234 Idem, p. 80.

235 See Klein, G., cit. and Coveri, L., cit.

236 Klein, G., cit., p. 57.

237 Terracini, B., "I rapporti tra i dialetti e la lingua", *Educazione nazionale*, 1927, p. 509 quoted in Coveri, L., cit.

238 Klein, G., cit.

239 Coveri, L., cit., p. 91.

240 De Mauro, T., cit., p. 131.

241 De Mauro, T., cit.

242 Corrà, L., Marcato, G., Ursini, F., Vigolo, M.T., "Dialetto e cultura", in Cortellazzo, M., (ed.), *Guida ai dialetti veneti*, Padua: CLUEP, 1981, pp. 233–309.

243 Tosi, A., *Language and Society in a Changing Italy*, Clevedon: Multilingual Matters, 2001, p. 68.

244 Cortellazzo, M.A., "Per una storia dell'italiano scolastico", in Cortellazzo, M.A., *Italiano d'oggi*, Padua: Esedra, 2000, pp. 91–109, p. 105.

245 Galli de' Paratesi, *Lingua toscana in bocca ambrosiana. Tendenze verso l'italiano standard: un'inchiesta sociolinguistica*, Bologna: Il Mulino, 1984 p. 166.

246 Baroni, M.R., *Il linguaggio trasparente. Indagine socio-linguistica su chi parla e chi ascolta*, Bologna: Il Mulino, 1983.

247 Archive of the Primary School "Gian Enrico Pestalozzi", Register by I.R., III grade, female class, Main Site, 1963/64.

3 Southern children and special education

The main aim of the previous chapter was to investigate the articulation of post-war discourse on Southern migrants' 'otherness' within the field of primary education. From the press to primary school teachers, the idea that Southern pupils represented a problem in Turin primary schools in the 1950s and the 1960s was generally accepted as a fact.

Post-war primary school education, however, was characterized by the growing intervention of experts, such as, for instance, child psychiatrists and psychologists, over issues regarding pupils' performance and, more generally, their well-being. There was also an unprecedented expansion of special education. As will be discussed in the section "Italian special education" of this chapter, the interest of these experts in primary education dated back at least to the beginning of the century. In the 1950s and 1960s, though, their role in relation to the social transformations witnessed by Italian society and by the education system acquired increasing prominence. Problems including the high rates of failures were interpreted as symptoms of children's maladjustment to be solved and prevented through the organization of an effective special education system.

The collaboration of the experts with primary schools offered the former an enormous amount of 'raw material' for studying and identifying different categories of maladjusted children. Southern migrant children attending Northern primary schools were one of these categories. The question was approached in different ways, depending on the author. Overall, however, these studies contributed to the scientific legitimation of Southern migrant children's 'otherness'. This process influenced day-to-day practices in Turin primary schools, including the "Margherita di Savoia" and the "Gian Enrico Pestalozzi". In these schools – as well as in others – from the 1950s (and increasingly in the next two decades), it was not uncommon for Southern pupils to be referred to special education classes called *classi differenziali*. Though not all Southern students were sent to these classes, the classes themselves consisted mostly of pupils born to Southern families. At the "Gian Enrico Pestalozzi", for example, in a 1962/63 *classe differenziale*, twenty-six out of thirty pupils were born in the South.[1]

DOI: 10.4324/9781003100546-4

Since the 1970s, the over-representation of Southern children in the *classi differenziali* as well as the whole special education system started to be challenged as a result of a demand for thorough and substantial change in primary education.

The current chapter is devoted to the analysis of these issues.

3.1 Italian special education

Italian special education has been quite neglected by historians as a subject of study. The topic embraces several disciplinary areas, ranging from the history of psychiatry to that of eugenics and education. In the past decades, the increasing attention paid to the British and the French as well as the Northern American cases has resulted in the publication of several pieces of research.[2] The same cannot be said of Italy, however – with the exception of a handful of contributions which focus almost exclusively on the theoretical implications. The institutional, social, and cultural aspects of the matter, not to mention the educational practices enacted in special education classrooms, are still unknown. Before turning attention to the post–Second World War period, it is worthwhile briefly to sketch the history of special education and the *classi differenziali* in particular.

3.1.1 From the early twentieth century to Fascism

The concern for the education of mentally 'abnormal' children dates back at least to the early nineteenth century, when the first experiments were initiated in France by Jean Gaspard Itard and his disciple Edouard Seguin, commonly considered the father of special education. In Italy, psychiatrists started to deal with the issue around the 1870s, but it was only at the turn of the twentieth century that it acquired prominence, becoming the crossroads of different interests and tendencies.

The new century was indeed the 'century of the child', one in which children's well-being began to be viewed as crucial for society as a whole. Childhood was thus "recognized as a distinct phase of life",[3] whose peculiarities became an object of scientific study with the aim of influencing policy-making and forging a new parental attitude towards children. As Hugh Cunningham has pointed out, "science, it was believed, could improve life chances for children; more than this, science could help to unlock the mysteries of how children's minds worked, could measure the intelligence of children, and could provide guidance for children whose development or behaviour did not conform to the standard norms".[4]

New awareness of the importance of children as the source of prosperity and well-being in society created the opportunity for experts to arise and make claims for the institutional recognition of their professional roles. According to Patrizia Guarnieri, there were three branches of science involved in the study of the child: the bio-medical field (including paediatrics), the psychiatric-psychological field, and the anthropological field. The borders between different disciplines were not clear-cut, though, and the establishment of university Chairs varied from place to place. If clinical paediatrics was officially declared a compulsory subject in 1906 – though the organization of the classes throughout the peninsula was far slower – the first professorships of child neuropsychiatry were set up only in 1960.[5]

School thus turned out to be an "ideal and privileged observatory" for studying children as the army had been for the observation of adult men.[6] The anthropologists had been the first to carry out surveys on the school population: Paolo Ricarda, for instance, from the University of Bologna, had conducted research in the 1880s, collecting anthropometric data as well as information on the social and psychic condition of Bologna and Modena primary school pupils. His main aim was to contribute to the renewal of pedagogy which was to be founded on the observation of children and their families in order to ascertain the links between physical health, economic and social background and school performance. For this reason, he sought close collaboration with the teachers and heads of those schools which took an active part in the survey. In 1886, Giuseppe Sergi proposed the introduction in primary schools of the so-called *carta biografica*, a biographical chart in which teachers could make notes on pupils' and their families' physical and psychological conditions.[7]

From the beginning of the twentieth century, spurred on particularly by the eugenic and mental hygiene movements, schools were indicated as sites for the identification and selection of 'abnormal' children to be referred to the educational institution best suited to their needs. An advocate of this role for schools was the periodical *Infanzia anormale* (Abnormal Childhood), founded in 1911 and with major contributions from Sante De Sanctis, one of the most prominent figures of Italian experimental psychology.[8] De Sanctis had already set up in 1899 in Rome the so-called *asili-scuola* for the education of the feeble-minded, and in 1906, he had obtained one of the three professorships of experimental psychology just established by the then Minister of Public Instruction, Leonardo Bianchi, who was himself a psychiatrist.[9] A year after the opening-up of the first *asilo-scuola*, another important initiative was taken with the foundation, again in Rome, of the *Scuola Magistrale Ortofrenica* (Orthophrenic School) whose mission was the training of teachers for mentally 'deficient' children. The school was officially directed by the psychiatrist Clodomiro Bonfigli, but its leading lights were Giuseppe Montesano and Maria Montessori.[10] It was within this institution that, in 1906, Montesano opened a class intended for pupils who had failed the first grade and, according to their teachers, needed special treatment. This class together with others designed for children whose performance had been judged inadequate since their very first schooldays (*alunni tardivi*) and opened in the following years in the Rome primary school "Principessa Jolanda" have been identified as the first *classi differenziali*.[11]

The First World War was a turning point. The thorough reorganization of production to sustain the war effort reinforced the leading and central-izing role of the State in the management of all the resources of the nation. Moreover, it offered the psychiatrists an extraordinary opportunity to reinforce the relevance of their science and their profession for the realiza-tion of this goal. The war indeed represented an enormous 'laboratory' for them: they were engaged in the observation and selection of soldiers and in experimenting with new techniques for the rationalization of the military forces to ensure maximum efficiency.[12] The separation of the 'normal' from the 'abnormal' was thus deemed essential and the debates on the use to be made of the latter were intense: some recommended their segregation, others advocated their reutilization. In the post-war period, this approach was transferred to the whole society which needed to regenerate itself after the disaster of the conflict. The selection was to be conducted within the school, conceived of as a peacetime "eugenic laboratory".[13] From the psy-chiatrists' point of a view, a widespread prophylactic action conducted in primary schools would prevent further growth in the number of patients in the asylums. On the other hand, early selection of 'abnormal' children could guarantee the possibility of sending them to the most appropriate kind of school or institute, thus making them productive.

This stance was supported, among others, by De Sanctis, who promoted the "scientific organization of mental work" inspired by the principles of taylorism.[14] In his view, schools were to be considered as factories: they were part of the production process and needed to be organized in a scien-tific way. In this context, society could reclaim the 'abnormal' by offering a specific training in the most appropriate educational institution depending on the degree and the kind of 'abnormality', to be measured through men-tal tests.[15] According to the complex classification set up by De Sanctis, the *classi differenziali* were intended for the so-called *falsi anormali* (false abnormals), children whose behaviour and/or intelligence were only tempo-rarily defective owing to "exogenous causes such as deafness, malnutrition, poverty, an inadequate familial environment", but who could be sent back to normal classes after being provided with proper care and treatment.[16] In 1924, De Sanctis participated in the setting up of the *Lega Italiana di Igiene e Profilassi Mentale* (LIPIM, Italian League of Mental Hygiene and Prophylaxis), which, influenced by the international mental hygiene move-ment, aimed at preventing mental illness mostly through the creation of a network of psychiatric dispensaries and school selection.[17] In 1926, he became the head of the Rome provincial federation of the newly formed ONMI and continued to support the importance of selecting and separat-ing those who could be reclaimed, and be productive for the community, from those whose recovery was impossible. This view informed ONMI pol-icies, for, as an internal 1928 circular established, only the individuals who could be useful to the nation were entitled to benefit from the assistance provided by the agency.[18]

As for the *classi differenziali*, their first official recognition also came during Fascism, though in an ambiguous and inconsistent way. The educational legislation enacted by the regime established that a Medical Faculty would be commissioned to study the "anomalies" of children's growth and propose to the Ministry of Instruction a set of norms regulating the organization of the *classi differenziali*.[19] The University of Genoa was appointed in 1925 by the Minister Pietro Fedele to accomplish this task, since the endocrinologist Nicola Pende, "who had long been championing and encouraging a comprehensive reform plan for the re-education of abnormal children", had just been transferred there.[20] The following year, the *Istituto Biotipologico Ortogenetico* (Biotypological Orthogenic Institute), based at the University of Genoa and directed by Pende, was inaugurated by Fedele himself.[21] Pende's theory, which he labelled 'biotypology', was based on the assumption that it was possible to reach a thorough understanding of the individual – including all his/her physical, psychological, moral, and intellectual characteristics – through endocrine biology and that the latter could be the foundation of State organization. Biotypology thus provided Fascism with a "biological justification for the totalitarian control" of the individual, also to be exerted in primary schools.[22] Pende's Institute screened thousands of Genoa primary school pupils and *Balilla*, organized the functioning of local *classi differenziali*, and ran training courses, attendance at which provided a qualification for teaching in special education classes. The ministerial primary education official publication divulged the principles and methods of the Institute and praised its contribution to the "realization of that essential postulate of modern social life, which requires the defence of race and the physical and psychic improvement of the new generations who are to be given every care".[23]

Moreover, in 1928, it was ruled that when "acts of permanent indiscipline are such as to suggest they might arise from psychic abnormalities", the teacher, after having sought the advice of the health officer, could propose that the pupil should be permanently removed by the head of school, who would have to refer him to a *classe differenziale* or, in agreement with the family, to an institute for young offenders.[24] Given the current lack of historical studies, it is not possible to explain here the reasons why the issue of the *classi differenziali* – and more generally of special education – which had been intensely debated for so many years was regulated in this way. The question seems to have been considered in terms of public order, as had already been the case with the 1904 law on asylums, strongly criticized by the psychiatrists themselves. This law established that the criteria to decide if someone should be mandatorily admitted to an asylum were if they posed a danger to themselves or others and constituted a "public scandal".[25] Similarly, "permanent indiscipline" was now the yardstick for deciding whether a child should be referred to a *classe differenziale*. Furthermore, the teacher and the health officer seemed the only ones involved: no mention was made of any other specialist.

3.1.2 The post-war period

After the Second World War, the lack of a comprehensive school reform also influenced the regulation of special education. The Fascist legislation remained in force, but, at the same time, the issue was regulated by an almost infinite number of circulars. Moreover, the most important feature of post-war special education, and particularly of the *classi differenziali*, was their enormous expansion: not only did the number of classes grow, but also the number of pupils attending them. State funding for special education also rose in an unprecedented manner.

The renewed interest in special education was linked, in the immediate aftermath of war, to the collective anxiety and moral panic over children and youth that has been already discussed in Chapter 1. The fear that the conflict had physically and morally damaged children, as well as the wave of activism that it engendered, involved psychiatrists, psychologists, and social workers. The phenomenon was not peculiar to Italy: it was fairly widespread in other countries, at least in Western Europe. The connections between doctors, psychologists, and, more generally, child experts were close. In 1946, for example, six Italian delegates, among whom were prominent figures such as Giovanni Bollea and Maria Elvira Berrini, participated in the first training course of the *Semaines Internationale d'Etudes pour l'Enfance victime de la Guerre* (SEPEG, International Study Weeks for Children Victims of the War) in Lausanne, which gathered people from twelve different European countries and was characterized by a multi-professional approach.[26] Associations, committees, and periodicals, in which older and younger names joined forces, were set up or restarted. In 1948, the *Società Italiana per l'Assistenza Medico-psico-pedagogica ai minorati dell'età Evolutiva* (SIAME, Italian Society for the Medico-psycho-pedagogical Assistance of Developmental Age Defectives), whose president was Giuseppe Montesano, was founded.[27] In 1953, the periodical *Infanzia anormale* resumed publication after more than twenty years in order to promote the differentiation of child neuropsychiatry from other disciplines and obtain its institutional recognition within universities.[28] One of the greatest novelties was represented by the opening of the first *Centri Medico-Psico-Pedagogici* (CMPP, Medical-Psycho-Pedagogical Centres) in Milan, Rome and Naples between 1947 and 1949.[29] In some cases, they were funded by the Councils or alternatively by State agencies such as the ONMI, still active in the post-war period, and the *Ente Nazionale per la Protezione Morale del Fanciullo* (ENPMF, National Agency for Children's Moral Protection), founded in 1945 by the criminologist Benigno di Tullio. The CMPP most commonly were organizations formed by a psychiatrist, a psychologist, and a social worker whose structure and mission were modelled on the tradition of the American and British Child Guidance Clinics, dating back to the interwar period.[30] Among their several functions was that of participating in the selection of children to be referred to special education. As the leading child neuropsychiatrist Giovanni Bollea made very clear during the 1954 National Conference of the SIAME, the early selection of 'abnormal' children, to be conducted in the first grade, was indispensable. It could prevent "incapable children, who force teachers to slow down the pace [of teaching]", from becoming a "deadweight", especially considering that "those most in need swelled the number of failing pupils", which was particularly high in Italy during the 1950s.[31] In the first grade, teaching activities had to start after Christmas vacations: "the selection has to take place from October to December".[32] Teachers had to be the first to observe their pupils, but they would soon be assisted by the experts of the CMPP, whose task was to study and assess "the whole child's personality".[33] This procedure would ensure that the organization of the *classi differenziali* was based on "scientific and rather probative elements [avoiding] hurting either the feelings of children or their parents".[34] The pedagogue Maria Teresa Rovigatti – who for many years had been a teacher at the Rome *Scuola Magistrale Ortofrenica* – also stressed that the *classi differenziali* could relieve normal classes of the "burden of slightly defective, nervous, difficult, unstable, troubled children who are not interested in school life and work" and prevent the appalling phenomenon of school failure.[35] These pupils would not stay permanently in the *differenziali*, but just long enough to allow them to recover and go back to a normal class.

School failure was, according to Bollea, a symptom of maladjustment. It is worth noting that an agreed scientific definition of maladjustment did not exist. That proposed by Bollea, commonly accepted by many of his colleagues, was extremely cryptic and wide-ranging: individuals rated as "maladjusted" were those unable to "assimilate external reality [and, at the same time,] to modify themselves to comply with external reality and to modify external reality and adjust it to themselves".[36] The array of subjects it affected was incredibly broad: "from psychomotility disorders to the vast field of mental deficiencies; from mild irregularity of conduct to the general field of asociality, antisocial behaviour and to that of juvenile delinquency in particular; from minor childhood nervous pathology to neurosis, psychosis, and child dementia; from brain lateralization disorders to dyslexia, anorthography, and the serious phenomenon of school failure; from hospitalism to the multifarious outcomes of affective lack".[37] A particular form of maladjustment constituted, however, a more pressing problem than others to the extent that Bollea defined it as the "the number one problem of our century".[38] Its main symptom was the "abnormality of conduct and character" and it was characteristic of failing pupils as well as of "young delinquents, teddy boys, pilferers".[39] Maladjustment was therefore related not only to poor school performance, but also to antisocial behaviour and delinquency. The huge and rapid transformation witnessed by Italian society had made it more difficult for the young to adjust themselves to the environment, which led to a "disturbing increase of these syndromes".[40] In this context, the role assigned to child neuropsychiatry was an almost

urgic one. The solution that Bollea proposed at an educational level
the realization of a model of "integral primary school complex", in
a problem pupils could be grouped into different classes correspond-
ing to the nature and degree of their maladjustment.[41] The *differenziali*
were reserved for those who could be redeemed and could return to normal
classes, while all the others would be referred to a few special classes. The
selection was to be carried out by the school doctors and the experts of the
CMPP, who had to acquire the status of full members of the class council
(*consiglio di classe*) together with teachers and the head of school. This new
type of school would guarantee a "functionally and scientifically complete
educational organization".[42]

Such stances were supported by statistical data supposed to prove that the
rates of maladjustment amongst Italian children were at their peak. The figures
were based on mere hypothesis, since, as the psychiatrists themselves declared,
in Italy "precise statistical surveys have not been done".[43] Moreover, there
was no agreement even on the estimates. According to the neuropsychiatrist
Franco De Franco, for example, in 1961, the number of "maladjusted" in the
entire Italian child population amounted to three million, while 271,000 primary school pupils were nebulously defined as "in need of particular teaching
and assistance".[44] Three years later, Giovanni Bollea affirmed that between
800,000 and 1,000,000 primary school pupils were maladjusted.[45]

The demands of the experts were only partially met in the 1960s and
their technocratic utopia was not destined to be realized. However, they
achieved some success. In 1960, Bollea was awarded the first Italian Chair
of child neuropsychiatry at the University of Rome.[46] The 1962 reform
provided for the setting up of *classi differenziali* also in middle school.[47]
Moreover, State expenditure for special education grew as never before in
the course of the decade. In 1962, up to 1,800 million liras were allocated
to finance the whole section – in both primary and middle school – and, as
was spelled out, to allow the "increment of primary school *classi differenziali*".[48] This figure rose to the extent that the provision for 1970 alone was
9 billion and 500 million liras.[49]

These huge investments, however, were not matched by adequate criteria
for approaching the question. The "disarray and inadequacy" of the legislation as well as the fact that the Ministry of Public Instruction simply
"recorded and legitimated" initiatives taken by a plurality of both public and private agencies at a local level was denounced even by the 1962
Special Commission of Enquiry on State Education.[50] The ministerial circulars, besides being a clear symptom of the lack of long-term projects,
were largely prescriptive and extremely confusing. Interestingly enough, in
January 1962, the Ministry asked primary schools to communicate within
thirty days the number of existing special education classes and of those
still to be established in the course of the school year. Schools were also
requested to indicate the amount of money they needed for the setting up
of these classes.[51] Only in July – and solely because schools had failed to

"indicate the criteria that they intended to follow" to form special education classes – the Ministry eventually gave some general indications, which,
however, substantially disregarded what the experts used to suggest. For
example, teachers to be assigned to special schools were compelled to hold
a diploma issued by a *Scuola Magistrale Ortofrenica* or to have attended
specific training courses. However, these qualifications were not deemed
indispensable for those employed in the *classi differenziali*. Furthermore,
the examination of children by the CMPP, for instance, was not mandatory
but just "recommended".[52] As for the didactic methods to be adopted, the
Ministry declared itself confident about the "initiative and inventiveness"
of teachers and referred them to "institutions having proven tradition and
experience" in the field in order to obtain "precise indications".[53]

This attitude represented a breeding ground for the uncontrolled growth
of the *classi differenziali* and for the further enactment of practices already
established in primary schools. During a 1961 conference on "The Issue of
School Mental Hygiene", co-organized by the Lazio branch of the LIPIM
and the SIAME, Bollea himself had complained that "the majority of
today's *classi differenziali* are a desperate jumble of heterogeneous elements
and this discredits an ortho-pedagogical tool worthy of the highest consideration and absolutely necessary".[54]

3.2 The scientific discourse on Southern children

In the post-war period, psychiatrists and psychologists were also largely
involved in the study of the prominent social phenomenon of internal
migrations. A complex and multifaceted debate unfolded, particularly in
the 1960s, and was characterized by a great variety of approaches, depending on the scientific background of the different authors.

The interest of psycho-sciences in migrations was not a novelty. In the
early twentieth century, for example, psychiatrists had dealt extensively
with the connections between transatlantic emigration and the incidence
of mental disease. Both in Italy and the United States, the construction
of migrants' marginality and deviance was "turned [by psychiatry] into a
scientific paradigm".[55] The decision to migrate was considered a symptom
of a pathological state and the whole experience was thought to create or
worsen mental diseases.[56]

In the post-war period, the resumption of emigration abroad and the huge
internal population movements offered the opportunity for new research.
Those focusing on internal migrations, in particular, showed a determina-
tion to offer a framework for the management of the deep social and cultural transformation the country was experiencing as well as of the various
problems they were supposed to cause. Not only did the experts analyse the
supposed pathologies affecting internal migrants, but they also proposed
the establishment of preventive measures and structures – so ensuring relevance to their professional competence and skills.

Southern migrants were accorded particular attention and their presumed 'otherness' was not only taken for granted but received scientific legitimation. The way in which the issue of migrants' so-called integration was approached was influenced by the sociological literature on internal migration. During the 1950s and 1960s, the latter enjoyed a considerable popularity and it almost exclusively focused on the questions of the cultural distance between the newcomers and the 'host' society and how the migrants integrated themselves into this allegedly different environment. Filling the cultural gap and adjusting to the values and rules of the place of arrival were normatively seen as their main goals.[57] Psychiatrists and psychologists relied on this model in a generally uncritical manner and interpreted any supposed deviation from it in psycho-pathological terms.[58]

3.2.1 School maladjustment

As far as Southern children were concerned, what was claimed to be their more pronounced tendency to school failure was interpreted as the result of their maladjustment to the more developed North-Western environment. The issue was analysed, between the 1950s and the 1960s, by psychiatrists, psychologists, and social workers employed in the CMPP of the industrial triangle cities, whose surveys of the school population they examined were frequently published in specialized periodicals. One of the most cited works was that carried out, between the second half of the 1950s and first half of the 1960s, by two neuropsychiatrists, Marcella Balconi and Maria Elvira Berrini. The aim of their investigation was to identify the causes of school failure in normally intelligent children in the first, the third, and the fifth primary school grades. The authors were then employed respectively in the CMPP of Novara *Ospedale Maggiore* and in the Milan Communal CMPP, where a thousand first-grade and a hundred third- and fifth-grade pupils had been referred by their teachers. School failure was, in their view, the effect of "intellectual poverty" originating from a low cultural environment, as well as from the unskilled jobs of the breadwinners, educational neglect by the parents, and "immigration from depressed areas of the South, the Veneto and the countryside".[59] In these cases, with the pupils intellectually and psychologically normal, Balconi and Berrini pointed out that the problem was not to be solved by doctors or special education, but through the organization, teaching methods, and programmes of primary schools which had to be revised in conformity with the "psychological and environmental conditions of all the pupils compelled to attend [them]".[60] Moreover, school failure was only one of the consequences of "school maladjustment" which, above all, was responsible for negative relationships with teachers and schoolmates and made it more difficult for children to accept and follow the school rules. The percentages of Southerners in Milan, and of those from the South and the Veneto in Novara, among these children were considerable, owing to precarious economic and housing conditions and to "totally dissimilar habits and cultural models".[61] This situation was further worsened by the "incapacity of our schools to integrate pupils who, beyond the deficiency of their own living environment, carry the burden of a school 'deficiency', linked to the inadequacy of the school in their place of origin".[62] On the one hand, educational reform was sought in order to meet all pupils' needs; on the other, the living environment, habits, culture, and even the school preparation of two specific groups, namely the Southerners and those from the Veneto, were understood as lacking in comparison with those of the locals.

The data collected by Maria Elvira Berrini were also discussed by the psychiatrist Virginio Porta, director of Milan Communal CMPP, during the Fifth Congress of the LIPIM held in Milan in April 1961. A session of the two-day conference was entirely devoted to internal migrations, owing to the "unexpected impressiveness" of the phenomenon and to the need for psychiatry – which was becoming "one of the most important branches of social medicine" – to deal with it.[63] The sample was formed of 500 schoolchildren, of whom 323 were born in Milan or Lombardy and 123 were of Southern origin. The analysis focused on the socio-economic condition of the families and was nothing more than a simple report of what had been observed. Despite the pretence of scientific neutrality and objective detachment, the study reproduced the most common stereotypes on Southern migrants in a far less nuanced way than that of Balconi and Berrini. It is significant, for example, that in relation to the bad housing conditions of Southern migrants – which in Milan as well as in other areas of the North-West were extremely problematic, and certainly not due to a deliberate decision of the migrants – Porta stated that they showed a "preference" for particular types of houses, such as "buildings under demolition, basements, shanties, back-shops and warehouses".[64] Southern mothers, in particular, were described as "segregated" from the surrounding community and characterized more than fathers by "indifference and incapacity" towards the education of their children. This view was perfectly consistent with the dominant image of Southern women as passive, subjugated by their husbands and confined to the domestic sphere. Moreover, they were depicted as not corresponding to the required standards of good mothering and maternal love. Southern children's intelligence quotient, unlike that of those from Lombardy, was, in the majority of cases, "at the lower end of normal limits".[65] As a result, the review of the data led to an ideal-typical representation of Lombard and Southern families implying the existence of a hierarchy among the two "ethnic groups": the former were described as "well-off, attending to the education of their one or two children, but dominated by anxious insecurity and neuroticism"; the latter were instead "completely ill-adjusted to their living environment, which is dominated by overcrowding, uncertain income and above all by an intense, and, it might be said, incurable incapacity to react to the new living environment".[66] Lombard families were thus fully integrated into the affluent society, whose most typical neurosis they had already developed, while the Southerners, on the contrary, were constitutionally unable to adjust themselves to it.

Southern families and the South in general were sometimes explicitly labelled less evolved and inferior and an unequivocal cause-and-effect relationship between this feature and children's poor school performance was drawn. This was the case in a report on the work carried out during the school year 1959–60 by the Psychiatric Institute of Milan Province with twenty-six first- and second-grade schoolchildren attending the *classi differenziali* of the primary school of Paderno Dugnano, a town close to Milan where, since the early 1950s, thousands of migrants from both the Veneto and the South had settled. The area, it was explained, had been renamed 'Corea' and the authors considered the appellation extremely indicative in itself of the "miserable economic condition and of the low standards of its inhabitants".[67] The local school was attended by a large number of migrant pupils, who constituted ninety percent of the population of special education students. Throughout the report, schoolchildren were generically defined as "immigrants from depressed areas". The great majority of them, however, were from the South (a Southern psychiatrist had joined the team in order to approach them better). The main assumption on which the work had been based was that "these subjects, though not being very gifted, can integrate themselves into primitive ethnic groups [...] but they necessarily fail if faced with the cultural demands of modern and more advanced countries, with consequences for both the individual and the society".[68] Hostile towards school and marked by inferiority feelings, children were reported to be frightened even by the school building. The latter, though it was "sober and without any pretensions, [appeared] luxurious and impressive" to children used to the "awful hygienic conditions of their rural schools".[69] Children's frustration, arising from their awareness of living in a "more demanding and difficult world" than that from which they originated, was exacerbated by the distress their parents experienced in the "effort of assimilation and inclusion into a more advanced social structure".[70] Moreover, the mothers especially were blamed for their "hostile, resentful and prejudiced" attitude toward special education and for their incapacity to understand its relevance to their children's recovery.[71] Teachers, on the contrary, were praised for their "innate insight" – which had allowed them to grasp their pupils' "subculturality" – and for having adapted their teaching methods to the learners' "mediocre resources".[72] At the end of the school year, both doctors and teachers claimed to have seen the results of their efforts: children's behaviour and performance had changed so much that they no longer looked as "special" as before.[73] The fact that just ten students out of twenty-six were declared able to return to a normal class while all the others were simply allowed to attend the following grade in a *classe differenziale* was judged an outstanding success. "Decisive" for such an outcome was supposed to have been the contribution of the Southern psychiatrist. Not only had his light-hearted tone and knowledge of their dialect made children feel at ease, but above all he was a living example for the children and their families of "how it was possible for one to integrate" into the new environment.[74]

Probably taking their cue from the Paderno Dugnano experiment, two years later, in 1964, the child neuropsychiatrist Amelia Maderna and the psychologist Silvio Valseschini proposed the setting up of *classi differenziali* specifically devised for Southern children in need of special education, to be taught by Southern teachers. The proposal followed the presentation of statistical data concerning 208 children they had examined in a Milan child neuropsychiatric dispensary during 1962. The majority of children, 146, were born in Milan or Lombardy and 62 were from other regions. This category included subjects born in "Southern Italy" and others from "central and Northern Italy". It is interesting to note, though, that the former were grouped in the category "immigrant" while the latter were classified as "non immigrant" together with those born in Lombardy and Milan. Southerners were therefore the only ones to be branded as "immigrants". The condition of the families and of their accommodation as well as the "overall evolutionary level [were] unfavourable to immigrant children" and even the evaluation of the intelligence quotient "shows a slight difference" from the non-immigrants.[75] Immigrants had shown up as less clever owing presumably to a "general difficulty in communicating which constitutes the external manifestation of immigrant minors' maladjustment".[76] Their presumed communication impairment could thus have altered the results of the intelligence tests. On the other hand, however, the "educational and cultural deficiencies characteristic of the environment where they have spent their early childhood" were thought to have "impoverished their cultural patrimony", thereby affecting their intelligence.[77] As a result, a "rather high percentage" of immigrants needed to be referred to special education. For this sub-category, Maderna and Valseschini proposed to "establish [...] some *classi differenziali*" possibly led by Southern teachers, to be chosen from those who were already "well integrated into the Northern environment".[78] The measure was meant to prevent "feelings of insecurity and frustration [as well as] inferiority complexes which would boost the affective isolation experienced by immigrant pupils and would obstruct their integration in the new school".[79]

The discussion of the data and the proposal itself were somewhat ambiguous and controversial. Maderna and Valseschini were not simply reaffirming the by then widely accepted notion that Southern migrant children were 'others' who still had to cross the border dividing their pre-modern and backward world from the advanced and complex Northern society in which they could only be maladjusted. They were recommending the creation of *classi differenziali* designed for Southerners only to be taught by already integrated Southern teachers. If their declared aim was to help the integration of Southern children, at the same time they were assuming that any contact with native schoolmates and teachers would have harmed them. The solution proposed was hence the ethnically homogeneous *classe differenziale*.

Fierce criticism came from the child neuropsychiatrist Mario Scarcella, then based at the University of Messina. He dismissed the idea of establishing *classi differenziali* "for *all* the immigrant schoolchildren from Southern regions" as exceeding the "limits of common sense and good taste".[80] His main arguments were that placing Southern children in classes intended exclusively for them would certainly have increased their isolation and hindered their integration. Furthermore, he claimed that not only the immigrants but also "the autochthonous" would benefit from coming into mutual contact, since the former, though different, also had *some* positive qualities.[81]

In reality, Scarcella's remarks were directed above all to the methods recommended by Maderna and Valseschini, but his view of the causes of Southern migrants' maladjustment was substantially consistent with that of his colleagues. He had indeed authored some studies on mental hygiene and internal migrations in which he himself had sketched an essentialized portrait of the Southerners. Their "vivacity of imagination, their impressionability, their personality as well as ethnic, historical and environmental factors, their primitive life, their poor cultural development, their isolation" – Scarcella pointed out – made it particularly difficult for them to "accept new conceptions, to conform to a completely different social reality, to modify hierarchies, values, prejudices and strongly rooted convictions".[82] Nonetheless, alongside these "handicapping circumstances", some positive features including a "spirit of sacrifice, industriousness, discretion, seriousness" could "often counterbalance" their negative traits.[83] He also endorsed the creation in Southern regions of an "especially devised agency" whose main task was to be the "selection of aspiring emigrants".[84] In the North instead, migrants would be "assisted and guided in order to favour their gradual and full settling into the new social environment".[85] The "mentality" of Southern populations, "less evolved in certain respects", indeed required "adequate operative methods".[86]

In Turin, instead, the educator Ferruccio Deva and the head of school Maurizio Pepe recommended referring Southern children to camouflaged *classi differenziali*, to be renamed *classi di recupero* (remedial classes). The two had carried out a study on the adjustment of migrant primary school children in Turin that had been published in 1963 in *Scuola e città*. Though the title of their article seemed to refer generically to the "immigrant[s]",[87] they stated that they were exclusively concerned with those from the South, excluding the others from other areas of Piedmont or from different Northern or Central Italian regions. The reason for this choice was twofold. First, integration into the new city and the new school was fast and easy for the Piedmontese, owing to their "socio-cultural affinity" with the Turinese; those from the Veneto or the Emilia did not "form separate groups in our city, but try to amalgamate with the local population".[88]

The "problem" arose when the "massive immigration from Southern Italy and the islands" started and was due to the insufficient adjustment of Southern pupils.[89] Their failure rates were very high, as the statistical data collected in four Turin primary schools demonstrated. During the school year 1961/62, 18.69% of pupils from the South and the islands did not pass to the next grade, while the percentages were considerably lower – 4.10% – for the "other pupils".[90] What kind of subjects formed part of the latter category was not further specified. Moreover, the authors asserted, teachers had reported that many Southern children were excessively shy, aggressive, and undisciplined. Such behaviour was branded as clearly symptomatic of "difficult adjustment, often brought about by lack of self-confidence whose causes are hereditary, social and environmental".[91] Their families were indeed generally poor and too big: their fathers, though declared to be factory workers, were usually employed in unskilled jobs; the number of children per family was high and negatively influenced the level of intelligence, which in several cases was below the average. At the "Carlo Boncompagni" primary school, of which Pepe was the head, the issue had been addressed through the creation of a remedial class (*classe di recupero*) gathering all the first-grade pupils who, at the beginning of the school year, had not performed well and seemed not to be well-adjusted. Not only were these children described as untidy and disruptive, but they were also dirty: "the first didactic tools [to be used with them] were soap and towel", Deva and Pepe emphasized.[92] The recourse to special teaching techniques had proved successful in improving their reading, writing, and counting abilities as well as the quality of their "expressive activities", which, before the treatment had revealed the "poverty of their world".[93] The free school meal service and the after-school activities – the so-called *doposcuola* – both provided by the Council to low-income pupils had also helped them to acquire good "behavioural habits that could not always be established in the families"[94]: they were trained to wash their hands before lunch, to put their towels back in a tidy way and to go to the refectory in an orderly manner. Likewise, the families, who "sometimes do not need less guidance and assistance than the schoolchildren", benefited from the "educational interventions of the teacher".[95] Remedial classes were henceforth recommended by the authors as "the most effective solution", but on the condition that they "appeared to be normal classes" and thus were not clearly labelled *classi differenziali*, that teachers received special training and that the maximum number of children per class was eighteen.[96]

3.2.2 *Social maladjustment*

The studies conducted on the school population thus created an image of Southern migrant children as maladjusted and underachieving owing to the inherent difference in the culture and living environment of their families. For this reason, their integration into a fully developed society and its schools could take place only through a separate educational channel, such as that of the *classi differenziali*, more suited to their reduced abilities and where they could be provided with special treatment and assistance. The use of scientific terminology and methodology as well as the professional authority of the experts, bestowed an aura of objectivity on these assumptions.

The designation of Southern migrant children as maladjusted was not restricted to the realm of school, though. Great account was taken of the burgeoning scientific literature on the links between Southern migrations, maladjustment, and juvenile delinquency. Although in many cases the studies on juvenile delinquency focused on subjects older than primary school children, their social maladjustment – equated with delinquency or antisocial behaviour – was seen as closely connected to school maladjustment. The latter, if not treated appropriately, was believed to lead to the former. Special education and particularly the *classi differenziali* were indeed meant to prevent not only school failure but also its moral consequences, including youth delinquency. Moreover, one could be referred to a *classe differenziale* because of mere indiscipline as the legislation established.

It was not a matter of chance that *Ragazzi d'oggi*, the official monthly of the ENPMF dealt extensively with school and special education issues.[97] The ENPMF had been founded in the immediate aftermath of the Second World War on the initiative of the criminologist Benigno di Tullio and its main aim was the prevention and treatment of the corruption (*traviamento*) of minors. A student of Salvatore Ottolenghi – inspirer and first director at the beginning of the twentieth century of the "School for Scientific Policing" – Di Tullio had adhered to Fascism and become one of the leading figures of what Mary Gibson has defined as the third generation of criminal anthropologists. The pioneers of the discipline, including Cesare Lombroso, Enrico Ferri, and Raffaele Garofalo, had attached great importance to the connections between childhood and crime.[98] Children were indeed believed to occupy "the same evolutionary stage as primitive peoples" and to be inherently morally depraved.[99] Criminals were hence identified as those whose development from childhood to adulthood had been arrested. In comparison with their predecessors, Di Tullio and his contemporaries provided criminal anthropology – according to Gibson – with the "theoretical evolution" without which it "could not have retained its pre-eminence in Italy".[100] These changes consisted mainly in focusing on "inborn psychological rather than physical abnormality [and] hormones and body types as the predictive bases for criminology".[101] As Claudia Mantovani has pointed out, the principles of traditional criminal anthropology were combined with Nicola Pende's biotypology and Sante De Sanctis's psychological studies on 'abnormal' children.[102] More importantly, such a newly shaped criminal anthropology exerted a considerable – though not defining – influence on Fascist juvenile delinquency policy and its proponents occupied important positions in the State apparatus. Di Tullio, for example, had been an enthusiastic supporter of the establishment of the so-called *Centri di Osservazione* (Observation Centres) where "any child who exhibited physical or psychological anomalies" could be examined in order to receive adequate treatment.[103] The Centres were officially set up by the 1934 law on juvenile courts whose main principle was that deviancy and delinquency in minors were a matter of bio-psychic 'abnormality'.

The prestige and authority of at least some of the criminologists collaborating with the regime were evidently not much damaged by its fall. Di Tullio was able to create the ENPMF in the post-war period, though he could not retain its presidency owing to a funding scandal. The first national conference of the agency, held in the Campidoglio in September 1946, was opened by the then Minister of Public Instruction, Guido Gonella, and it subsequently obtained official State recognition and economic support.[104] Moreover, in 1963, he obtained what was reported to be the first Italian Professorship of Criminal Anthropology at the University of Rome.[105] Though the importance of biological heredity for the study of young offenders was downgraded in favour of a stronger emphasis on environmental and cultural factors, a strongly deterministic approach continued to be adopted and references to the biological causes did not disappear completely. As a result, the construction of certain categories of subjects as different and prone to delinquency was still possible even within this changed interpretative framework.

As for Southern migrant children, the first assessment of their deviancy did not concern the industrial triangle, but early 1950s Rome – which witnessed a large number of people moving from other regions – and it came from the social worker Elio Ruocco, then employed at the *Centro Distrettuale di Servizio Sociale per i Minorenni* (District Centre of Social Work for Minors) of the Ministry of Justice. Ruocco's main argument was that there existed a close relationship between juvenile delinquency and family's maladjustment and that this was the case of Southern families and children living in Rome. In his view indeed, "Southern populations were 'different' from the others, different in economic-social-political conditions, but also in their way of thinking, behaving, reacting, in a word 'psychologically' different".[106] By visiting the houses of an unspecified number of Southern families and talking with their members, he had come to the conclusion that "the South presents a particular organization", which had allowed the survival of "structures that elsewhere had already been overcome a very long time ago".[107] Southern families were hence characterized by the complete dependence and submission of women, excessively strict education of children, limited occasions for entertainment, and strict sexual morality. The role of women, parent-child relationships and sexual mores which they had found in Rome were completely different and almost none had been willing to change their living habits. Their way of "educating children, of cultivating friendship, of having fun, in other words of living, was the same as in the small villages of Sardinia and Sicily".[108] Southern children and youth thus easily understood that they had to conform themselves to a set of rules which their local peers ignored. This awareness served Ruocco as a basis for an apocalyptic prediction. He envisaged children hating their parents, becoming aggressive and infringing all the norms – the negative as well as the positive – imposed upon them. This "breach of the orders" already contained in itself the "germs" of future "corruption".[109] It was thus necessary to help the family to reach a "better understanding of the surrounding culture and, as a result, of the youth's attitude" through an "effective social therapy" and to consider the possibility of removing them from their environment.[110]

During the 1960s, the debate focused instead on North-Western urban areas. The research on "Delinquency and minors' maladjustment" coordinated by the educator and director of the juvenile prison "Cesare Beccaria", Piero Bertolini, and published in 1964 devoted a specific chapter to the effects of internal migrations on juvenile delinquency in Milan.[111] The increase in the rate of crimes committed by minors in the North, which had been observed since the late 1950s, was interpreted in different ways. Bertolini challenged the stance taken by the consultant of the Ministry of Justice Gino Faustini, who had affirmed that internal migration alone could not account for what he saw as an extremely complex phenomenon. It was certainly true – Faustini maintained – that the growth of youth criminality in the regions affected by migrations was "largely due to the immigration of populations traditionally carrying high rates of youth crime".[112] On the other hand – he noted – only a minority of the migrants came from the South and the "ethnic" features of these people, including the "greater disposition" of the youngsters to commit crimes could only offer a partial explanation.[113] It was thus necessary to look at the cultural, economic, and social transformation witnessed by the whole country to achieve a more comprehensive outlook. According to Bertolini, however, not only had Southern young offenders moved to the industrial triangle – there had occurred what he defined as a "delinquents' emigration" – but migration itself was a "new source of maladjustment".[114] Between 1958 and 1961, a growing percentage of Southern minors had been reported to the Milan juvenile court for penal code offences, while only a few had been reported by their families as needing re-educational treatment and assistance. It could thus be supposed that migrants and particularly the Southerners were "more prone to cross the *criminal threshold*", probably because of the multiple problems they had to face. However, it was also possible that migrant parents were much more reluctant than the locals to call for the institutions to intervene in their children's behavioural disorders. This lack of "pedagogical sensitivity" was generally due to the fact that migrant parents were not aware of the existence of medical-psycho-pedagogical services and of the possibility of referring youths to juvenile courts. Moreover, their children, though "irregular", often were a source of income for the family and their sense of honour made them ashamed of having their children in a reformatory or labelled as "corrupted". Some regions contributed more than others to the increase in juvenile delinquency. The rates of young offenders coming from Apulia, and particularly from the province of Foggia, as well as from Calabria, Sicily, and Sardinia, had more than doubled as a result of the "persistent socio-economic depressions" of those areas.[115]

For the second half of his survey, Bertolini discussed the results of the interviews conducted with twenty Southern minors aged twelve or over. The group was hence rather small and consisted of boys only. As he had already pointed out, antisocial or aggressive behaviour was quite rare among young females whereas "sexual maladjustment" and "prostitution" were more frequent especially for subjects older than fourteen.[116] The majority of Southern boys came from small towns or villages and all of them had had an "extremely poor family life from the moral, cultural and economic point of view".[117] All the families were characterized by "despotic and authoritarian" fathers, while mothers were usually "meek and submissive".[118] Parents' work experience and cultural level were defined as "modest" and minors' school performance as "negative": all of them had repeated some grades more than once and none had completed primary school education as a result of the "negligence or even hostility of their parents toward this activity".[119] Their IQ was generally low, the electroencephalogram had revealed that their brains had suffered from some diseases, and their personalities were substantially "disturbed".[120] His conclusion was then that migrants, especially if less gifted, were more prone to maladjustment and juvenile delinquency. Migrant boys sensed that their families were at the very bottom of the social ladder in the new place of residence, so that theft – the offence they committed most frequently – was their way of reacting to this humiliating situation as well as of identifying themselves with local and better off peers. The implementation of "preventive interventions", to be conducted not only in Northern cities but, above all, in the South, could ensure – it was suggested – that internal migrations, which were already causing socio-economic problems, did not become a breeding ground for the "alarming spread of maladjustment and Italian juvenile delinquency".[121] Bertolini's analysis was shared by Tommaso Senise, Director of the medical-psycho-pedagogical office of Lombardy minors' re-educational centres. His proposal for the prevention of maladjustment and delinquency among young migrants was, however, slightly different. In his view, the early diagnosis and treatment of migrant children younger than fifteen years of age was to be made in primary schools. Each migrant child would be tested by its teacher and its living conditions assessed by a social worker. The creation of special education classes would allow children to receive the most appropriate kind of education, while the families would be assisted by the social services.[122]

The issue of internal migrations and youth crime was also deemed relevant in Turin and discussed by social workers and doctors employed by the local juvenile court. In this case too, old and new approaches and terminology coalesced into an alarming picture whose main subject were the Southerners. The high rates of juvenile delinquency were considered "disturbing" by the head of the social service office, Amelia Parmentola, especially when compared with the national average: crimes against the person, for example, were reported to have increased by 60.5%, whereas at a national level, by only 10.6%.[123] In the first instance, Parmentola stated that Turin juvenile delinquency had a "profoundly uniform character" and the causes of "immigrants' irregular behaviour [were] the same as those of the Piedmontese".[124] It was the "forceful development of the city", not followed by an adequate improvement in public services and building provision, together with the myths of easy success spread by cinema, television and songs, which were to be held responsible for the distress of the youth.

On the other hand, the whole of the second half of Parmentola's survey focused entirely on the peculiarities of migrants' maladjustment and on the "degenerative phenomena" characterizing migrations.[125] It is interesting to note that throughout the investigation, the term "immigrants" was used interchangeably with "Southerners", thus suggesting that this was the only group involved in juvenile delinquency. The presumed distinctive features of Southern culture – the economic and social backwardness of that portion of the country – served once more as the basis of the construction of a stereotyped image of the migrant, whose destiny appeared to be fixed and inescapable. Many youngsters – Parmentola reported – were recruited by adult criminal organizations and pushed towards illicit activities by sentiments such as group solidarity, honour, and friendship still persisting in the *Mezzogiorno* owing to "feudal residues".[126] Despite industrialization and the improvement of the communication network witnessed in those years by Southern regions, it was impossible to believe that these habits would disappear soon:

"for years in the South brother will still defend brother, even though wrongly, fellow villager will defend fellow villager, even at the cost of bypassing laws and institutions which are traditionally alien, for historical and political reasons, to the fundamental values of Southern culture, since they are inspired by the need to regulate the life of a wider society and transcend the group ethic to embrace a more universally human one".[127]

This mentality was believed to be uniform and common to all Southerners, who were unable to change it. It was because of their inability to "breach the borders of the group they belong to" that the young *magliari* (door-to-door clothes sellers) were willing to beat the members of other groups. The various types of criminal activities "typical of the immigrants"[128] were singled out, including pimping and the organization of the "cooperatives" for the recruitment of a cheap migrant workforce depicted as exclusively managed by Southerners. There was no reference to the fact that Turin firms relied on them for recruitment.[129] A confusing mixture of nineteenth-century moralism and more recent sociological concepts also informed the discussion of the causes of juvenile delinquency among migrants. It was indeed their "indigence [...] which contained the potential for maladjustment".[130]

Economic poverty could easily be turned into "moral misery"[131] and led them to develop forms of "clientelism" towards friends and relatives or to exploit welfare institutions, including the *patronato scolastico*. Even more importantly, their often unhealthy accommodation, concentrated in particular and circumscribed areas of the city, which Parmentola defined as "islands", made their "misery [...] become a forma mentis [...] engendering a wound difficult to heal in their ethical worldview".[132] For the youth, this "school of misery [made up of] small thefts, scepticism towards all ethical and civil values, and begging for help without any physical or intellectual effort" was of course detrimental.

An important contribution to the scientific legitimation of the stereotypes of young Southern delinquents living in Turin also came from Ennio Pontrelli, specialist in forensic medicine and director of the Ministry of Justice's local medical-psycho-pedagogical office. One of his principal assumptions was that the "immigrant mass" reaching the North from the South comprised individuals lacking the "capacity to integrate" and "structurally unsuited".[133] Interestingly enough, Pontrelli saw the origin of the host society's "racial prejudice" against the newcomers in the awareness of this feature.[134] The majority of the migrants "remain[ed] bound to archaic cultural patterns and [were] forced to enclose themselves in 'islands' uprooted from the rest of the environment".[135] Responsibility for the ghettoization of migrants was hence laid on the migrants themselves and the phenomenon was paradoxically explained by their supposed inability to abandon their primitive culture. Moreover, the migrants were even charged with causing what Pontrelli himself defined as the "racial prejudice" of the Turinese, which he made appear as the natural response to Southerners' unfittedness. However, migrants' "sense of honour, jealousy, sexual aggressiveness [which represented] the most disturbing elements of immigrants' personality" were not to be considered – Pontrelli went on – "racial defects", but the outcome of a particular "socio-cultural structure [that is] the ancient misery of the South".[136] In their own town, Southern minors had already had the opportunity to become aware of "their frailty and social insignificance, to be subjected to a merely executive and always subordinate role",[137] and to develop an oppositional attitude towards the outside world. Once in the North, they mistook Northerners' "indifference or pacific refusal" for a form of "aggressive hostility" towards them to which they reacted with "unstable work patterns, running away, thefts".[138] Furthermore, many of the youth examined by the office over which he presided had turned out to be slightly mentally defective and hence less able to adjust to a more complex society.

3.3 Southern children in Turin *classi differenziali*

The scientific discourse on Southern migrant children's school and social maladjustment provided 1950s and 1960s North-Western primary school

achers with a toolbox for understanding and managing the problem that
...ese pupils represented.

An increasing number of Southern children attending Turin primary
schools were referred, particularly throughout the 1960s and the 1970s,
to the *classi differenziali*. It is worth underlining once more that not all
Southern pupils were placed in the *differenziali*. However, in many schools –
including the "Margherita di Savoia" and the "Gian Enrico Pestalozzi" –
these classes comprised a large number of Southerners. It is also important
to add that not all the *classi differenziali* were officially recognized as such.
Quite commonly, mixed-sex classes were formed when the school year had
already started with the purpose of gathering pupils who, according to
their teachers, showed learning and behavioural problems.

3.3.1 The medicalization of teaching

In general, post-war primary school teachers seemed to be fairly familiar
with the most common psychiatric and psychological concepts and labels
concerning children. It is difficult to say in what ways this knowledge transmission had taken place, given the current lack of Italian scholarly studies
on this specific issue. The so-called medicalization of education, of which
special education formed a part, had been a long and complex process,
occurring in Western Europe and United States at least since the last two
decades of the nineteenth century. The term medicalization usually refers
to the process whereby "a problem is defined in medical terms, described
using medical language, understood through the adoption of a medical
framework or 'treated' with a medical intervention".[139] As Stephen Petrina
has remarked, the medicalization of education was not limited to the realm
of mental hygiene and special education but included physical education,
vaccinations, hygiene teaching, and many other areas.[140] These issues have
been almost completely neglected by the historiography of Italian education
and it is therefore impossible at the moment to offer even a rough overview
of their development and articulation. The very few studies available so far
suggest, however, that in late nineteenth and early twentieth century Italy,
the growing interest in the teaching of physical education and hygiene was
closely linked with the nation-building project, to be accomplished through
the shaping and control of healthy and disciplined bodies. Science hence
invaded the sphere of traditional pedagogy and, at the same time, was ped-
agogized.[141] In this context, the role of teachers became crucial: they were
expected to acquire notions of physiology, biology, and psychology; they
had to be aware of children's most common diseases and be the "promot-
ers of hygienic knowledge and habits".[142] Likewise, special courses and
training schools, such as the above-cited *Scuola Magistrale Ortofrenica* in
Rome, were set up during the first two decades of the twentieth century to
provide teachers with knowledge and skills to deal with 'abnormal' pupils
referred to special education. Moreover, teachers were the first to have the

opportunity to notice the symptoms of a child's mental or behavioural disease. Psychiatrists and psychologists, among whom was De Sanctis, thus stressed the importance of equipping them with specific knowledge on these subjects.[143]

How and if the project of making teachers aware of the principles of mental hygiene took place during the Fascist regime is still to be ascertained.[144] What can be argued, at least with reference to the two Turin primary schools examined for this research, is that, in the post-war period, labels such as 'of abnormal intelligence', backward, and maladjusted were commonly employed by teachers. Educational periodicals contributed to the spread and popularization of these concepts. *Scuola e città*, for example, informed its readers about foreign initiatives in favour of "maladjusted youth".[145] In addition, at the beginning of the 1960s, it published the text of a lecture on "Mental Hygiene and School" delivered by Eugenio Medea, at the *Centro Pedagogico Milanese* (Milan Pedagogical Centre), an institution organizing training courses for teachers.[146] Medea had been one of the co-founders of the LIPIM in the 1920s and in the post-war period was regarded as a sort of tutelary deity of Italian mental hygiene. In plain and accessible language, he illustrated the process of selecting children in need of special education: from the first school days, "the clever teacher starts the work of selection and takes into special consideration the child having difficulty concentrating, the child with clear symptoms of instability, the child who clearly cannot hear well or who cannot see well; and, if need be, the child having involuntary tics".[147] Teachers had thus to report these children to the school doctor, or to a medico-psycho-pedagogical centre, which would refer them to the most appropriate school. Those who were not "really abnormal, but owing to special health conditions, weakness or unfortunate conditions of the familial environment are in a condition of inferiority that we can define as temporary" had to be sent to the *classi differenziali*.[148] The measure – Medea underlined – was meant to be temporary. As a result, these classes had to be formed year by year, depending on the number of pupils deemed to need them. Teachers could not replace doctors in the evaluation of the degree of children's 'abnormality'. Mental tests, for instance, were to be handled by specialists in order to avoid wrong results. Nonetheless, especially considering how busy the medical-psycho-pedagogical centres were, "the clever and willing teacher can, even without the tests, form an idea of their little pupil's psychic conditions and, through repeated observation, formulate a judgement on the pupil's abilities".[149] Some easier tests could be administered by teachers: for instance, they could ask the pupil to cross out the vowels 'a' and 'o' in a printed text and could calculate the time taken to accomplish this task. Very useful also could be the tests for the measurement of the pupil's "moral value", such as those concerned with "cruelty, falsehood, theft and so on proposed by various authors".[150]

Other journals, such as *I diritti della scuola*, whose target readership were primary school teachers only, also tried to make teachers acquainted with the "evaluation of [pupils'] subnormality".[151] The outcome was, however, confusing and the classification provided rather arbitrary. 'Subnormal' children could be divided into three main categories – the journal reported – depending on their IQ. Those affected by severe 'subnormality' were "completely unable to see to their own physical and social needs [and] lacked any expressive, perceptive and ideational activity".[152] A second group comprised children who were "able, if carefully guided, to learn some basic activities and notions" including reading and writing, but could never recover completely. The last category comprised those whose "nervous system" presented only a "slight abnormality". These children could read, write, and count but, though they were able to "insert themselves into social and working life, [...] they would never be normal subjects".[153] A further group, the "psychic subnormals", was also introduced, without explaining how it would fit into the previously outlined categories, and included children "unable to adjust to the social environment".[154] Those who could "fully recover" were commonly referred to the *classi differenziali*, whose curriculum – it was underlined – was exactly the same as that of normal classes. It was thus up to the teachers to adapt learning activities to their pupils' abilities. This suggestion clearly contradicted the experts view about the absolute need for teachers of the *classi differenziali* to receive proper training and to employ special teaching methods in order to obtain the best possible results.

3.3.2 Turin classi differenziali

Recommendations on the organization and functioning of the *classi differenziali* directed to teachers and heads of school came also from local school officials. The implementation of these classes was believed to fuel the modernization of primary education. Their "remarkable development" in early 1950s Turin Northern District primary schools – which included the "Gian Enrico Pestalozzi" was praised by the inspector Riccardo Dal Piaz. In his view, the phenomenon was a clear symptom of teachers' "willingness to improve professionally and to upgrade their teaching methods [...] to new and more effective pedagogical and didactic standards". Both teachers and head of schools, by "accepting superior authorities' invitation to establish *classi differenziali*, [had proved to be] culturally and professionally mature enough to understand and face the new needs of primary schools". This attitude, together with the collaboration with school officials would ensure that "our school [could] accomplish its task for the total benefit of youth and society". The *differenziali* had to be intended for children who "were distinguished from their peers owing to a sort of atrophy or annihilation of the normal and common personal faculties". Their teachers were expected to gain a deep knowledge of their pupils' needs, of the reasons why they had been referred to that kind of class, to help and inform the school doctor of pupils' behaviour and performance. Dal Piaz also suggested the use of a data form for each child, to be completed by both the teacher and the doctor. In this way, the latter could obtain information useful for the diagnosis, but above all, teachers could *"improve their pedagogical orientation and didactic action on the basis of the medical report for the benefit of the learner"*. The doctor's pronouncement was thus the foundation of the educational practice of the *classi differenziali*. It was, however, recommended that the forms with their data were kept secret in order to prevent "the unpleasant gossip of parents [which would damage] this school beneficial activity".[155]

In the course of the 1950s, *classi differenziali* were generally well established in many Turin primary schools and their increase became progressively connected with migrations towards the city and the province. As has been mentioned above, in 1962, primary schools were asked by the Ministry of Public Instruction to provide information concerning their special education classes. At Ivrea – a town witnessing huge migrations in the 1950s and 1960s – all the twenty-two children deemed to need a *classe differenziale* were born to "recent immigrated families, coming especially from the Southern provinces". Though not affected by "severe physical and psychic anomalies", they were reported to be experiencing "great difficulty in settling into the [new] environment" and, for this reason, underperforming. The *classe differenziale* would "favour their adjustment much more effectively than a normal class could do".[156] At Chiaverano, not far from Ivrea, where "owing to the migratory flow the school population was constantly increasing", the head of school requested the setting up of a *classe differenziale* as a result of "the high percentage of backward and *falsi anormali* among local pupils and, in particular, the immigrants".[157]

Throughout the 1960s, Turin primary schools followed the same trend. A survey conducted at the end of the decade by the local branch of the *Amministrazione per le attività assistenziali italiane ed internazionali* (AAI, Administration for Italian and International Assistance Activities) concerning all the primary schools of both city and province underlined the increase in special education classes, including the *differenziali*. Even more importantly, the authors found that it was common to designate the latter "classes for failing pupils" or "classes for immigrants".[158] Many pupils were referred to these classes without being examined by any doctor. In some cases, teachers and heads of school had declared themselves unable to complete the questionnaire they had been given by the AAI, where they were asked to indicate the type of maladjustment affecting their special education pupils. Also significant was the answer of a head of school who did not hesitate to assert that he was able to recognize "by his science" the pupils needing special education treatment.[159] Such a claim seems to suggest that the experts were sometimes more or less clearly perceived by heads of schools as intruders impugning their professional competence and undermining their prestige. More generally, school personnel did not see themselves as a passive recipient of the psychiatrists' and psychologists' authority. On the contrary, teachers in particular expressed their agency in appropriating scientific labels and using institutions such as the *classi differenziali* to solve the problem that migrant children represented for them.

At the "Margherita di Savoia", a considerable number of the children placed in the *classi differenziali* had been examined and found to need them by the experts of the Communal Medical-Pedagogical Centre. Its director, Carlo Ferrio, was a renowned psychiatrist, teacher at the University of Turin and medical head of the Medical-Pedagogical School "Padre Agostino Gemelli", intended for children whose 'abnormality' was deemed particularly severe.[160] The examinations usually took place during the school year, when teachers were requested to draw up a list of pupils showing particular problems or 'abnormalities' and deemed in need of medical advice. Once a pupil had been referred to and diagnosed by the experts who, in the vast majority of cases, decreed that s/he needed to attend a *classe differenziale* or the Medical-Pedagogical School, his/her chances of passing the grade were much reduced. Teachers were indeed not only influenced by the report of the experts, but might, it seems, rely on it to legitimate their decision to fail the pupil. This was the case of N., born in Apulia and attending the second grade during the school year 1958/59. According to the medical report, he "was agitated and got emotional" during the examination, had shown "remarkable difficulty in verbal expression" and was an "immature subject, also owing to a frail constitution and lack of familial education". It was thus suggested that he should be referred to a *classe differenziale*.[161] At the end of the school year, his teacher adopted the same terminology to explain the reasons why N. had failed: "He is an immature subject, of a particularly frail constitution. He easily gets emotional and agitated. He has difficulty in verbal expression and his school performance has been inadequate".[162] As for another of her pupils, E. from Naples, she was even more explicit and reported that he could not pass because, throughout the year, he had been "dull, stubborn, inattentive, insensible and indifferent to everything and he has proven to be so while undertaking the mental tests of the Turin psycho-pedagogical centre".[163]

The following year, E. as well as N. were moved to a second-grade *classe differenziale*. The class comprised twenty-three boys and was entrusted to a teacher of proven experience. She had, indeed, taught at the Medical-Pedagogical School and, as a result of her "specific preparation" and of her "very maternal zeal", the *classi differenziali* of the "Margherita di Savoia" were usually assigned to her.[164] The pupils came from other second-grade classes and all but two had failed the previous year. Their teacher described them as "rascals" and was resolved to carry out a "study of the Southern Question to be sent to the Ministry of Public Instruction". It was the first time in her long career, during which she had "met a lot of problem children", that she had had to deal with pupils having so many different but extremely negative personalities: "from the violent to the bully, from the liar to the coward, from the stubborn to the careless". She tried to alternate "kindness" and "iron discipline", trying to be "as fair as possible, in order not to hurt their susceptibility, especially accentuated in the Sicilians". Furthermore, she expressed the need to "keep a school diary" of the ways in which they manifested their disinclination for "social life with the aim of evaluating what a ruinous contribution these children will give to society once they have grown up".[165] Pupils' troublemaking and potential for future delinquency were thus associated by the teacher with the Southern Question, as if they were direct outcomes of the latter. Interestingly enough, only ten children were born in the South though – as has been already pointed out – it is not possible to say with certainty whether the eight boys born in Turin belonged to Southern migrant families or not. What can be argued is that the moral panic about the antisocial behaviour and delinquency of young Southerners was so strongly felt as to make the 'ethnic factor' appear the only possible cause of youth deviance. The perception of teachers was, however, most probably also influenced by the gendered view of Southern migrants and their children. Women were usually portrayed as submissive and passive, whereas men were commonly represented as hot-tempered, oversensitive – especially about matters of honour and reputation – and prone to violence. Moreover, as has already been mentioned in connection with Piero Bertolini's study of Milan, the only form of young female deviance was then believed to be of a sexual kind, while disruptiveness was considered the prerogative of boys.

As far as the school performance was concerned, the teacher's expectations were low and the assessment extremely negative. She was not only convinced that "none [of the pupils] will go to the Polytechnic", one of Turin's most prestigious universities, but she also described them as "the most depressing ever because of the absolute indifference of both children and their families towards everything but free school meals and textbooks".[166] In other cases, however, bad school results were attributed to intellectual deficiency. The teacher F.G., for example, had been assigned a class of twenty-three third-grade girls, half of whom were born in the South and whose main characteristic was reported to be a "rather stubborn intelligence". This was not an official *classe differenziale*, but it had been formed four months after the beginning of the school year and comprised "subjects taken from other classes and needing particular care". Though they were "disciplined and attentive", they were underperforming and made "elementary mistakes". Verbal expression and vocabulary were deemed particularly poor, "probably because they are used to speaking dialect". Their teacher therefore tried to help them through a "mental gymnastic exercise", consisting in the "constant repetition" of the most basic notions, and struggled against "the absolute negligence of their families, which is sometimes really discouraging".[167]

The status of the *classi differenziali* was rather ambiguous in an even greater measure at the "Gian Enrico Pestalozzi". Proper *classi differenziali* were established, often in the middle of the school year. These initiatives

ere welcomed by some teachers with relief, since burdensome, under-
,erforming, and disruptive pupils could be sent there. A teacher, whose
1962/63 class was made up of thirty-six boys and who had asked for seven
of them to be moved, was adamant that without them "everything is going
better".[168] One of the main reasons for referring a pupil to a *differenziale* –
and this was especially the case with boys – was troublemaking, not
infrequently associated with familial 'deviance'. G., for example, an eleven-
year-old boy from Apulia still attending the third grade, was so turbulent
as to make the situation of his class "more and more difficult and serious".
His reactions to his teacher's reprimands were described by the latter as
"savage": he screamed, hid himself under his desk, and "refus[ed] to believe
in God". The cause of his behaviour was alleged to be the "squalid moral,
religious and educational abandonment" in which he and his brothers lived
as a result of their father's imprisonment and their mother's hourly work.[169]

Other classes, though not clearly labelled *differenziali*, were mixed-sex –
in contrast with the rigid and well rooted principle of single-sex education –
and assigned to temporary teaching staff. They were usually intended for
pupils "unwanted" by their teachers and their reputation was entirely negative.[170] As a teacher remarked, their "parents [were] not happy to send their
children to a mixed-sex class which is considered, I do not know whether
rightly or not, a *classe differenziale* gathering backward subjects".[171]
Throughout the 1960s, the majority of children placed in these classes were
Southern migrants: "they are particular pupils", an instructor noted of his
class, pointing out not only that their "needy families [were not] the most
fit to educate their children", but also that they had not been given an "adequate training" in the "small Southern villages" from which they came.[172]

Discipline also was seen as the most pressing problem in these classes.
As has been mentioned at the beginning of this chapter, during the school
year 1962/63, for instance, twenty-six out of thirty pupils attending a fifth-
grade mixed-sex class were born in the South. As well as underachieving,
they were described as "dirty, ill-mannered, hot-tempered, nervous, hys-
terical ... and schizophrenic" owing to the negligence of their families.
Working with children like these – their teacher reported – was not dissimilar to a "real mission". Teaching activities and aims were thus different
from those of normal classes and tailored to pupils' supposed abilities and
natural inclinations. In order to follow their "spontaneity", they were often
involved in artistic activities, including singing and dancing. One of them,
in particular, was able to "dance the tiwsit [twist]" with "such a nimbleness
and flexibility that he seemed a real African negro".[173]

At the "Pestalozzi" too, the examination of pupils reported as needing
investigation was carried out by the experts of the Communal Medical-
Pedagogical Centre. Southern children were often diagnosed as "primitive subjects", a label probably meant to indicate their developmental
retardation, which was often linked to their poor familial environment.
A.D., a boy from Apulia, who during the examination had maintained an

"indifferent, apathetic, superficial and suspicious attitude" and had shown himself "instinctual", was branded a "very primitive and immature subject, lacking familial education" and needing to receive "special treatment in order to overcome the wariness [preventing him from] adjusting to the new environment". It was thus suggested that he should be moved to the Medical-Pedagogical School in order "to favour his recovery, which is considered to be possible".[174] The following year, however, the boy, who was already attending a mixed-sex class at the time of the examination, was placed in another unofficial *classe differenziale*.[175] Paradoxically, a diagnosis was made even when the patient was reported to have resisted testing. This was the case of M.D. who, though having "answered randomly the majority of questions, refusing to apply himself with any care", was classified "severely abnormal" and recommended to attend the Medical-Pedagogical School.[176]

3.3.3 *"Turin poor immigrants' children are 'less clever'"*

Towards the end of the decade, the issue of Southern migrant pupils and of their over-representation in Turin *classi differenziali* started to attract a growing amount of attention, not only from school personnel and experts but also from local politicians and the public in general. The Council showed an interest in addressing the question which had been lacking before. Between 1968 and the beginning of the 1970s, on the initiative of the Socialist *assessore* (deputy mayor) for hygiene and public health Frida Malan, several new psycho-medical-pedagogical teams, including at least a psychiatrist, a psychologist, and a social worker, were established to carry out the "rational tracking" (*reperimento*) of pupils to be referred to special education in compliance with new ministerial instructions.[177] Each team had to be in charge of examinations and counselling for a limited number of schools in order to provide a more effective and complete service, as well as guaranteeing a continuous collaboration with teachers, heads of school, and families. The realization of this project, however, turned out to be much more difficult than had been expected. As the experts themselves reported, the number of teams – only five – was deemed insufficient for the needs of a primary school population that in October 1970 amounted to about seventy-nine thousand pupils. Furthermore, they had to face teachers' "attempts to obtain their endorsement for initiatives of 'exclusion'". Teachers indeed used to refer to the teams "always the same cases of disruptive children".[178]

At the same time, however, the work of the teams was given public prominence and presented as closely associated with the issue of Southern migrant children. In an interview with *Tempo Medico*, a renowned informative journal, doctor Graziella Olivetti, the teams' coordinator and new medical head of the Medical-Pedagogical School "Padre Agostino Gemelli", explained that the "overwhelming majority" of pupils referred to the service by their teachers were "Southern immigrants' children, all with the common denominator of being affected by severe socio-economic and hence pedagogic discomfort".[179] Olivetti's view of the question is particularly interesting and significant in revealing continuities and ruptures in dealing with what she defined as the problem of Turin "'different' children". On the one hand, she pointed out that pupils were placed in special education classes in a completely random way. Even more importantly, she criticized the "more or less conscious criterion" lying at the foundation of the system of the *classi differenziali* and according to which "in order not to hinder the development of the 'gifted', who will guarantee a good return for society, the 'troublemaker' is eliminated".[180] The most common practice was thus to separate the "'different' child" from the "'normal' ones" without considering that the problem was of a social kind. It was – she remarked – the education system which was "inadequate to the real situation of the population". On the other hand, her analysis of Southern migrants' living conditions and psychology was informed by old stereotypes and reproduced the stereotypical construction of Southern children and their families. In her view, indeed, "the sudden passage from a kind of culture (or non-culture) [...] to another one in which everything is radically different [led the adult immigrant to become] a maladjusted – frustrated and hyper-demanding toward his son". Fathers, in particular, wanted their sons "to get what they could never have achieved" and were for this reason held responsible for an "exacerbated climate of violence and prevarication". As a result, "the little immigrant" lacked "any familial educational support" and found himself "culturally and emotionally immature in a school where the punitive relationship was substantially repeated". She also indicated two different types of reaction: the "sound" child would "rebel" and become a troublemaker because his "feeling of inadequacy, his lack of real competitiveness would lead him to refuse the relationship with the teacher and to assault his successful schoolmates"; the "less sound" child, instead, "would end up appearing mentally defective".[181]

Alongside old stereotypes, the organicist approach continued to subsist and to exert its influence not only over the experts, but also over policy-making and public opinion. In September 1969, the *assessore* for work and social problems, Renato Valente, presented the results of a "medical-psycho-sociological survey" conducted in nine primary schools by the neuropsychiatrist Gastone Jacobbi and his team. The survey focused on one hundred and twenty pupils – boys and girls – and their families, of whom fifty-one, all from the South, had "recently" arrived in Turin: forty-two had been living there for five years and only four were "indigenous". The physical conditions of the children were reported to be extremely poor: "40% of the examined subjects are affected by more or less severe morbid syndromes (epilepsy, after-effects of encephalitis, skeletal alterations, heart disease, enuresis, weight and height deficit)". It was not only their physical conditions that were alarming, though. The IQ of 67.5% of them was "lower than average", while 87.5% were "neurotics, maladjusted, par-anormal, disturbed". The "familial environment" was deemed to play a "determinant role": inadequate housing and "promiscuity" of marriage relations often "shocked the little ones". The precarious economic situation of 67% of the families had allegedly provoked the weight and height deficit, whereas "immigration" and its related "housing, working and integration problems" were indicated as "another cause of maladjustment".[182]

The data disclosed by Valente were taken for granted by the council-lors, with the only exception of the Communist Angiola Massucco Costa. The latter was also a renowned psychologist and head of the *Istituto di Psicologia Sociale* (Institute of Social Psychology) at the University of Turin. Throughout the 1950s and 1960s, she had dealt with the issue of migrations from the South and particularly with the stereotypes and prej-udices with regard to Southerners. The research she had conducted on the students of the *Istituto Magistrale "Domenico Berti"* (Teacher Training School "Domenico Berti") in Turin, for example, had revealed "the exist-ence of a very clear stereotype of the Southerners, with a prevailing negative content".[183] It is worth pointing out that Massucco Costa did not question the 'difference' between the North and the South in terms of progress: she attributed this to the "age-old different acculturation" of the two areas of the country.[184] Her view was consistent with the classical Marxist inter-pretation of the backwardness of the South and its inhabitants as result-ing from the persistence of "feudal familial traditions".[185] This condition would have been overcome by the migrants in the North-West, for they were developing their "class consciousness", as was evident in their partic-ipation in "struggles which they had *learnt* to conduct".[186] Even women – she added – were "rapidly assuming a greater awareness of their rights and of many cultural and human needs that once they ignored".[187] Her research approach was, however, significantly different from that of the above-mentioned psychiatrists and psychologists, for her main subject of study was the 'host society' and what she defined as its stereotypes. At the end of the 1960s, as will be discussed in more detail in the next section, she joined the campaign against the *classi differenziali* and the practice of making of them 'classes for immigrants'. As for Jacobbi's survey, during the Council session she highlighted "the damage brought to these children by the fact of being considered mentally defective". It would have been "fairer" – she thought – "to evaluate them not with an abstract intelligence quotient [...] but with more-up-to date criteria of personality development [taking into account] the manifold social, economic, cultural and sanitary parameters which can provide more convincing and steady results". Moreover, she warned that the "usual consequence of this kind of evaluation" was chil-dren's referral to the *classi differenziali*.[188]

The outcome of the survey caused an outcry in the press too. A few days after the Council session, the local newspaper *La Gazzetta del Popolo* ran a full-page article, significantly entitled "Turin poor immigrants' children are 'less clever'".[189] The whole article sums up the inferiorization of Southern children and their families taking place in Turin in the 1950s and 1960s. The use of inverted commas for the words "less clever" did not mark the newspaper's will to distance itself from the results of Jacobbi's work. Their validity was not called into question throughout the article. The inverted commas, though suggesting awareness of the discrimination implied in the title, only served to emphasize it further. Moreover, the word "immigrant" was intended to mean Southerners. The piece indeed opened with the "tragic and dreadful" plea of a "Southern father" to Dr. Jacobbi:

"Doctor, take this daughter of mine with you. She is almost twelve and I fear that her brothers take advantage of her. For now there is no danger, but if at some points she gets a baby, what do I do? We are cramped here, eight people in two rooms, I can't control everything, take her away".

The squalor in which this family was alleged to live was total, ranging from overcrowding to the risk of incest, and was represented as threatening the whole city. As the journalist remarked, the "fact" had not taken place in "other times" or in "remote countries" where "sub-human conditions of life, preceding any form of civilization" still subsisted, but had happened "in May 1969, in Turin". In reality – it was revealed – the scenario depicted by Jacobbi's survey was common to "at least 15% of school-age children" to the extent that the number of the *classi differenziali* was insufficient, as the *assessore* Frida Malan was reported to have pointed out. The extreme poverty of the families produced mentally defective children: "the child of the poor is less clever than the child of the rich only because he is poorer". It was therefore necessary to "heal the [present] ills [...] without creating others day by day". The remedy proposed by Malan herself was to stop migration: "[we have] nothing against immigrants or against FIAT, but there exist tragic objective situations that call for the transfer of industrial development to other areas of the country". Otherwise – she warned – the development of Turin and FIAT would become "suicide". Her analysis thus did not take into account migrants' will and it implicitly reproduced the negative image of their presence in Turin. No less gloomy was the view of Giuseppe Turletti, head doctor of the Council health office, according to whom what was being built was a "city of barricades". The sense of anguish about the future and an indication of its origin also came from the picture accompanying the article which portrayed two little boys playing with slings. In front of them were blocks of flats and weed-covered fields. The caption read: "Immigrant children play on the fields of the outskirts of the metropolis. Who will take care of them?"

3.4 The 1970s: continuities and change

The 1970s can be taken as a turning point for the question of Southern migrant children and special education as well as for the education system as a whole, not only in Turin, of course, but at a national level. Under the impact of the late 1960s protest movements, the school, its organization, and its practices were shaken by a storm of criticism. In the context of an overall critique of the existing social order, the educational institutions became some of the key sites in which the struggle for change characterizing those years unfolded. As for primary school, the *classi differenziali*, were no longer commonly seen as a valid instrument for advancing maladjusted children. Instead, they became the symbol of the class-based selection process and of the exclusion from mainstream education of certain categories of pupil.

This shift did not take place all at once and in an abrupt manner. Especially at the beginning of the decade, the opinions on the *classi differenziali* were extremely varied, as will be discussed below in more depth. On the one hand, the *classi differenziali* were finally discredited as an effective pedagogical instrument. On the other, however, this did not automatically imply that specific groups of pupils referred to them, such as Southern migrants in Turin, ceased to be conceived of as 'different' and, as a result, in need of help and special treatment. The method by which their 'otherness' was addressed was dismissed, but it is far less clear whether their alleged 'difference' was disputed or not.

The following pages are thus meant to offer an overview of this many-sided and complex process, without any pretence at completeness. First, I will analyse the coverage of a Southern fifteen-year-old boy's suicide in Turin, which seems useful to illustrate the intricate mixture of old and new elements in the approach to the issue of Southern migrant pupils; and second, I will offer an insight into the development of new teaching practices and the reorganization of primary education, as well as of the unfolding debate on the *classi differenziali* in the early 1970s.

3.4.1 *"Turin failed him and he hanged himself"*

The 1970s opened with a tragic event which shocked Turin and, to a certain extent, the whole country. Ciriaco Saldutto, a fifteen-year-old boy, hanged himself in June 1972. The son of an Apulian family, who had moved to Turin a few years earlier, he had failed the second grade of middle school. In the absence of a suicide note, this was indicated by the media as the cause of his death – which became a metaphor for the predicament of Southern migrant children, alienated in the industrial North-West.[190]

The newspaper *La Stampa* ran several articles depicting Saldutto as the powerless victim of "a city which rejected him".[191] The "Apulian shepherd boy",[192] who was claimed to having been watching over grazing cows in his native town in the province of Foggia before arriving in Turin, had apparently been both surprised and upset by the big city way of life. There he had "'discovered' the tram" – one of his teachers said – as well as the street lamps which "in his town [he] had never seen".[193] At the same time, however, soon after boarding "one of those long Southern trains", he looked "shocked and was frightened, I don't know of what", his mother was reported to recall. Of his home town he missed the sky: "to see the sky I have to go in the centre of the courtyard", a neighbour had been told once.[194] It was above all the school, however, that was held responsible for not having helped the "rootless" boy.[195]

His school performance had been considered extremely poor as a result of his lack of previous preparation. As his teacher of French put it: "I often realized that I could not understand what he had written in Italian; in French incredible things came out". In Italian too, his scripts were judged "intricate, without connections", focusing always on the same topics, such as "his countryside, pastures, the stream where he could catch fish with his hands". He was described as a meek, passive boy: "it was as if I had a plant, an object in front of me", the teacher of French declared.[196] The psychologist Tilde Giani Gallino was convinced that "school [was] an obstacle to be overcome" and that it "repressed personality". This view was echoed by the head of the primary school "Giuseppe Mazzini", who deemed it necessary to go beyond "marks, curricula and selection" and try to "understand what children have 'inside'". It was urgent to "reform education deeply". The criticism of educational institutions did not necessarily entail the questioning of the cultural underdevelopment of the Southerners. Angelo Lusso, head of the psychiatric services of Turin province, on the one hand, called for teachers to show more "tact and sympathy" towards problem pupils, and on the other insisted that "in the areas of immigration thousands of children are forced to move from conditions of sub-culture to a culture which is abstract for them".[197] For their part, the teachers and the principals of Saldutto's middle school "Antonio Pacinotti" complained that there were among their pupils some "real hooligans". As a result of their allegedly typical "immigrant's awe", they usually reacted by "withdrawing into themselves, or with an exaggerated vivacity leading to hooliganism".[198]

The boy's family also blamed the education system. "The school has to understand our problems, not to kill", the weeping mother was reported to have exclaimed, while other women "made a chorus with high moans". Parents and relatives expressed their anger – it was remarked – "a bit in [Italian], a lot in dialect".[199] Pictures of the mother's and father's faces twisted with despair and looking like both a cry of pain and a public act of indictment accompanied two of the articles, as if their bodies could speak better than their words. The mother's photograph accompanying the article on the funeral, significantly entitled "Let's try not to forget why he died", portrayed the woman as a suffering "black veiled" Madonna, held up by a bare-headed lady in modern dress. Interestingly enough, the last words on the matter were those of a teacher. Though confirming the 'otherness' of Southern migrants, who "speak dialect, have others habits, a different way of life", the teacher asserted that "school [had] to adjust itself", to change assessment and teaching methods and even to abolish the *classi differenziali*.[200]

The magazine *Oggi* too covered the case with an article by Neera Fall which, taking its cue from the Turin episode, addressed the question the inadequacies of the school as an institution in meeting the increas demand for schooling from the lower strata of the population. Saldutto's figure was depicted following the stereotypical traits which *La Stampa* had already attributed to him: the bucolic childhood, during which "his eyes had not, in curiosity, scanned pictures on books, [but] had instead swept through the meadow where he herded the cattle to the pasture" and could catch fish with his hands; the homesickness, the fear of the traffic and the nostalgia for the sky; the "intricate and meaningless" scripts.[201] The article was also accompanied by some pictures, two of which were intended to make the reader "figure out the social environment in which Ciriaco Saldutto had grown up": one portrayed his native stone house, surrounded by green hills and trees; the other, instead, showed the two-room apartment where he had "ended up living" in Turin. Once again, however, the story became the metaphor for the fallacies of educational institutions. The number of failing pupils was too high and, as a result, many of these, who were most commonly born to poor families, left before finishing middle school. According to Gavino Sanna, principal of one of Milan's several middle schools and columnist for the magazine itself, the intelligence of the children of well-off and educated families was "like an already ploughed and hoed field" whereas that of the poor was "like a field which the school has to begin to plough and hoe before starting the seeding". The current school organization was, however, unfit to meet this kind of need. After four hours of school, children were sent back home where, if poor, nobody could help them with their homework. Who may have helped the "factory worker's child" – Sanna asked – if their parents "often do not know the orthography and, while reading, move their lips and follow the line with their finger so as not to lose their place?". The solution to be pursued was therefore full-time school (*scuola a tempo pieno*), where children would have to remain both in the morning and in the afternoon. Moreover, both Sanna and Fallaci wished for the abolition of the *classi differenziali*, seen as "instruments of selection".

It was, however, Ivan Della Mea's 1971 song, *Ballata per Ciriaco Saldutto* (The Ballad for Ciriaco Saldutto) which made the boy's death the symbol of the effects of a class-based education system to be vigorously and openly opposed along with the whole social order.[202] Della Mea had been a member of the *Nuovo Canzoniere Italiano* group (New Italian Song-Book), founded in Milan in the 1960s with the aim of rediscovering Italian folk music, and had already written songs inspired by real and often tragic events, linked to social and political issues.[203] As well as the title, the very first lines of the song made direct reference to Saldutto's suicide: "he is fifteen years old/surname Saldutto/middle school pupil/school 'Pacinotti'/ come from Apulia, immigrant 'terrone' /Turin failed him and he has hanged himself".[204] The lyrics made use of the most characteristic 1970s left-wing protest movement language. The purpose was to expose and denounce the injustice of a school deemed to be one of the capitalist bourgeoisie's instruments of power over the lower classes. As the refrain put it: "to make things clear we say: it's a crime/another crime of the repression/using the law, the gun and the school/to make us more servants of our master".[205] By transmitting the 'culture' of the bourgeoisie – it was claimed – the school ensured that the capitalist order was reproduced: "it is well known that the master/wants his workers instructed and well educated/with his culture and his discipline/he shapes the servants of every workshop".[206] Those who did not conform to this model, such as Saldutto and Southern migrants, were destined to fail: "but there is no struggle, there are no conditions/'terrone', you adapt yourself or it will happen/that the repression of all the masters/using school marks as a weapon will exclude you".[207] Saldutto, the powerless victim of a society to be held responsible for his death, was left with no choice but to kill himself: "So at fifteen years old/they've also taken the sky away from you/and in return they gave you/a void of nothing/and the last toy they've left you/is a piece of rope/and you've hanged yourself".[208]

3.4.2 The full-time experiment

The representation of the case of Ciriaco Saldutto by the media, as well as by Della Mea's song, illustrates an important shift in the way in which the educational problem of Southern migrant children was viewed. On the one hand, it seems that the possibility that the boy's suicide could stand as an act of free will and an expression of agency was not contemplated at all. Furthermore, the media did not object to Southern migrant pupils' presumed need to receive special care and treatment, as well as their 'otherness'. On the other hand, however, the education system as a whole, including the *classi differenziali*, was called into question and held responsible for what had happened.

Such a change is to be seen in the wider context of the late 1960s and 1970s protest movements, whose main targets included educational institutions. Though the most prominent arenas of struggle were university and high schools – or at least the latter have been accorded greater attention by historians – primary education was also deeply involved in the debate over a school system deemed authoritarian and based on class selection ideology and practices from the lowest to the highest level.[209] It was not a matter of chance that the "single most influential text in the student movement", *Lettera a una professoressa*, written by the dissident priest Don Lorenzo Milani and eight of his pupils in the Tuscan rural village of Vicchio Mugello, focused on the mechanism of exclusion of poor students from compulsory education.[210] The inadequacies of reform in a period of change, the increasing demand for instruction and the appearance of a new generation of teachers made it imperative to question the *status quo* and offer alternatives. The calls for change did not come from full-time students and teachers only, but also from the working class and, later on, from the feminist movement. The experience of the so-called "150 hours" of paid educational leave, first granted to metalworkers and subsequently extended to other workers' categories, including housewives, is an indication of the new social and political meaning attached to education as well as of the will to renegotiate the relation between the masses and the school system.[211]

As for special education, the anti-psychiatric movement considerably undermined the prestige and authority of psychiatry. In 1974, in Turin, a psychiatrist, Giorgio Coda, was tried and condemned to five years imprisonment for having abused his patients. During his long career, Coda had been working in the local CMPP run by the ONMI. He had been a director in the Turin province, and had been working in the Collegno asylum until he became head of the Grugliasco child medical-pedagogical institute "Villa Azzurra". Finally, he had even been appointed honorary judge of Turin juvenile court. He was accused of and condemned for having used therapeutic methods for punitive purposes, as many former asylum patients testified in the course of the trial. The case was brought by the *Associazione per la lotta contro le malattie mentali* (ALMM, Association for the Struggle against Mental Illnesses), an organization set up in Turin in 1967 in the wake of the experience of Franco Basaglia's team at Gorizia, which had been since then denouncing the condition of the psychiatric hospitals' inmates.[212]

There were several actors involved in the dispute over the primary education system, including grassroots organizations, teachers, and educators. The demands included the abolition of the *patronato scolastico*, the rejection of marking and of the *classi differenziali*, the setting up of full-time school and the adoption of different teaching materials and methodologies. One of the most influential and well organized teachers' organizations on the frontline was the *Movimento di cooperazione educativa* (MCE, Movement for Educational Cooperation). Inspired by the ideas of the French pedagogist Célestin Freinet, whose innovative teaching techniques – such as the study of the human and natural environment outside the classroom, the production by students and teachers of class-newspapers, and the correspondence between pupils of different schools, to cite but a few – had become known throughout the world, the MCE had been operating in Italy since the early 1950s. It was, however, towards the end of the following decade that it gained growing prominence as it promoted and helped spread the protest movements' demands among teachers.

The Turin group of the MCE was among the most active and, at the turn of the 1970s, some of its adherents led one of the first Italian experiments in full-time school in the peripheral neighbourhoods of *Le Vallette – Santa Caterina*. The initiative was supported by the local *comitato di quartiere* (neighbourhood committee). In December 1969, during a meeting between teachers and the committee itself, it was decided to extend the full-time system – which was already in place in two classes – to the whole local primary school "Nino Costa". "Our children" – it was reported in the cyclo-styled paper *La voce delle Vallette* (Vallette's Voice) – "need a 'full-time' school, that is a school where they may spend morning and afternoon". The document contained a sharp denunciation of the situation of primary schools in the area and of its negative impact particularly on migrants:

"We are told that children cannot go to school in the afternoon because there is a shortage of teachers: but we have found out [as a result of the meeting with the teachers] that in Italy there are 100.000 unemployed teachers; we are told that there is a shortage of classrooms, but we have found out that at the "Nino Costa" there are five empty classrooms, which nobody is using. [...] Moreover this school (the school which should be for workers' children) very often fails children. [...] We had a look at the statistics of our neighbourhood schools and found out that all [failing pupils] are the children of recent immigrants: it means that they fail because they are still not able to express themselves in the masters' language, because they can't keep themselves still at their desks, they can't accept that discipline to which the masters have wanted to educate them since they were little. We have also found out that a few years ago the *classi differenziali* have been set up at the *Vallette* primary school. The authorities send to these classes the most vivacious, restless and naughty children; they keep them separate from the others (so that they 'do not damage' the best behaved and clever)".[213]

The collaboration between MCE teachers and parents was, however, not always harmonious. Full-time school did not mean just a prolongation of the time children spent in school and the possibility of having two teachers rather than one. It also entailed a new didactic approach, to which parents were not always keen to conform. Fiorenzo Alfieri, one of the leading figures of the MCE and teacher at the "Nino Costa", complained about the unwillingness of "working-class families" to consent to the most modern teaching methods. As he pointed out, "the most aware and advanced working-class families do not find it hard to appreciate that their children undertake new kinds of school activities dissimilar from the traditional ones".[214] They thus seemed to be happy that their sons and daughters "spent many hours debating, writing freely, painting, working in groups, breeding animals and cultivating the vegetable garden". What they refused to accept were the changes in their children's behaviour coming as a result of the anti-authoritarian pedagogy practised in the classrooms. Children whose "creative abilities [were] respected and developed" by their teachers became "troublesome beings [for their parents], who discuss before obeying, want to know the reason for everything, object to the behaviour of teachers and parents that they do not consider appropriate". Once at home, children found "insurmountable walls erected by adults who have no intention of putting in doubt the more or less stable balance of familial relationships" and their reaction was often "violent and troublesome", as the parents themselves had reported to teachers.[215] Another subject of contention was teachers' approach to sexuality, meant to pose – in Alfieri's words – a challenge to the "sexual taboos imposed by our repressive soci ety". Parents complained not only about "children's freer behaviour", bu also about school debates and research on topics such as abortion, homo-sexuality, and prostitution. It was thus necessary for working-class families to "understand how the current system cannot be thrown into crisis only in some fields and preserved in others; one has to have the courage to change it completely and forever".[216]

Other teachers' associations, such as the Turin branch of the Catholic AIMC, were far more moderate and somewhat ambiguous towards full-time school. On the one hand, the association recognized that compul-sory school was "deeply unfair [because] it gives more to those who have more" and that there were many "reasons to ask for full-time" school.[217] On the other, however, it warned that "a well qualified group of teachers [was] using school for precise political purposes" and could for this reason cause the failure of the experiment of full-time school, which the Minister of Public Instruction had officially started in eighty-two primary school classes of four different primary schools in 1971.[218]

Among the teachers themselves, full-time school was the object of intense debate and sometimes of harsh confrontations between those for and against. This was the case of the "Gian Enrico Pestalozzi", which was among the handful of schools involved in the starting of full-time edu-cation. Not all the teachers had decided to make their classes full-time, though. During the school year 1971/72, a head-on clash took place with the teaching staff split into two opposed factions. According to the teacher E.T., who had been working at the "Pestalozzi" at least since the 1960s, full-time classes were nothing more than a source of problems for the school, whose lack of classrooms had already led to the two-shift system. The fact that some classrooms were going to be occupied in the morning and in the afternoon by the same group of pupils – the full-time ones – would have worsened the situation for all the others. Furthermore, he claimed that "older teachers" had not been informed of the experiment whose architects had been "a very small minority of teachers (3 or 4 out of 35) who in the past had distinguished themselves by aggression and by their pronounced political character".[219]   Others explained in their registers that "such an innovation required facilities and a didactic preparation which the majority of teachers [did] not possess".[220] Someone suggested that "immigrant fam-ilies [living in the area] with so many children and poor culture [...] [were] easily tempted by the prospect of keeping their children at the school for the whole day" and it was not difficult to convince them that "the work-ing class is no longer to be exploited by the ruling class and that all that has been done so far in schools relates exclusively to the 'masters' caste'". School – it was remarked – was meant to improve pupils and "not to make them maladjusted, anarchic and ill-mannered".[221]

The solution adopted was to move the full-time classes to another building. Nonetheless, even teachers who were adhering to the experiment were not satisfied by the way in which it was handled by the authorities, to the extent that they organized a strike which took place in February 1972.Besides the revision of the old-fashioned primary school curriculum and more funding for teaching and playing facilities, they requested the "presence in *every building* of a psycho-medical-pedagogical team in order to guarantee to all children showing adjustment difficulties a real and constant therapy address-ing the problems of the individual and of the group, instead of the mere diag-nosis [which is meant] exclusively to select and marginalize them and does not solve problems".[222]The medical-psycho-pedagogical teams did, however, provide advice and treatment to some pupils at least. This was the case of the second-grade boy, N.M., who, according to his teacher, was "introverted and intolerant of any form of discipline" and, for this reason, had been recom-mended by "the psychologist and the social worker" to be moved to a full-time class.[223] This occurrence was not isolated. Two grade-three teachers reported that on the one hand, during the first school days, there had been a "continuous exodus" of pupils from their full-time class owing to the "deni-gration of full-time", which had been taking place in the neighbourhood; on the other, several "backward children, with severe didactic and social defi-ciencies" had arrived from other classes "where they often were not wanted". As a result, teachers, together with the psycho-medical-pedagogical team, tried to investigate their pupils' "environmental and familial conditions and their intellectual and psychic possibilities" in order to help the "recovery of [those] showing major difficulties in settling in" within the class. The interest in the lives of families was also linked, however, to teaching activities, espe-cially to history teaching. Children themselves had carried out a "survey" concerning their families, whose outcome had proved to be useful for "stud-ying working conditions and the phenomenon of immigration", which many of them had experienced.[224]

The attempts to get an 'objective' knowledge of pupils' living conditions were not uncommon among full-time teachers. Two of them, for exam-ple, drew up an extensive "sociological and environmental profile" of their third-grade class. The report seems to suggest that, alongside an alternative view of teaching and, more generally, of the role of school and education, there persisted some continuities in the way in which migrant pupils were viewed. Spurred on by the will to analyse the "objective conditions in which [they] performed [their] didactic activities and make these consistent with the former", the teachers had used a set of different parameters, such as, for example, "the failure rate [and] the emigration rate". The "failure index" was indicated as "very high", as it amounted to 39%: out of eighteen pupils, three had already repeated two years and four had already been failed once. The "emigration index" too was considerable: only three children were not reported to be "immigrants", whereas ten were of "second emigration, that is to say that their parents emigrated first and had been in Turin for a gen-eration [and] five [...] had emigrated recently". The latter were reported to be experiencing the "psychosocial consequences of this phenomenon", summarized as "difficulty in passing from the previous living condition (often of an agricultural or artisanal kind, of which they have retained habits and mindset) to a radically different condition". This had led the "most fragile subjects" to develop a "permanent lack of self-confidence [causing] a situation of maladjustment". Such a condition manifested itself in many different forms, but the "most severe difficulties" were alleged to be the "linguistic ones". Many children were native speakers of "several dialects" and their command of Italian was reported to be limited to few "verbs and keywords (for instance, the verb 'to do') which they use in a constant and repetitive manner". The main didactic aims were thus the "gradual recall of these subjects to the Italian language [and] a patient and constant work on orthography through continuous exercises".[225] At least in this case, dialect was seen, as had happened in the past, as proper to migrants and even a symptom of their maladjustment. Furthermore, these teachers seemed to place it in a subordinate position with respect to Italian and, by focusing on orthography, revealed a strictly normative approach to language teaching. The importance attached to orthography and the devaluation of dialects were indicated by the linguists who, in 1973, had set up the *Gruppo di intervento e studio nel campo dell'educazione linguistica* (GISCEL, Group for Action and Research in Language Education), as one of the main characteristics of what they referred to as the "traditional language pedagogy". The GISCEL had indeed produced a manifesto, known as *Dieci tesi per l'educazione linguistica democratica* (Ten Theses for Democratic Language Education), in which they criticized the then current and well-entrenched language teaching methods. They also proposed a new language pedagogy based on the recognition by teachers of the importance of spoken language – up to that time secondary to the written one – and of all the linguistic varieties.[226] This new approach was promptly followed and spread by several teachers' association, including the MCE. Nonetheless, as has been recently remarked, its impact on day-to-day language teaching practice has been limited, mostly because teachers have not been provided with adequate training.[227] A study conducted at the end of the 1990s by the Institute of Philology of the University of Palermo of one hundred and sixty-seven primary schools throughout the country has shown how the prejudice towards dialect is still widespread among schoolchildren themselves, owing, among other reasons, also to teachers' persistent belief that "dialect is a poor language, the expression of a degraded and marginal world".[228]

3.4.3 *"The great maladjusted"*

The setting up in the early 1970s of some full-time classes in a limited number of primary schools did not involve the sudden disappearance of the *classi differenziali*, whose function in the context of a changing approach to education was intensely debated. In this case too, the stances were extremely varied. On the one hand, the *differenziali* were the object of a strong wave of criticism and were viewed as the clearest expression of the exclusion of lower-class children from mainstream education. On the other hand, some continued to defend their role in helping problem pupils or to call for continuing their existence at least until a new model of primary school had been organized.

The debate that unfolded in the Communist Party educational journal, *Riforma della scuola*, between 1969 and the early 1970s, was significant and hard-hitting. The controversy was sparked by the publication of an article summarizing the outcome of a screening of all first-grade pupils attending primary schools in Ferrara carried out by the local centre for mental hygiene – and with the collaboration of the authors themselves – in order to evaluate the intelligence of each child and, if required, refer them to special education.[229] The testing revealed that the intelligence quotient of 251 pupils out of 1714 was below average and that 36.58% of these were from "families of unskilled workers and farm workers, that is to say families from the lowest economic level". They lived in "isolated rural homes" and could only speak the local idiom, *ferrarese*, a "dialect of Celtic origin whose links with Italian are few and uncertain". Another 33.33% were instead generically indicated as "subproletarians" without providing any further details. The high percentage of "mental subnormals" even in Emilia, an "economically and socially advanced region", was defined as alarming and requiring immediate intervention[230]. The authors called for early testing of children soon after their "school debut" and suggested that those referred to the *classi differenziali* should remain there from the first primary school grade to the end of compulsory education.[231]

The article was bitterly criticized in one of the following issues of the periodical by the child neuropsychiatrist Michele Zappella.[232] He challenged the fact that Ferrara children had been screened through tests written in a language – that is Italian – which, as the authors themselves had underlined, they did not know or speak habitually. In his view, the authors were "giving a pseudo-scientific basis to some basic contradictions of compulsory school", which was only officially open to everybody, being in reality a "class-based, authoritarian, transmission belt of the bourgeoisie's traditional values, centred on the enhancement of verbal abilities to the detriment of practical aspects of intelligence, unable to understand and accept the various subcultures of the various regions and substantially unsuited to subproletarian classes, made not for them but against them".[233]

It was, however, for the pedagogist Bruno Ciari to reverse completely the traditional perspective on the *classi differenziali* and, more generally, on special education by asserting that it was the education system that was "maladjusted".[234] In the early 1950s, Ciari had been among the founders of the MCE and was one of its most prominent figures. His criticism was addressed not only to the authors of the article on the Ferrara school population, but to what he saw as a more general tendency toward the creation of "permanent and differentiated school channels", which had found expression also at a legislative level.[235]

In July 1969, a bill on the reorganization of social services for "psychically, physically, sensorially and socially maladjusted" people had been presented to the Chamber of Deputies and was backed by more than a hundred members of Parliament.[236] The so-called *disegno di legge Foschi* (Foschi bill) – so named after its first signatory – relied on a series of data, including those presented by Giovanni Bollea in the early 1960s and mentioned above, which depicted an alarming scenario: 5–10% of the Italian population was affected by a form of maladjustment and, with regard to schoolchildren, the percentage amounted to 20–25%. It thus called explicitly for an "organized tracking (*reperimento*) of maladjusted subjects" to be carried out "through a systematic and periodic research on the whole population".[237] Moreover, maladjusted children, for whom co-education with normal subjects was not recommended, were to be referred to "special classes" where they had to remain from the first primary school grade up to the last one of middle school.[238] According to Ciari, the underlying logic of projects like this was to meet the needs of the Italian productive system of the time: to have at its disposal a small minority of graduates and a vast reserve of unskilled workers. School – as he pointed out – was "traditionally intended to pick out from the mass of pupils the most efficient minority [while tending] fatally to marginalize and reject those who do not meet, within certain precise time limits, the required levels of efficiency and competitiveness".[239] Failing pupils, who constituted a heavy burden for teachers, were to be directed towards special education so that they could contribute to the productive system, though in a "subaltern" way, without damaging normal children's productivity.[240] The creation of separate educational channels, though, needed to be provided with the "scientific backing" of psychiatrists and psychologists who relied on mental tests, whose only aim was to ascertain the extent to which a child had "adjusted them to certain models of behaviour imposed by the dominant class" and not to measure their intelligence or abilities.[241] Experts such as those working in Ferrara considered test results "as gospel" and did not take into account the fact that the school as an institution was the "great maladjusted". It was indeed failing to accomplish its most important tasks, such as offering adequate space to satisfy pupils' "needs for exploration, adventure, conquest", giving children the opportunity to express themselves freely and to develop their "expressive and creative potential". On the contrary, they were shut into a "narrow parallelepiped [that is to say the school building] often intolerably overcrowded". It was hardly surprising that children adjusted themselves only with great difficulty to this situation and it was time to start wondering if indeed the "recalcitrant and resistant [were] the more 'normal'".[242]

The debate was also joined by Marco Cecchini, a psychologist working at the Institute of Psychology of the *Consiglio nazionale delle ricerche* (CNR, National Research Council) and author of a study on school failure among primary and middle school pupils and *classi differenziali*.[243] Cecchini argued that, according to his analysis of official statistical data, between 1959 and 1967, at a national level, the rate of failure of primary school pupils had "remained high and almost constant (1959: 34%, 1967:30%)".[244] Moreover, once failed, a primary school pupil had a 45% probability of being failed again. This meant – Cecchini pointed out – not only that to fail a student was useless but, above all, that "exclusion creates exclusion".[245] As for the social class of failing pupils, the majority were "proletarians and peasant sub-proletarians".[246] An analysis of regional trends showed that "failure affected 'Southerners' in a very selective way": the percentage of failing students had remained the same between 1959 and 1966 and it had dropped only "in the regions of central and Northern Italy where Southern immigration had *not* taken place (except the Veneto)".[247] The situation was not different for middle school whose "selective structure was practically unchanged" in spite of the 1962 reform. The data clearly demonstrated – in Cecchini's view – that the registered growth of failure rates in Northern regions could "be explained *only* by taking emigration into due account and recognizing that school selection has massively affected the children of Southern immigrants [as a result] of cultural and linguistic differences and of a different school structure between the North and the South".[248] The pressure engendered by the high number of failing students was eased through the "diffusion and enhancement of the classi differenziali". The latter were particularly widespread in "'poor neighbourhoods', in areas where two cultures come into contact (city and countryside) and where teachers are driven to continuous comparisons between 'two kinds of pupil'; in other words *classi differenziali* are intended to exclude pupils with socio-cultural learning problems".[249]

The issue of Southern migrant children and the practice of referring them to the *classi differenziali* was addressed with specific reference to Turin by Angiola Massucco Costa.[250] This was to be numbered "among the most urgent problems affecting [Turin] schools".[251] To the *differenziali* – she argued – were sent pupils with the "most varied forms of maladjustment", tested by the medical-psycho-pedagogical teams in a "superficial" manner when the school year had already started.[252] Furthermore, the tests measured the "level and the type of performance required by the social environment in which schools were located" and thus were not "culture-free". Her approach was, however, characterized by some contradictions. For example, she warned against the negative effects on pupils' personalities which could arise from the habit of "repressing peculiarities and cultural qualities proper to traditions and attitudes [whose importance] is not recognized in primary schools, as well as dialects and other expressive forms peculiar to cultural sub-groups which are not recognized". However, her proposal for starting to sort out these questions was the establishment of "summer courses for immigrants" in order to help the recovery of "children who had just undergone a settling-in trauma, and are not to be treated as sub-normal".[253]

The *classi differenziali* became in Turin an increasingly vexed question for the authorities too. In 1970, the Council organized a roundtable aimed – according to the *assessore* for Public Instruction, Vinicio Lucci – at "clarifying the ideas on this topic" and offering suggestions for those "initiatives that our Society is demanding and expecting".[254] The speakers included, among others, one of the most prominent advocates of post-war *classi differenziali*, Giovanni Bollea. Interestingly enough, Bollea declared himself forced to make "a sort of self-criticism".[255] The *classi differenziali* had indeed proved to be a failure: of the 5,600 classes then existing in Italy, not one – Bollea argued – was a "real *classe differenziale*".[256] The subjects who had up to then been referred to special education had instead to be kept in a "normal class" and followed by experts working with them for a certain number of hours in order to favour the recovery of "their deficit".[257] The local primary school inspector Andreina Loreti Ricci also advocated alternative solutions. The *classi differenziali* had progressively turned out to be safety valves" where teachers could place "problem pupils". These usually were children with "transitional behavioural disturbance", those with "slightly below average intelligence", as well as children who, owing to "recent immigration [and a] situation of moral and material misery", were "anti-social".[258] Furthermore, the number of psycho-medical-pedagogical teams was too low to ensure an effective service. Even more importantly, she underlined how problem pupils would have better recovered in a "normal class, not only with good understanding and sensitive teachers but also with classmates [able to] stimulate them".[259] Being referred to a *classe differenziale* was instead a "humiliation", since, in spite of all the attempts at disguise, it was commonly considered a class of "different" pupils.[260] Her proposal thus was the abolition of the *differenziali* and the implementation of full-time schools, where "especially children living in a difficult, narrow and insufficient environment" could find adequate space and support for their personal development.[261]

Full-time school and the abolition of the *differenziali*, with the consequent integration of children who had once attended them into normal classes, constituted the cornerstone of the so-called *documento Falcucci*. The latter, presented to the Parliament in 1975, contained the results of the work carried out by a special commission, chaired by Senator Franca Falcucci, whose main task had been to investigate and propose alternative solutions to the issue of special education.[262] The document provided the basis for the official suppression of the *differenziali*.[263] The early 1970s debate on special education and the initiatives for the setting up of a new system of primary education certainly led in this direction.

Notes

1 Id., Register by R.M., Main Site, V grade, mixed sex, 1962/63.
2 For a general overview, see for example, the special issue of the journal *History of Education*, XXIV, 2, 2005 edited by Annemieke Van Drenth and dedicated to special education.
3 Marland, H., Gijswijt-Hofstra, M., (eds), *Cultures of Child Health in Britain and the Netherlands in the Twentieth Century*, Amsterdam: Rodopi, 2003,

p. 7. See also Cooter, R., (ed.), *In the Name of the Child. Health and Welfare 1880–1940*, London: Routledge, 1992.

4 Cunningham, H., *Children and Childhood in Western Society since 1500*, London: Longman, 1995, p. 165.

5 Guarnieri, P., "Un piccolo essere perverso. Il bambino nella cultura scientifica italiana tra Otto e Novecento", *Contemporanea*, IX, 2, 2006, pp. 253–84. On the birth of Italian paediatrics see also Guarnieri, P., "E la mamma dov'è? Medici, donne e bambini nell'Ottocento", *Bollettino di Demografia Storica*, 30–1, 1999, pp. 95–117; Caroli, D., *Day Nurseries and Childcare in Europe, 1800–1939*, London: Palgrave, 2017.

6 Babini, V.P., *La questione dei frenastenici. Alle origini della psicologia scientifica in Italia (1870–1910)*, Milan: Angeli, 1996, p. 43.

7 Idem.

8 Arzenati, P.M., *La Rivista 'L'Infanzia Anormale' (1911–1925)*, Unpublished MA Dissertation, Faculty of Letters and Philosophy, University of Milan, 2005–2006.

9 Cenci, S., "Profilo biografico di Sante De Sanctis", in Cimino, G., Lombardo, G.P., (eds), *Sante De Sanctis tra psicologia generale e psicologia applicata*, Milan: Angeli, 2004. The *asili-scuola* were day schools intended for poor children, while for those belonging to well-off families De Sanctis founded *Villa Amalia*, a nursing home. See Babini, *La questione dei frenastenici*, cit. p. 63.

10 On the early work of Maria Montessori as well as on her activity as a feminist campaigner, see Babini, V., Lama, L., *Una donna nuova. Il femminismo scientifico di Maria Montessori*. Milan: Angeli, 2003.

11 Rovigatti, M.T., "Le classi differenziali in Italia", *Infanzia anormale*, XXIV, 5, 1954, pp. 65–82.

12 Gibelli, A., *L'officina della guerra. La Grande Guerra e le trasformazioni del mondo mentale*, Turin: Bollati Boringhieri, 1991; Scartabellati, A., *Intellettuali nel conflitto. Alienisti e patologie attraverso la Grande Guerra (1909–1921)*, Bagnaria Arsa: Edizioni Goliardiche, 2003.

13 Mantovani, C., *Rigenerare la società. L'eugenetica in Italia dalle origini ottocentesche agli anni Trenta*, Soveria Mannelli: Rubettino, 2004, p. 186.

14 De Sanctis, S., "L'organizzazione scientifica del lavoro mentale", *Rivista Italiana di Sociologia*, XX, 5–6, 1916, pp. 496–530 cited in Arzenati, P. cit.

15 Mental tests, meant to measure the psychological and intellectual 'abnormality' of the individuals, were first introduced in Italy at the end of the nineteenth century by Giulio Cesare Ferrari. De Sanctis, however, proposed his own version of mental tests – known as *reattivi De Sanctis* – in 1905 at the International Congress of Psychology in Rome. See Ferreri, A.M., "Sante De Sanctis", in Cimino, G., Dazzi, N., (eds), *La psicologia in Italia. I protagonisti e i problemi scientifici, filosofici e istituzionali (1870–1945)*, Milan: LED, 1998, pp. 255–96 and Cimino, G., Lombardo, G.P. (eds), cit.

16 Lombardo, G.P., Cenci, S., "La concezione differenziale di Sante De Sanctis negli studi di psicologia applicata", in Cimmino, G., Lombardo, G.P., (eds), cit., p. 198.

17 On the history of LIPIM, see Mantovani, C., cit. and Cassata F. *Molti, sani e forti. L'eugenetica in Italia*. Turin: Bollati Boringhieri, 2006. For an overview on the mental hygiene movement, see Thomson, M., "Mental hygiene as an international movement", in Weindling, P., (ed.) *International Health Organizations and Movements, 1918–1939*, Cambridge: Cambridge University Press, 1995, pp. 283–304.

18 Cassata, F., cit., pp. 137–8 and Mantovani, C., cit., p. 317.

19 The measure was first included in the Royal Decree 31 December 1923, no. 3126 on compulsory schooling, which was extended to deaf and blind

children, and subsequently into the Royal Decree 5 February 1928, no. 577, a comprehensive text containing all the regulations concerning elementary and post-elementary education.

20 Arcamone, G., "L'Istituto biotipologico-ortogenetico di Genova", *Annali dell'Istruzione Elementare*, V, 2, 1930, p. 38.

21 Cassata, F., cit., p. 193. On Pende and his Institute see also Mantovani, C., cit.

22 Idem, p. 192.

23 Arcamone, G., cit., p. 44. Other articles included: "Le finalità scientifiche e i mezzi d'indagine dell'Istituto biotipologico di Genova", *Annali dell'istruzione elementare*, V, 3–4, 1930, pp. 18–53; Gualco, S., "Forme di crescenza accertate e curate nella scuola in un quinquennio", *Annali dell'istruzione elementare*, XI, 4–5, 1936, pp. 134–61; Idem, "Il controllo della crescenza ad uso degli educatori", *Annali dell'istruzione elementare*, XI, 4–5–6, 1936, pp. 224–33.

24 Royal Decree 26 April 1928, no. 1297.

25 On the 1904 law and the criticism coming from psychiatrists see Moraglio, M., "Dentro e fuori il manicomio. L'assistenza psichiatrica in Italia tra le due guerre", *Contemporanea*, 1, 2006, pp. 15–34.

26 See Bollea, G., "Evoluzione storica e attualità della neuropsichiatria infantile", *Infanzia anormale*, 37, 1960, pp. 141–63. On Bollea see Fiorani, M., "Giovanni Bollea (1913–2011). Per una storia della neuropsichiatria infantile in Italia", *Medicina&Storia*, 21–22, 2011, pp. 251–276. The SEPEG was a transnational organization whose work focused on the consequences of the war on children from a multidisciplinary perspective. See Boussion, S., Gardet, M., Ruchat, M., *L'internationale des républiques d'enfants (1939–1955)*, Paris: Anamosa, 2020.

27 On its history and mission see Montesano, G., "La S.I.A.M.E.", in *Infanzia anormale*, 2, 1953, pp. 131–38.

28 See De Sanctis, C. "Il Comitato Italiano per la Psichiatria Infantile", *Infanzia anormale*, 1, 1953, pp. 15–29.

29 Giordano, G.G., "Significato e Funzioni del Centro Medico-Psico-Pedagogico", *Infanzia anormale*, 6, 1954, pp. 207–18.

30 There is a growing amount of literature on this topic. On the United States and Canada see Richardson, T., *The Century of the Child. The Mental Hygiene Movement and Social Policy in the United States and Canada*, Albany: State University of New York Press, 1989; on the British case see Stewart, J., "The scientific claims of British Child Guidance, 1918–1945", *British Journal for the History of Science*, 42, 3, 2009, pp. 407–32.

31 Bollea, G., "La selezione scolastica. Principi teorici e organizzazione pratica", *Infanzia anormale*, n. 6, 1954, p. 222.

32 Idem, p. 221

33 Idem, p. 223.

34 Ibidem.

35 Rovigatti, M.T., "La classe differenziale", *Infanzia anormale*, 6, 1954, p. 234.

36 Bollea, "Evoluzione storica e attualità della neuropsichiatria infantile", *Infanzia anormale*, 37, 1960, p. 151. The concept of maladjustment had already been employed and acquired growing prominence in other European countries during the interwar period. On Britain see Hayes, S., "Rabbits and Rebels. The Medicalization of Maladjusted Children in Mid-Twentieth Century Britain", in Jackson, M., (ed.) *Health and the Modern Home*, London: Routledge, 2007, pp. 128–52. On France see Chauvière, M., *Enfance inadaptée, l'héritage de Vichy*, Paris: Éditions Ovrière, 1980 [L'Harmanattan, 2009].

37 Ibidem.

38 Idem, pp. 159.

39 Idem, p. 160.

40 Ibidem.

41 Bollea, G., "Le pedagogie speciali nelle scuole elementari". Problematiche del 'depistage' e del trattamento dei disadattati", *Annali della pubblica istruzione*, n. 12–13, 1964, p. 290.

42 Ibidem.

43 De Toni, G., "Importanza medico-sociale del problema della tardività mentale", in *Atti del Primo simposio nazionale sul recupero dei bambini ritardati e difficili. Quaderni di Infanzia anormale*, 2, 1962, p. 27.

44 De Franco, F., "Per una legislazione organica in materia di igiene mentale infantile", in *Igiene mentale*, 1962, p. 287.

45 Bollea, G., "Le pedagogie speciali nelle scuole elementari", cit., p. 287.

46 Bollea, G., "Evoluzione e attualità della neuropsichiatria infantile", cit.

47 See Chapter 2.

48 Law 24 July 1962 no. 1073, "Provvedimenti per lo sviluppo della scuola nel triennio dal 1962 al 1965", *Gazzetta Ufficiale*, 8 August 1962. About this bill see also Chapter 2.

49 Law 31 October 1966 no. 942, "Finanziamento del piano di sviluppo della scuola nel quinquennio dal 1966 al 1970", in *Gazzetta Ufficiale*, 15 November 1966.

50 Ministero della Pubblica Istruzione, *Relazione della commissione d'indagine sullo stato e sullo sviluppo della pubblica istruzione in Italia*, Vol. I., *Testo della relazione*, Rome, 1963, p. 342. On the commission see chpater 2.

51 Circular 4 January 1962 no. 103, *Classi differenziali*, in Zanobini, L., *Raccolta delle circolari della Pubblica Istruzione*. Vol. I: *Istruzione Primaria*, Milan: Giuffrè, 1965, p. 815.

52 Circular 9 July 1962 no. 4525, in Idem, pp. 817–9.

53 Circular 2 February 1963 no. 934/6, in Idem, p. 822

54 Bollea G., "Il medico scolastico come psico-igienista", *Igiene mentale*, 1962, p. 418.

55 Molinari, A., "La salute", in Bevilacqua, P., De Clementi, A., Franzina, E., (eds) *Storia dell'emigrazione italiana. Arrivi*, Rome: Donzelli, 2002, p. 378.

56 On this topic see also Molinari, A., *Le navi di Lazzaro. Aspetti sanitari dell'emigrazione transoceanica italiana: il viaggio per mare*, Milan: Angeli, 1988 and Frigessi Castelnuovo, D., Risso, M., *A mezza parete. Emigrazione, nostalgia, malattia mentale*, Turin: Einaudi, 1982.

57 For a general overview see Liguori, M., "Fenomeni migratori e sociologia. La letteratura sociologica sulle migrazioni interne nel triangolo industriale (1958–1968)", *Rassegna Italiana di sociologia*, XX, 1, 1979, pp. 109–46. A critical approach to the sociological concept of internal migrants' integration is in Foot, J., *Milan since the Miracle*, cit.

58 Pizzolato, N., "'Una situazione sadomasochistica ad incastro'. Il dibattito scientifico sull'immigrazione meridionale", *Quaderni Storici*, 118, 2005, pp. 97–120.

59 Balconi, M., Berrini, M.E., "L'analisi del disadattamento dell'alunno normodotato nel corso degli studi elementari", in Bollea, G., (ed.) *Disadattati e minorati. Ricerca sulla scuola e la società italiana in trasformazione*, Rome-Bari, Laterza, 1964, p. 17. The first part of this study focusing on first-grade school maladjusted pupils had already been published and more widely discussed between 1958 and 1960 in the periodical *Infanzia anormale*. The book was published as a result of the conference on "School and Italian Society in Trasformation", held in 1960 and co-organized by the Milan *Centro di*

prevenzione e difesa sociale (Centre of Prevention and Social Defence) and by the *Consulta dei professori universitari di pedagogia* (Committee of University Professors of Pedagogy) .

60 Idem, p. 35.
61 Idem, p. 58.
62 Ibidem.
63 Porta V., "Migrazione interna ed igiene mentale. Quadro psicologico e psico-patologico", *Igiene mentale*, 1962, p. 728.
64 Idem, p. 734.
65 Idem, p. 736.
66 Ibidem.
67 Maderna, A., Leone, B., "Interferenze affettive nel disadattamento di scolari immigrati da zone depresse", *Igiene mentale*, 1962, p. 1190.
68 Idem, p. 1191.
69 Idem, p. 1193.
70 Idem, p. 1194
71 Ibidem.
72 Idem, p. 1195.
73 Idem, p. 1196.
74 Ibidem.
75 Maderna, A., Valseschini, S., "Alcuni aspetti della situazione scolastica dei figli degli immigrati", *Minerva medicopsicologica*, V, 4, 1964, p. 238.
76 Ibidem.
77 Ibidem.
78 Ibidem.
79 Ibidem.
80 Scarcella, M., "Rilievi su una proposta di classi differenziali per i figli di meridionali emigrati nel Nord", *Infanzia anormale*, 1, 1965, p. 88.
81 Idem, p. 93. Emphasis is mine.
82 Scarcella, M., "Igiene mentale delle migrazioni interne", *Minerva medicopsicologica*, II, 1, 1961, p. 11.
83 Ibidem.
84 Ibidem.
85 Ibidem.
86 Idem, p. 12.
87 Deva, F., Pepe, M., "L'adattamento dei ragazzi immigrati nella scuola elementare", *Scuola e città*, XIV, 7, 1963, pp. 340–6.
88 Idem, p. 340.
89 Ibidem.
90 Idem, p. 342.
91 Ibidem.
92 Idem, p. 345.
93 Idem, p. 345.
94 Idem, p. 346.
95 Ibidem.
96 Idem, p. 346.
97 See for example Rovigatti, M.T., "Le classi differenziali", *Ragazzi d'oggi*, III, 11–12, 1952, pp. 6–9; Giaccone, E., "Il servizio sociale nella scuola", *Ragazzi d'oggi*, IV, 4, 1953, pp. 3–6; Groppelli, A., "I Centri-medico-psico-pedagogici e la scuola", in *Ragazzi d'oggi*, VI, 6, 1955, pp. 6–9; Faustini, G., "La programmazione dei 'depistages' nella scuola dell'obbligo in una prospettiva scolastica di sanità mentale e di educazione alla società", *Ragazzi d'oggi*, XIII, 4, 1962, pp. 9–20.

98 Gibson, M., *Born to Crime*. cit.

99 Idem, p. 181.

100 Idem, p. 210. On Di Tullio see also Patriarca, S., *Race in Post-Fascist Italy 'War Children' and the Color of the Nation*, cit.

101 Idem, p. 211.

102 Mantovani, C., cit., p. 318.

103 Gibson, M., cit., p. 197.

104 Gonella, G., *Salviamo il fanciullo. Discorso tenuto in Campidoglio per l'inaugurazione del convegno nazionale dell'Ente per la protezione morale del fanciullo*, Rome: Istituto Poligrafico dello Stato, 1946.

105 The text of his first lecture was published by the long-lasting periodical *La Scuola positiva*, which proudly announced: "criminal anthropology has won". See Di Tullio, B., "L'opera del medico nella lotta contro la criminalità", *La Scuola positiva*, 1964, pp. 389–402.

106 Ruocco, E., "Incidenza dell'ambiente sull'inadattamento sociale dei giovani, 1", *Ragazzi d'oggi*, III, 3, 1952, p. 8.

107 Ibidem.

108 Ruocco, E., "Incidenza dell'ambiente sull'inadattamento sociale dei giovani, 2", *Ragazzi d'oggi*, III, 5, 1952, p. 9.

109 Idem, p. 11.

110 Idem, p. 12.

111 Bertolini, P., *Delinquenza e disattamento minorile. Esperienze rieducative*, Bari: Laterza, 1964. The book was published – as well as Bollea's *Disadattati e minorati* – following the conference on the "School and Italian Society in Transformation".

112 Faustini, G., Conte, M.T., "La delinquenza minorile in Italia dal 1958 al 1963", *Esperienze di rieducazione*, XI, December 1964, p. 51.

113 Idem, p. 54.

114 Bertolini, P., cit., p. 36.

115 Idem, p. 44.

116 Idem, p. 27.

117 Idem, p. 48.

118 Ibidem.

119 Idem, p. 49.

120 Ibidem.

121 Idem, p. 51.

122 Senise, T., "Disadattamento e criminalità negli adolescenti maschi compresi tra il dodicesimo e il tredicesimo anno di età, immigrati nel territorio di giurisdizione del Tribunale dei minorenni di Milano", in *Atti del convegno internazionale di studio su immigrazione, lavoro e patologia mentale. Milano, 23–24 marzo 1963*, Milan: Zanolla, 1963, pp. 179–84.

123 Parmentola, A., "Giovani immigrati a Torino", *Esperienze di Rieducazione*, IX, March 1962, p. 25.

124 Idem, p. 26.

125 Parmentola, A., "Fenomeni degenerativi dell'immigrazione a Torino", *Esperienze di Rieducazione*, IX, May 1962.

126 Idem, p. 37.

127 Idem, p. 38.

128 Idem, p. 39.

129 Idem, pp. 40–1. On the cooperatives, see Chapter 1

130 Idem, p. 46.

131 Idem, p. 45.

132 Idem, p. 48.

133 Pontrelli, E., "Immigrazione e dissocialità minorile", *Minerva medicolegale*, LXXXV, 5, 1965, p. 170.

134 Idem, p. 169.
135 Idem, p. 170.
136 Ibidem.
137 Ibidem.
138 Idem, p. 171.
139 Conrad, P., *The Medicalization of Society: On the Transformation of Human Conditions into Treatable Disorders*, Baltimore: John Hopkins University Press, 2007, p. 5.
140 Petrina, S., "The Medicalization of Education: A Historiographic Synthesis", *History of Education Quarterly*, XLVI, 4, 2006, pp. 503–31.
141 Bonetta, G., *Corpo e nazione. L'educazione ginnastica, igienica e sessuale nell'Italia liberale*, Milan: Angeli, 1990.
142 Idem, p. 313.
143 Arzenati, P.M., cit.
144 For some interesting indications on physical education, see Motti, L., Caponeri Rossi, M., (eds), *Accademiste a Orvieto. Donne ed educazione fisica nell'Italia fascista, 1932–1943*, Ponte San Giovanni: Quattroemme, 1996.
145 Oneto, R., "Per la gioventù disadattata", *Scuola e città*, XII, 2, 1961, pp. 62–4. Other articles included Id., "Fanciullezza in difficoltà", *Scuola e città*, XI, 12, 1960, pp. 471–3; Segrue, B., "Un coraggioso esperimento di lotta contro la delinquenza minorile", *Scuola e città* XII, 9, 1961, p. 357.
146 Medea, E., "Igiene mentale e scuola", *Scuola e città*, XIII, 9, 1962, pp. 334–339.
147 Idem, p. 335.
148 Ibidem.
149 Idem, p. 336.
150 Ibidem.
151 Sauro, M., "Valutazione della subnormalità", *I Diritti della scuola*, LXV, 9, 1 February 1965, pp. 15–16.
152 Idem, p. 15.
153 Idem, p. 16.
154 Ibidem.
155 Archive of the Primary School "Gian Enrico Pestalozzi", Folder "Scuole differenziali", *Istituzioni e funzionamento delle classi differenziali o di recupero, 16 November 1951*.
156 TSA, Provveditorato agli Studi, Folder 617, *Proposta di istituzione di posti in organico per classi differenziali presso le scuole "Massimo D'Azeglio" e "Costantino Nigra" di Ivrea, 20th January 1962*.
157 Id., *Classi differenziali: proposta di istituzione, 18 January 1962*.
158 Central State Archive (CSA), MI, AAI, Documentazione, Folder 49, Amministrazione per le Attività Italiane e Internazionali. Ufficio Proviciale di Torino, *Indagine sull'entità del fenomeno del disadattamento nella provincia di Torino e sulle relative strutture diagnostiche e di trattamento esistenti. Relazione sulle indicazioni generali dello studio e prime valutazioni di carattere particolare sui problemi*, 1971, p. 23 . The AAI had been created in the immediate aftermath of war for the management of aids coming from the United Nations Relief and Rehabilitation Administration (UNRAA) and, later on, continued its activity as a public assistance agency dependant from the Ministry of the Interior. Its president was the Catholic Ludovico Montini, brother of Pope Paul VI. On its history see Ciampani, A., (ed.) *L'Amministrazione per gli Aiuti Internazionali. La ricostruzione dell'Italia tra dinamiche internazionali e attività assistenziali*, Milan: Angeli, 2002.
159 Central State Archive (CSA), MI, AAI, Documentazione, Folder 49, Amministrazione per le Attività Italiane e Internazionali. Ufficio Proviciale di

Torino, *Indagine sull'entità del fenomeno del disadattamento nella provincia di Torino e sulle relative strutture diagnostiche e di trattamento esistenti*, cit., p. 27.

160 Garbero, C., *La Scuola Medico-Pedagogica "Padre Agostino Gemelli" di Torino*, Turin, 1967. Ferrio had also authored a widely acclaimed volume on the history of psychiatry. See Ferrio, C., *La psiche e i nervi: introduzione storica ad ogni studio di psicologia, neurologia e psichiatria*, Turin: UTET, 1948.

161 Archive of the Primary School "Margherita di Savoia", Folder *Consultorio Psico-Pedagogico anno 1958/59*, medical report of N.M., 12 May 1959.

162 Id., *Relazione relativa all'alunno N.M.*

163 Id., *Relazione relativa all'alunno E.O.*

164 Archive of the Primary School "Margherita di Savoia", Personal Folder of the teacher V.F., *Verbale di visita, 20 February 1959*.

165 Archive of the Primary School, "Margherita di Savoia", Register by V.F., Main Site, II grade, males, 1959/60.

166 Ibidem.

167 Archive of the Primary School "Gian Enrico Pestalozzi", Register by F.G., Main Site, III grade, females, 1959/60.

168 Archive of the Primary School "Gian Enrico Pestalozzi", Register by A.M.A., Via Ceresole branch, III grade, males, 1962/63.

169 Archive of the Primary School "Gian Enrico Pestalozzi", Folder Scuole Differenziali, *Relazione sul comportamento dell'alunno B.G. 18 January 1962*.

170 Id., Register by G.P., Via Ceresole branch, III grade, mixed sex, 1961/62

171 Id., Register by I.G., Corso Vercelli branch, I grade, mixed-sex, 1956/57.

172 Id., Register by G.P., cit.

173 Id., Register by R.M., cit.

174 Id., Folder *Scuole differenziali*, Medical Report of A.D., 30 March 1962.

175 Id., Register by R.N., Via Ceresole branch, IV grade, mixed sex, 1962–63.

176 Id., Folder *Scuole differenziali*, Medical Report of M.D., 9 April 1962.

177 ATCC, Ufficio Igiene e Sanità, cat. IX, cl. 2, fasc. 4, 1971, Circular no. 5521 8 October 1970, *Programma 1970/71 per il razionale reperimento e l'assistenza igienico-sanitaria-didattica di alunni di scuola speciale e classi differenziali*, in ; Id., Deliberazione della Giunta Municipale, *Assistenza psico-pedagogica e igienico-sanitaria-didattica di alunni di classi differenziali e speciali*. 1 December 1970 .

178 ATCC, Ufficio Igiene e Sanità. cat. IX, cl. 2, fasc. 4, 1971, *Promemoria: Servizio specialistico (medico-psicologico-sociale) per la popolazione scolastica di Torino.*

179 Istituto Piemontese per la Storia della Resistenza e della Società Contemporanea, Fondo Frida Malan, busta CFM 20, fasc. 57., "La malattia sociale del piccolo immigrato", *Tempo Medico*, p. 34.

180 Id., "Olivetti: la terapia tecnica non basta", in *Tempo Medico*, p. 37.

181 Ibidem.

182 "Relazione dell'Asssessore al lavoro e problemi sociali della città di Torino – Dott. Renato Valente al Consiglio Comunale", *Atti del Consiglio Comunale di Torino*, 15 September 1969, pp. 1–2.

183 Massucco Costa, A., "La dimensione storica nella formazione della coscienza individuale e sociale: Nord e Sud", *Rivista di Psicologia Sociale*, VIII, 2, 1961, p. 136.

184 Id., "Lo stereotipo del meridionale", *Rivista di Psicologia Sociale*, XI, 1, 1964, p. 56.

185 Idem, p. 51.

186 Id., "La dimensione storica nella formazione della coscienza individuale e sociale: Nord e Sud", cit., p. 140. Emphasis is mine.
187 Ibidem.
188 Massucco Costa, in *Atti del Consiglio Comunale di Torino*, 24 September 1969, p. 20. The same remarks are in Massucco Costa, A., Rizzo, G., "Condizioni oggettive e moventi soggettivi nelle migrazioni interne", *Rivista di Psicologia Sociale*, XVI, IV, 1969, pp. 295–312.
189 Natoli, V., "Sono 'meno intelligenti' i bambini figli di poveri immigrati a Torino", *Gazzetta del Popolo*, 26 September 1969.
190 "Ragazzo di 15 anni respinto a scuola lascia uscire i familiari e si impicca", *La Stampa*, 13 June 1972.
191 "Un'insegnante dello studente: 'Lo ha ucciso lo scontro con la città che lo respingeva", ibidem.
192 "Il pastorello pugliese era uno sradicato forse la scuola avrebbe potuto aiutarlo", *La Stampa*, 14 June 1972.
193 "Un'insegnante dello studente: 'Lo ha ucciso lo scontro con la città che lo respingeva'", cit.
194 "Ora ci si domanda: di chi la colpa?", *La Stampa*, 14 June 1972.
195 "Il pastorello pugliese era uno sradicato forse la scuola avrebbe potuto aiutarlo", cit.
196 "Quel che dicono della vittima il preside, le insegnanti di lettere e di francese", *La Stampa*, 14 June 1972.
197 "Il pastorello pugliese era uno sradicato forse la scuola avrebbe potuto aiutarlo", cit.
198 "Questi teppisti della Pacinotti", *La Stampa*, 15 June 1972.
199 "La madre: quando andavo a parlare del figlio mi mandavano via", ibidem.
200 "Cerchiamo di non scordare perchè è morto", *La Stampa*, 16 June 1972.
201 Fallaci, N., "I ragazzi che la scuola perde", *Oggi*, 1 July 1972.
202 Della Mea, I., "Ballata per Ciriaco Saldutto". Song originally contained in the LP album *La Balorda* (Dischi dello Zodiaco VPA 8165, 1971) reprinted in Ivan Della Mea *Venne Maggio* (1969–1971 integral and critical rerelease of *Il rosso è diventato giallo* and *La Balorda* - NOTA BN 2CD594, 2019) ISBN 9788861631939.
203 On the *Nuovo canzoniere italiano* see Bermani, C., *Una storia cantata, 1962–1997. Trentacinque anni di attività del Nuovo canzoniere italiano*, Milan: Jaca Book, 1997. See also Pivato, S., *La storia leggera. L'uso pubblico della storia nella canzone italiana*, Bologna: Il Mulino, 2002.
204 "Lui ha quindici anni/cognome Saldutto/alunno alle medie/scuola Pacinotti/ venuto di Puglia/"terrone" immigrato/ Torino lo boccia e lui si è impiccato".
205 "Per fare chiarezza diciamo: è un delitto/un altro delitto della repressione/che usa la legge, il fucile e la scuola/per farci più servi del nostro padrone".
206 "Si sa che il padrone le sue maestranze/le vuole istruite e ben educate/con la sua cultura e la sua sua disciplina/lui plasma i servi di ogni officina".
207 "Ma non c'è battaglia, non c'è condizioni/'terrone', ti adegui oppure accadrà/ che la repressione di tutti i padroni/con l'arma del voto ti escluderà'".
208 "Così a quindici anni/ti han tolto anche il cielo/e in cambio ti han dato/un vuoto di niente/e l'ultimo gioco che ti hanno lasciato/è un pezzo di corda e ti sei impiccato".
209 The bibliography on the students' movement is huge. See Lumley, R., *States of Emergency: Cultures of Revolt in Italy from 1968 to 1978*, London: Verso, 1990; for a more recent overview see Cornis, I., Waters, S., *Memories of 1968. International Perspectives*, Bern: Peter Lang, 2010.
210 Lumley, R., cit., p. 82. See also Scuola di Barbiana, *Lettera a una professoressa*, Florence: Libreria Editrice Fiorentina, 1967.

l On the "150 hours" see Tornesello, M.L., *Il sogno di una scuola. Lotte ed esperienze didattiche negli anni Settanta: contro scuola, tempo pieno, 150 ore*, Pistoia: Petit Plaisance, 2006; Fuhrmann, I., Montanari, G., *Scuola, storia e memoria del sindacalismo torinese. Negli anni di movimento sessanta e settanta*, Turin: Angolo Manzoni, 2005. On the role of the feminist movement see Caldwell, L., "Courses for Women: The example of the 150 hours in Italy", in *Feminist Review*, no, 14, 1983, pp. 71–83.

212 On the activity of the ALMM see Associazione per la lotta contro le malattie mentali (sezione autonoma di Torino), *La fabbrica della follia*, Turin: Einaudi, 1971; see also Lasagno, D., "Il faló delle cinghie. Lotte nei manicomi a Torino nel 1968–1969", in *Zapruder*, 16, 2008, pp. 24–37. On Coda's trial see Papuzzi, A., *Portami su quello che canta: processo a uno psichiatra*, Turin: Einaudi, 1977. In December 1977, Coda was kidnapped by a terrorist group linked to the organization *Prima Linea*. See Tranfaglia, N., Novelli, D., *Vite sospese: le generazioni del terrorismo*, Milan: Baldini Castoldi Dalai, 2007.

213 The document was published in Gruppo Torinese, "Lavoro di Quartiere alle Vallette-S. Caterina", *Cooperazione Educativa*, XIX, 6, June 1970, pp. 6–8.

214 Alfieri, F., "Le cose difficili da far accettare anche alle famiglie operaie", *Cooperazione Educativa*, XXII, 8, August 1973, p. 23.

215 Ibidem.

216 Idem, p. 25.

217 Passalacqua, C., "Il 'Pieno Tempo': una soluzione per una scuola migliore", *Vita Nostra*, XIII, October 1970, p. 4.

218 Il 'Tempo pieno' a Torino", *Vita Nostra*, XIV, October 1971, p. 1.

219 Archive of the Primary School "Gian Enrico Pestalozzi", Register by E. T., Main Site, IV grade, males, 1971/72.

220 Id., Register by A.C., Corso Vercelli branch, III grade, mixed sex, 1971/72.

221 Id., Register by C.S., Main Site, II grade, mixed sex, 1971/72.

222 Id., Register by D.D.G. and E.C., Main Site, III grade, mixed sex, 1971/72, *Situazione delle scuole a tempo pieno al momento dello sciopero del 1 febbraio 1972*. Emphasis is in the text.

223 Id., Register by P.C.E., Main Site, II grade, mixed-sex, 1971/72.

224 Id., Register by A.B. and P.B., via Figlie dei militari branch, III grade, mixed sex, 1971/72.

225 Id., Register by D.D.G. and E.C., Main Site, III grade, mixed sex, 1971/72.

226 The ten theses were approved by the GISCEL in 1975 and have been reprinted several times. The text is also available on the official website of the association: https://giscel.it/dieci-tesi-per-leducazione-linguistica-democratica/ [last time accessed: 22/9/2021].

227 Lavinio, C., "Per un rilancio dell'educazione linguistica democratica", in Pistolesi, E., (ed.) *Lingua, scuola e società. I nuovi bisogni comunicativi nelle classi multiculturali*, Trieste: Istituto Gramsci, 2007, pp. 29–45. See also Tosi, A., *Language and Society in a changing Italy*, Clevedon: Multilingual Matters, 2001.

228 Ruffino, G., *L'indialetto ha la faccia scura. Giudizi e pregiudizi linguistici dei bambini italiani*, Palermo: Sellerio, 2006, p. 71.

229 Cannella, S., Poletti, M., Cattani, L., "La scuola e l'igiene mentale", *Riforma della scuola*, XV, 10, 1969, pp. 33–5.

230 Idem, p. 35.

231 Idem, p. 33.

232 Zappella, M., "Un paese di deficienti?", *Riforma della scuola*, XV, 12, 1969, pp. 21–23.

233 Idem, p. 22.

234 Ciari, B., "La grande disadattata", *Riforma della scuola*, XVI, 4, 1970, pp. 16–22.

235 Idem, p. 16.

236 *Atti Parlamentari*, Camera dei Deputati, V Legislatura, Proposta di Legge N. 1676, 7 July 1969, "Organizzazione del settore dell'assistenza sociale e interventi per le persone in condizione o situazione di incapacità e, in particolare, per i disadattati fisici, psichici, sensoriali e sociali".

237 Article no. 9.

238 Articles no. 18 and 20.

239 Ciari, B., cit., p. 18.

240 Idem, p. 19.

241 Idem, p. 20. Emphasis in the text.

242 Idem, p. 21.

243 Cecchini, M., "Ritardo e differenziali", *Riforma della scuola*, XVI, 6–7, 1970, pp. 9–16.

244 Idem, p. 9.

245 Idem, p. 10.

246 Idem, p. 11.

247 Idem, p. 12.

248 Idem, p. 14. Emphasis in the text.

249 Idem, p. 15.

250 Massucco Costa, A., "Ragazzi immigrati nelle scuole di Torino", *Riforma della scuola*, XV, 6–7, 1969, pp. 43–5.

251 Idem, p. 43.

252 Idem, p. 44

253 Idem, p. 45.

254 Città di Torino-Assessorato all'istruzione, *Atti del dibattito sulla validità delle classi differenziali nella scuola dell'obbligo*, Turin, 1970, p. 2.

255 Idem, p. 27.

256 Idem, p. 28.

257 Ibidem.

258 Idem, p. 9.

259 Idem, p. 10.

260 Idem, p. 11.

261 Idem, p. 12.

262 Trainito, G., "Il dibattito parlamentare sul problema degli handicappati", *Annali della pubblica istruzione*, XXII, 2, 1976, pp. 219–23.

263 Law 4 August 1977 no. 517.

4 Talking to grown-up children

Chapters 2 and 3 have addressed the main issues of this book. The sources that have been relied upon are archival documents, school registers, educational journals, scientific publications, mainstream newspapers, and magazines. The voices of children, however, have hitherto been absent. This chapter aims to fill this gap through the use of oral history. Fourteen people – seven men and seven women – have been interviewed for this purpose. All of them were born to Southern parents and attended primary school in Turin between the 1950s and the 1970s. The majority of the interviewees came from a working-class background. Only two – a man and a woman – belonged to middle-class families. They were selected randomly, mostly through networks of friends and acquaintances.

Interviews are not used as objective accounts to confirm what has been discussed in previous chapters. They are instead intended to be a partial, though no less interesting, attempt to analyse the school and childhood memories of the interviewees and of the way in which they have made sense of their past. Given the novelty of using the tools of oral history to investigate the memories of the children of post-war Southern migrants, the following analysis cannot reach any firm conclusions.

A brief introduction to oral history and its connections with history of children constitutes the topic of section "History of children and oral history". Some key concepts that I have employed for the analysis of the content of the interviews will also be introduced. Section "Fourteen grown-up Southern children" provides an overview of the narratives produced by the subjects, focusing on the most frequently recurring topics. In the third and last section "Five stories" of the chapter, the focus is restricted to the comparison of the narratives of five people with the aim of deepening the analysis.

4.1 History of children and oral history

Historiography on children and childhood dates back to the 1960s. One of the first pieces of work to be published was Philippe Aries' *Centuries of Childhood*. In his landmark book, Aries showed how, far from being natural and immutable, childhood and, particularly the way in which

DOI: 10.4324/9781003100546-5

humans conceive it, changes over time.[1] In the following decades, the field enjoyed an increasing amount of attention from the scholarly community. Historical research on children and childhood now possesses a consolidated tradition. Some disputes concerning its sources are continuing. It is worthwhile devoting a few lines to them.

4.1.1 From history of childhood to history of children: the problem of sources

Historian Harry Hendrick has emphasized the reluctance of many of his colleagues to make a proper distinction between childhood as a cultural construction and children as people and consequently as historical actors. "Historians" – Hendrick has pointed out – "have tended to focus on the *concept* of childhood rather than on the lives of children".[2] As a result, according to Hendrick, children have not been considered as social actors and "in much of the published work to date [they] have been denied both a voice and, an essential feature of human identity, a rational standpoint".[3]

The American scholar Steven Mintz has noted that the history of children is usually seen as a marginal subject and that "it is especially difficult to write, [as children] leave fewer historical sources than adults".[4] The neglect of the history of children has influenced the way in which the few historical sources produced by them have been looked at and kept. As educational historian Joshua Garrison has stressed referring to the United States, researchers working on the history of education "may indeed face insurmountable barriers in trying to locate the voices of children in American educational history".[5]

The situation is not different in other countries. In Italy, for example, even in the few cases in which school archival documents have been properly preserved, pupils' exercise books and essays have been thrown away. Attempts have been made to safeguard exercise books when, in 2002, the *Istituto nazionale di documentazione per l'innovazione e la ricerca educativa* (INDIRE, National Institute for Educational Innovation and Research) launched a project aimed at the reorganization of its collection of exercise books. The collection had been started during Fascism. Juri Meda, one of the project leaders, has explained that in the early 1930s, the Ministry of National Education established that all Italian schools had to provide evidence of their classroom activities. Teachers sent exercise books and other kinds of work undertaken by their pupils. They continued to do so even after the war and up to the mid-1960s. The collection currently contains about 1500 documents.[6] In 2007, an international conference on exercise books as sources for educational history was organized by the University of Macerata.[7]

Another remarkable case is that of the *Quaderni di San Gersolè*, a collection of notebooks written by pupils themselves between the 1930s and the 1950s. San Gersolè is a small Tuscan village, not far from Florence.

The then young teacher Maria Maltoni started to teach in the local primary school in the early 1920s. Born to a socialist family, she did not embrace the pedagogic methods of the time. Inspired by the educator Giuseppe Lombardo Radice, Maltoni started a method on her own, based on the observation of real life. Over the years, she managed to collect more than 1600 exercise books, 2400 drawings, and 600 journals currently constituting the *Fondo Maria Maltoni* (Maria Maltoni Collection) of the Impruneta Library near Florence.[8] In 1959, a selection of notebooks and drawings was published by the publishing house Einaudi with a preface by Italo Calvino.[9]

It is interesting to note that the *Quaderni di San Gersolè* have been employed by the anthropologist Giovanni Contini to study Tuscan sharecroppers' culture. Throughout many years of study and research, Contini has used the documents produced by the children of San Gersolè not only to analyse their education, but also to understand their role within sharecropping society and culture and how they made sense of the world around them. In the introduction to one of his most recent books, Contini defines the *Quaderni di San Gersolè* as an "invaluable source" to get an inside view of the life of sharecroppers.[10] Children were, indeed, asked by their teacher to write about every aspect of their lives as well as that of their families. The *Quaderni* thus offered the opportunity to look at that world from their perspective.

Another means which historians can use to listen to children's voices is constituted by oral interviews. In my case, oral interviews were the only option available to bring the views of Southern children into this research and to avoid treating them like objects instead of subjects. It was, indeed, impossible to locate any kind of written sources produced by pupils. Oral history thus proved to be an essential resource, whose historiographical and theoretical background deserve attention.

4.1.2 The difficult beginnings of a new approach to history

It is extremely difficult to establish a date and a location for the birth of oral history. According to one of its more renowned practitioners and theorists, Paul Thompson, "oral history is as old as history itself [having been] the *first* kind of history".[11] Up to the nineteenth century – Thompson argues – oral history was popular. Things had started to change, however, when the role of the historian became a profession and historians started to be recruited through education. They acquired social status, legitimated by the training curriculum they accomplished in academia. Thompson indicates German historian Leopold von Ranke, appointed Professor of History at Berlin in 1825, as the initiator of professional historical training based on archival documents.

By the end of the nineteenth century, written documents were considered the only possible reliable sources for history. In Thompson's view, "the documentary method [...] offered [...] three key advantages to the professional historian".[12] It made it possible to test junior scholars through the writing of monographs. It provided the discipline with its own specialism, which the use of oral sources, seen as available to everyone, could diminish. It offered historians what Thompson refers to as "an invaluable social protection": not only could historians isolate themselves from the rest of the world, but they "could also pretend to an objective neutrality, and thence even come to believe that insulation from the social world was a positive professional virtue".[13]

It was in the second half of the twentieth century – even though relevant projects had been carried out especially in the United States – that oral history started to be practised more extensively. The impact of oral history on more traditional forms of history was dramatic. Although it was a subfield of a comprehensive and multifaceted discipline, it contributed to changing the meaning and aims of the latter. It posed a challenge to the community of historians and, at the same time, an extraordinary opportunity for renewal. As Robert Perks and Alistair Thomson have pointed out,

> "the most distinctive contribution of oral history has been to include within the historical records the experiences and perspectives of groups of people who might otherwise have been 'hidden from history', perhaps written about by social observers or in official documents, but only rarely preserved in personal papers or scraps of autobiographical writing".[14]

From the United States to Europe, particularly throughout the 1960s and the 1970s, oral history projects flourished, allowing subaltern groups – the working classes, women, black people – to find a prominent place on the historical stage. Oral history also offered the opportunity to look differently at the histories of former European colonies. This was the case of the African continent, for instance, traditionally considered excluded from historical process before the arrival of the white colonizer. Historians like Jan Vansina – who during the 1960s had to battle to avoid inclusion in the category of anthropologist – started to focus on the history of Africans through a careful collection and analysis of local oral traditions.[15]

Given the extent of the innovation brought about by oral history, criticism was inevitable. The old guard accused oral historians of using unreliable and unrepresentative sources and of neglecting facts. They reinstated the primacy of written sources and particularly of archival documents. Oral historians, however, did not lack arguments to defend themselves and their methodological choices. In a well-known essay, Alessandro Portelli made a strong case against criticism by pointing out at the specificities of oral history. Portelli explained that "the first thing that makes oral history different [...] is that it tells us less about *events* than about their *meaning*".[16] Unlike the traditionalists, oral historians were – according to Portelli – forced to interrogate themselves about the meaning their interviewees gave to facts and on the manner in which they did it. "What informants believe" – Portelli explained – "is indeed a historical *fact* (that is, the fact that they believe it) as much as what really happened".[17] It was not difficult for Portelli to produce evidence that many accredited written sources were nothing but transcriptions of oral sources. This was the case of trial or Parliamentary minutes. Such documents proved that "orality and writing, for many centuries now, have not existed separately".[18] To those accusing oral sources of lacking objectivity, Portelli replied that no sources are objective. The peculiarity of oral sources resided in the fact that they were "artificial, variable and partial".[19] The primary sources with which oral historians worked were always the product of their relationship with the interviewee. The published work itself was to be considered the result of the complex interaction between the researcher and the informant. However, Portelli concludes,

> "the control of historical discourse remains firmly in the hands of the historian [...] who selects the people who will be interviewed; who contributes to the shaping of the testimony by asking the questions and reacting to the answers; and who gives the testimony its final published shape and context".[20]

A valuable contribution to the debate came from another Italian scholar, Luisa Passerini, whose criticism was addressed not to traditional historians but to oral history practitioners. Passerini warned about the "risk of constructing oral history as a merely alternative ghetto, where at last the oppressed may be allowed to speak".[21] She opposed the "predominantly factual use of oral sources" made thus far by scholars. Such use did not accord proper weight to the "specificity of oral material [which] consists not in factual statements, but is pre-eminently an expression and representation of culture, and therefore includes not only literary narrations but also the dimensions of memory, ideology and subconscious desire".[22] The lack of awareness of these inherent characteristics of oral sources had led oral historians to simply "[juxtapose] oral history to the customary tradition of European historiography", without channelling the criticism towards the positivist approach to history into novel methodologies and, ultimately, a new sense of history. Passerini thus urged the community of oral historians to stop treating their sources "as fragments through which the past 'as it really was' may be reconstructed".[23] On the contrary, as she proposed, "oral sources refer to and derive from a sphere which I have chosen to call subjectivity".[24] The term subjectivity, Passerini pointed out, indicated "that area of symbolic activity which includes cognitive, cultural and psychological aspects".[25] It was not to be confused with

> "mentality, ideology, culture, world-view and consciousness, [as it was] sufficiently elastic to include both the aspects of spontaneous subjective (*soggettività irriflessa*) being contained and represented by attitude, behaviour and language, as well as other forms of awareness (*consapevolezza*) such as the sense of identity, consciousness of oneself, and more considered forms of intellectual abilities".[26]

Passerini's article marked, according to historian Lynn Abrams, the beginning of the second wave of oral history characterized by "a more critical approach to the issue of empowerment".[27] The spur came from feminist scholars who remarked upon the "power imbalance between researcher and subject".[28] The former was seen as the person holding the power to ask questions and controlling the equipment for the registration of the interview. Feminist researchers, thus, clamoured for a more collaborative attitude towards the interviewing process which could lead interviewees, and particularly women, to regain control over their own history. More recently, however, these claims have been revised, Abrams continues. Growing scepticism has been expressed about the possibility of putting into practice the ideal of an interviewing process based on a mutual and equal relationship. Joan Sangster, for example, has been adamant in asserting that she is using interviews with women "for the purpose of writing books which are often directed, at least in part, to academic or career ends"; her position as "professional historian" is hence a privileged one.[29]

Sangster's point sheds light on another flaw in the traditional feminist approach to oral history, namely, in Abrams' words, the "downplay[ing] of other structural relationships such as class or race". To make her point, Abrams relies on the observations of Diane Reay and Sondra Hale.

Reay was well aware that, even though she was a woman and her research was focused on the lives of a group of women, class differences between her and the latter affected the outcome of her work. In addition, social class mattered for the women she interviewed. As she pointed out, "raising issues of social class within feminism [was considered] an act of disloyalty or a display of ignorance".[30] Social class, though, continued to be, in her view, "one of the major filters through which individuals make sense of their world".[31]

Hale reported that during her long fieldwork in Sudan, she had struggled with feminist scholarship, having had the feeling that she was seen by Fatma Ahmed Ibrahim, a famous Sudanese women's activist, as a "mere listener" and not as a "sister feminist".[32] Ibrahim's detachment was the result, Hale argued, of her patronizing Western attitude in conducting the interview which nullified feminist solidarity.

A third wave – that of advocacy – followed, as a result of the debates outlined above. It was characterized by a further change in the relationship between the oral history practitioner and the interviewee. As Abrams reports, "in this kind of practice, the practitioner is the person using the oral history in order to act as advocate on another's behalf but at the same time those telling their stories also develop abilities in the sharing of information about past practices and experiences within their own community".[33] The advocacy method has been successfully employed in several projects across the globe and is testimony to the importance of oral history well beyond the narrow confines of the academia.

It is, of course, impossible to mention here all the numerous and multifaceted research lines followed by an ever-growing number of scholars, as well as their reflections on the concepts underpinning their findings. Nonetheless, some of these concepts need to be examined because of their relevance to the analysis of the interviews with grown-up Southern children which follows.

4.1.3 Key concepts

Oral history is first and foremost concerned with memory. Respondents are asked by their interviewer to recover their memories about specific events or, more generally, about their lives. Though seemingly straightforward, the issue of memory is theoretically articulated. Memory is related not just to what a person recalls, but also to what s/he, more or less voluntarily, forgets. In addition, there is an individual and a public memory which, far from being like parallel lines, intersect in often complex ways. Categories, such as class, gender, race, and age, shape the contents and the forms of memory. Memory is directly connected to the present.

Historian Michael Frisch has pointed out that "memory – personal and historical, individual and generational – [is] the object, not merely the method of oral history". The main questions to which oral history tries to find answers are thus, in his view, "what happens to experience on the way to becoming memory? What happens to experience on the way to becoming history?"[34] These questions entail a concept of memory as a process, regardless of its truthfulness. The aim of oral historians is indeed not to verify whether or not memories of certain events are true, but to understand, through a comprehensive analysis of their narratives, how people have made sense of those events and how they see them in the broader context of their lives. Oral history, according to Frisch, "[shows] people trying to make sense of their lives at various points in time and in a variety of ways".[35]

Another concept which has become increasingly important in the field of oral history is that of narrative. As Lynn Abrams puts it, "a narrative is a story told according to certain cultural conventions".[36] Interest in narrative is not peculiar to oral history. On the contrary, many disciplines, from psychology to sociology and anthropology, have focused on it. Nor it can be said that a narrative is expressed only through words – be they oral or written. The French semiologist Roland Barthes famously wrote:

> "There are countless forms of narrative in the world. First of all, there is a prodigious variety of genres, each of which branches out into a variety of media, as if all substances could be relied upon to accommodate man's stories. Among the vehicles of narrative are articulated language, whether oral or written, pictures, still or moving, gestures, and an ordered mixture of all those substances; narrative is present in myth, legend, fables, tales, short stories, epics, history, tragedy, *drame*, comedy, pantomime, paintings [...] stained-glass windows, movies, local news, conversation. [...] Narrative starts with the very history

of mankind; there is not, there has never been anywhere, any people without narrative".[37]

Autobiography is a common genre of narrative. It is a narrative of life in which, as narrative theorist Barbara Czarniawska explains, "actions acquire meaning". It is indeed "in order to understand their own lives [that] people put them into a narrative form – and they do the same when they try to understand the lives of others".[38] This process is never unilateral. In constructing their life narratives, people are influenced by their audience. Czarniawska gives the example of a new Head of Department introducing herself to her colleagues: "she tells them how she wants to be perceived [and] their reaction will tell her how much of this has been accepted or rejected [...] and how the members of the group want to be perceived by their new boss".[39]

By telling their life stories, people express their subjectivity. This term has already been mentioned above, along with the definition provided by Luisa Passerini. More recently, Lynn Abrams has defined it as the way in which the "interviewee constructs an identity – or subject position – for him or herself by drawing upon available cultural constructions in public discourse".[40] The interviewee, however, is not the only subject taking part in the interview. The historian is a subject too. He or she can influence the answers of the interviewee and the process by which the latter constructs his or her self, even just with a simple gesture or an expression. This interaction is referred to as intersubjectivity. The notion of intersubjectivity – Abrams continues – "describes the way in which the subjectivity [of the interviewer and of the interviewee] is shaped by the encounter with the other".[41]

Closely related to the issue of intersubjectivity is that of composure, which has been discussed by historian Alistair Thompson in his work on the Australian and New Zealand Army Corps (ANZAC) veterans. As he has pointed out, "'composure' is an aptly ambiguous term to describe the process of memory making".[42] According to Thompson, on the one hand, people compose their memories "using the public languages and meaning of [their] culture"; on the other, composing memories helps them "to feel relatively comfortable with [their] lives and identities".[43] Penny Summerfield has added that "composure occurs when a teller composes a story about him- or herself, so [...] composure refers to the *composition* of the narrative".[44] The narrative can thus be composed in different ways according to the audience or to the context in which it is produced, for example. Through composure, the narrator selects the content and the form of his or her narration in order to offer an image of his- or herself that he or she wants to project onto the listener. At the same time, he or she uses composure as a means to satisfy his or her sense of self and to feel at ease. Oral interviews are thus performances and as such, it is impossible to conduct the same interview twice. These elements are to be carefully taken into account when it comes to analysing oral interviews and using them as a source for historical research.

4.2 Fourteen grown-up Southern children

The interviews with grown-up Southern children, who had attended primary school in Turin in the years considered, are fourteen. By Southern children, I mean either children born in the South or children born in Turin to families who had moved from the South. Most of the interviews were conducted at the interviewees' homes. Only four were conducted in public places. As mentioned above, the interviewees were selected randomly, through informal networks. They were all friends or relatives of people I met during my fieldwork in Turin.

4.2.1 Nuanced memories

All the interviews were conducted during my last research stay in Turin, in May and June 2009. I had collected almost all my written sources and I had expectations about what people would tell me. It was the first time I had practised oral history. In spite of the large amount of literature, I had read on the topic, I was inexperienced. I naively expected to hear stories of educational discrimination and suffering told by people proud of their places of origin and criticizing the stereotypical view of the South, which is still so common in Italy. To my surprise, my interviewees' memories were much more nuanced.

The first thing that struck me was that, at least in the first phase of the interviews, people were more eager to talk about their parents' experiences than about their own. In addition, their narratives followed similar patterns. They started from the decision to migrate. The most commonly indicated reason was the need to find a job or, for those who were already working, to get a better one. In all the cases, the decision had been taken by the adults only, without the participation of the interviewees. The latter were children or, in some cases, they were not yet born. Nobody complained, however, about the decision to leave, not even those who were born in the South. All of them, more or less explicitly, stated that such a decision had been taken in the interests of the whole family. This is consistent with the commonly held belief that only adults can be expected to make choices in the best interests of children.

The search for a job was thus the starting point of many narratives:

> "Like all the Southerners, in the post-war period, there was the problem of jobs. They came up here to look for a job" (Lorenzo, Turin,1954, factory worker)[45]
>
> "They came here to get a job, like everyone else. A job for my father" (Monica, Troia – Apulia, 1957, housewife)[46]
>
> "My father came here to get a job. He hoped to give us a better future" (Pasquale, Palermo, 1959, postman)[47]

The difficulties faced by the parents, especially by fathers, in the first period after the arrival were also described by many interviewees:

> "My dad worked wherever he found something. He did everything, whatever he could get; he shovelled snow, he downloaded boxes at the fruit market. My mum was, instead, a seamstress. She could only get a job in a shirt-maker's shop and she made shirts." (Lorenzo)
>
> "My father was paid on a daily basis. He was a bricklayer. But in Calabria he worked with stones. When he moved here, because they did not have money, he found out that bricklayers worked with bricks. And he toiled a lot. He had to learn everything from scratch. He was not used to the local methods." (Mauro, Crotone, 1964, caretaker)[48]

Another problem on which many memories focused was that of housing:

> "When [my father] arrived here… there was along the river… the *canile municipale* (municipal dog shelter) rented these metal huts. He had a breakdown because in his town, in the South, he had his own house; it was poor, with few things, but it was a house. So he had this break-down; he wanted to rent a proper house, also to bring his family here, but he was asked to pay a year's deposit, because they did not rent to Southerners. So he came back to his town, he sold some properties. He had to sell properties to rent a decent house for his family" (Angela, Salerno, 1951, teacher)[49]
>
> "There were the signs 'Not for rent to Southerners'" (Mauro)
>
> "That was the time of the signs 'Not for rent to Southerners'" (Immacolata, Turin, 1958, shopkeeper)[50]

The insistence on the signs, which no interviewee admitted to have seen with his or her own eyes, as well as the central role assigned to the fathers' job search in the decision to migrate, are indicative of the connections between individual narratives and public memory. As was examined in Chapter 1, the image of the Southern man moving to North-Western cities to find a job in the local factories is one of the pillars on which the public memory of post-war internal migrations has been constructed. At the same time, the signs 'not for rent to Southerners' have become a fixed image reproduced in all sorts of narratives concerning the issue, from books to movies to newspapers and magazines articles. This is not to say, of course, that these signs did not exist or that housing was not a major problem for Southern migrants. However, a selection process is at work at an individual and a public level. As I will discuss in more detail later in this section, the *classi differenziali*, though being a relevant phenomenon, have been almost completely forgotten.

In some cases, individual narratives contain elements that have been excluded from public memory. This is the case of Southern working women. As has been pointed out in Chapter 1, Southern migrant women were most commonly represented as completely submissive to their husbands and relegated to the domestic sphere. This image prevailed not only in the 1950s and 1960s, but also in the historiography. The previously mentioned research on extra-domestic work among Southern migrant women in Turin conducted by Anna Badino was the first to dismantle this myth. My interviewees' memories followed the same path. The majority of them remembered their mothers as working both in and outside their houses:

> "My mother made bags, she constructed…she made bags. She worked with another person. This man had a shop and so he bought the leather, my mother made the bags and then he sold them […] She earned more than my dad […] She worked like a crazy" (Michele, Turin, 1948, teacher)[51]
>
> "My mum was a seamstress, she managed to get a job in a small shirt factory and later she continued to be a seamstress"
>
> GDM "Always in the factory?"
>
> "No, by herself, because when she got children, me and my sister, there was no chance to leave us somewhere, so like many other women, she was forced to stay at home to look after her children. As a result, she started to make dresses for her friends or acquaintances, she cut and sewed, but even now that she is eighty-three she continues to make dresses, but just for the family"
>
> GDM "It's more like a hobby, is it?"
>
> "Yes, whilst once she did it to earn something. I remember I was little, and to earn something, we got some enormous boxes containing valves, they were electric valves and they had a small wire which had to be pulled out with tweezers and you got paid depending on how many valves you did, one thousand, two thousand, and so my mum did it to earn something more, because my dad's salary was that of a factory worker and it was a good salary, but for a family with two children it was not enough" (Lorenzo)

School memories, especially those concerning the first years of school, were much vaguer:

> "I started school…but I do not remember it well…I do not even remember the name of the school. It was in Corso Grosseto. We lived there, but when my parents got an eviction order we moved to my grandma's, so for a while I went to a school nearby, but again I don't remember its name. I only remember two big entrances, one for males and the other for females, because that's how it was at that time, males and females were separated. After Italia '61, my father got a house and we moved

to the *Vallette* and there was a school there, just in front of our house. I think it was called Leopardi" (Lorenzo)

"We lived in *Borgo San Paolo*, a nice neighbourhood. There was everything there. I remember my mum walking me to school...and..."

GDM "Do you remember the name of the school?"

"The school was in via Luserna and it was called....it was called... no, I don't remember its name" (Giovanna, Turin, 1954, retired)[52]

Women more than men remembered the strict division among the sexes:

"Boys had women teachers only in the first two years at primary school, when they were little, from the third year they got men. We, the girls, got a white apron with big blue ribbons. We were rigorously separated. We met only when we went to the toilet" (Assunta, Turin, 1955, civil servant)[53]

"There were two different entrances: one was for the girls and the other for the boys. We never met each other" (Alfonsina, Turin, 1955, accountant)[54]

Certain practices of control over pupils' bodies were recalled by women only. This was the case of personal hygiene inspections. Teachers or school doctors used regularly to inspect pupils' heads in search of lice. Pupils who had lice were treated with petroleum jelly. The procedure, which took place in front of classmates, was remembered by women interviewees as particularly shameful. Having lice meant being dirty. Southern children, as has been discussed in Chapter 2, were considered by their teachers dirtier than the other pupils, regardless of whether they were boys or girls. Only the latter, however, have retained the memory – once grown up – of the inspections and of the bad feelings associated with them as a result of the importance attached to hair and its cleanliness as a symbol of femininity. Even the simple suspicion of having lice was remembered by one interviewee as a trauma:

"I remember when the doctor came and they inspected our heads. I didn't like it, because, you know, if a girl has lice you look at her differently. And I remember once that there was this woman doctor and we were in a row. It was always the same doctor coming every year, and she asked me my name. She usually asked the names of the girls who had lice and so my classmates started to murmur and I went back home crying and I told my mum, 'Mum she asked me my name, she will put petroleum jelly on my head'; and my mum said, 'That's not possible'; and she did not find anything, but my classmates in the following days continued to say that they were going to put petroleum on my head too. In the end, they put petroleum on other girls' heads but not on my hair and I have never understood why the doctor had asked my name but I still remember it because I felt really bad, because you were pointed at and, you know, it is normal, if you saw a girl with petroleum on her head you thought that she had lice, that she was dirty" (Monica)

Another woman remembered the shame she felt when, after having been scolded by her teacher for her dirty ears, she heard a classmate refer to her origins:

> "We were in a row. I did not like this form of militaristic control. They said my ears were not clean enough and I was sent to the toilet to wash them better and someone said: "She is the daughter of Southerners"
> GDM "Who said so?"
> "Another girl. I felt really ashamed and sad" (Giovanna)

4.2.2 *"When they arrived they were dull"*

Monica's words about how the girls treated with petroleum jelly were pointed at and seen as dirty are noteworthy: "if a girl has lice, you look at her differently [...] it is normal". She remembered how bad she had felt because of the simple suspicion of having lice, and thus, being deemed dirty. However, this experience had not spurred her to question the cultural construct about lice and dirtiness. On the contrary, this cultural construct informed the meaning she had given to the episode. Something similar happened, in some cases, when it came to the way in which Southern children were treated by their teachers:

> "The Southerners were always put by the teacher at the back of the classroom because they were not interested in learning and they were the more...needy. They had never got pens, pencils, so a teacher had no choice, and also because there was a difference in their brain, I mean their culture, when they arrived they were dull, it was as if going to school was killing them" (Mauro)
> "I did well at school, I mean, I wasn't a genius because, you know, my parents were from the South I didn't do as well as other children who were from Turin, they did better in Italian [...] yes, they did better than me and you could see that they were different" (Monica)

The narrative of one interviewee showed open criticism of education methods and of teachers' attitude towards Southern pupils, defined as "racist". Still, criticism seemed to occur as a result of particularly traumatic circumstances experienced by the subject rather than as an effect of a change in public discourse over the disadvantages of being Southerners:

> "The first thing they did when I arrived from Palermo was that they wanted to move me back to the second grade while I already was in the third. And I remember this scene: I clung to the banister and I said 'I won't go back to the second grade'. So they allowed me to attend the

third grade but of course I was failed. So I was sent by my parents to a boarding school and that was the biggest mistake. Of course I could understand the whole situation only when I was grown up; you know, you are a child, you've been failed, your parents send you to a boarding school run by nuns. And I was failed again, but this time my father was angry, he asked the teacher why she had failed me. I think it was because of racism. My father told her to test me in front of him but she refused to. There wasn't all the care children get now at school, they were ignorant. I didn't like their way of teaching, I refused it, because I was a curious child and I had this uncle [he cries] he explained me everything I wanted to know. If I asked a question at school, the teacher thought I was an idiot because they did not want us to think critically, to ask questions. Never ask 'why'!" (Pasquale)

The descriptions and perceptions of the South reported by the vast majority of the interviewees indeed reflected the stereotypical view of that portion of the country, referred to as "*il meridione*", and its inhabitants:

"We went to the village every year during the summer. The beaches there were wonderful because they were totally wild. You could find everything on the beaches. They were dirty. I felt like an explorer. It was a wild, primitive place. I remember this blooming pinewood"

GDM "And what about people?"

"They had a strong smell, because when I arrived they kissed and hugged me and they got this smell because houses were not comfortable, they smelled of food, their behaviour was always sensational, they didn't live in their houses, but outside. They were emotional, without filters. Their faces were burnt by the sun, their hands were big" (Marcello, Turin, 1964, entrepreneur)[55]

"I would never adapt to living down there. The mentality is too different, not because mine is better than theirs, but it's just that they have different habits. In certain respects, maybe, they live better than us, they live hand to mouth, their lives are not as hectic as ours, but they mind too much what people say. I can't stand it." (Giovanna)

"I love Naples and the Neapolitans. I like the people. The city is problematic and I think it's difficult to live there. Here it's better because there is much more petty crime there, but I like the people. You know, in the streets people say 'hello' even if they don't know you, you get on the bus and you say 'hello' to the driver. Here nobody does it, the attitude is different. It's true that they don't mind their own business, but they are happy, the Neapolitans tell you their lives as if they were actors, they talk about adversities in a funny way. I call them Neapolitans because I know them more than the others, maybe the Sicilians are nice too"

GDM "But aren't your parents from the province of Benevento?"

"Yes, but by Neapolitans I refer to the whole region" (Alfonsina)

The use of categories like "us" and "them" did not imply the identification by the interviewees with one group or another. Many of them indeed confessed to feeling neither Turinese nor Southern. Some lamented the attitude of local people during their occasional stays in their parents' places of origin:

"I no longer know who I am, if I'm a Southerner or not" (Mauro)

"Here the Turinese didn't like us, but then you went down there and they didn't like you either. They made fun of us. They said, 'why do you come here?', that we were bothering them, so you felt out of place both here and there" (Monica)

"We went back during the summer, but I didn't like it not because I bite the hand that feeds me. I'm proud of my origins; but it was the way they saw us. They stayed seated outside their houses and you went to buy an ice-cream and they said 'Look at her, look how she is dressed', they didn't have anything else to do. Or the way we talked, they said 'talk your parents' language' and I answered 'I cannot speak Southern dialect', because I really cannot speak it, and I would have never spoken it there because I would have been mocked. They did not like us to go there for holidays, they were annoyed, really annoyed" (Giovanna)

Another noteworthy aspect of the narratives produced by the interviewees is, as has been mentioned above, the almost unanimous absence of memory concerning the *classi differenziali*. This was not the case of other school-related institutions, such as the *patronato scolastico*:

"I remember the *patronato*, they gave food to children. I remember they give them jelly fruit and I was jealous" (Assunta)

"The *patronato* distributed books, pens, rubbers and also some factories gave things for free, including books, to the children of their workers" (Roberto, Turin, 1947, factory worker)[56]

"I ate at school. Food was nice, it smelled really good, I was happy to eat there, not because my mother wasn't a good cook, but they gave us things we didn't have at home" (Monica)

The *classi differenziali*, on the contrary, had been erased from their memories. Only in a small minority of cases, people remembered what they were and, even in these few cases, I had to ask them explicitly about these classes:

GDM "Have you ever heard of the *classi differenziali*?"

"I have seen them with my own eyes…yes, there were those classes but, let's stay calm, the classes were so…in my school for instance there were the children of all the desperate people living in the area so…yes, some of them studied, but the rest was like me. I can see the difference when I talk with my wife, she has a school friend who is a doctor now, they all went to university, almost none of my school friends did" (Michele)

GDM "Do you remember the *classi differenziali?*"

"There were some *classi differenziali* in my school, my class was not a *classe differenziale*; but yes, I remember them, they were for turbulent kids, I remember teachers' complains about these classes. The teachers who taught in these classes were not fully qualified, they were in the lowest ranks". (Giovanna)

Apart from few exceptions, the most common answers were negative:

GDM "Do you remember something about the *classi differenziali?*"

"No"

GDM "Haven't you ever heard about them?"

"Yes...yes...but I don't remember them. Maybe there were some in my school, but I don't remember. What were they exactly?"

GDM "They were classes intended, at least in theory, for 'abnormal' children..."

"No, they did not exist in my school" (Assunta)

GDM "Did you ever hear of the *classi differenziali* when you went to primary school?"

"No, never"

"And what about middle school?"

"No, I don't think so ... maybe I didn't realize, no I never heard of this stuff. No, there weren't handicapped children" (Mauro)

It is interesting to note that Mauro linked the *classi differenziali* to "handicapped children". It is possible that, even if in his school there were no *classi differenziali*, a fragment of the 1960s and 1970s public discourse on the issue remained in his mind.

4.3 Five stories

The last part of this chapter is devoted to the stories of five different people. Focusing on them and employing a comparative approach will offer the opportunity to broaden the analysis and to make it more detailed.

The stories presented will be as follows: I will first examine the differences and similarities in the memories of two sisters, Alfonsina and Immacolata; the stories of Angela and Rosario will instead provide the opportunity to discuss how categories such as class and gender intersect and contribute to shape narratives and sense of self; lastly, the story of Marcello will shed light on the reasons why people may sometimes prefer to forget.

4.3.1 Two sisters

Alfonsina was born in 1955 in Turin. Her parents had moved there from a small village in the province of Benevento soon after their marriage. She has a sister, Immacolata, who is three years older. Their father had worked first as a bricklayer and, after a few years, had been hired by the then renowned tyre company CEAT. Their mother worked as a hotel maid. The family lived for about twenty years in an area of Turin city centre, the so-called *quadrilatero*, almost completely inhabited by migrants during the 1950s and the 1960s. When Alfonsina was 18, they moved to the *Barriera di Milano*. Alfonsina re-met there a former neighbour, a migrant herself too, who had earlier moved from the *quadrilatero* to *Barriera di Milano* and married the woman's nephew. At the age of eighteen, after having completed vocational training, Alfonsina found an administrative job in a private company. Her sister Immacolata, instead, obtained a high school qualification in accountancy and, along with her husband, started a business.

Alfonsina's and Immacolata's school and childhood memories are interesting because, although they are sisters and close in age, their narratives conflict. Listening to their interviews, I had the impression of having been talking to two persons who had lived in different times and places. Historian Isabelle Bertaux-Wiame, who has been working on internal migrations in France in the first half of the twentieth century, has suggested that "every biographical account takes place in the present time, and *in relation to the present*".[57] As a result, those of her interviewees who had been "socially successful" told her about their hard childhoods. Those who, on the contrary, had not been able to improve their position in the social ladder, refused to talk or were reticent about their bad childhood memories.[58] Both Alfonsina and Immacolata – as will be explained below – have been able to advance socially. Still, if the former composed the narrative of a happy childhood, the memories of the latter were, on the contrary, negative.

I met Alfonsina in her house. She is still living in *Barriera di Milano*. I was introduced to her by her daughter, Laura, who was present during the interview, which took place in their living room. She answered my questions with a firm voice and short sentences.

> "We lived in the *quadrilatero* which then was not as posh as it is now. It was different then. The entire area was populated by Southern immigrants. I attended a primary school not far from our home".

During the whole interview, Alfonsina repeatedly drew comparisons between past and present. "There was the *maestro unico*", she remembered – referring to the vexed issue of the re-introduction of the single teacher per class model by the Minister of Instruction Maria Stella Gelmini in 2008.

Since the early 1990s, Italian primary school classes had been taught by teams composed of at least three teachers as a result of a long-term pedagogical debate. As Marco Pitzalis has pointed out, "the plan was presented as a 'media event'" and a heated public debate followed.[59] The term "*maestro unico*" was not in use at the time when Alfonsina attended primary school. By using it, she is thus establishing a link between the past and present.

Alfonsina's memory of primary school was positive:

> "There were all the social classes in my school: there were rich children and poor ones, like me, but I do not remember ever having been abused or discriminated against because I was a Southerner, because there were a lot of Southerners in my class. I liked reading and, since I never got books as gifts, I used to borrow them from the class library".

Her mother, however, never allowed her daughter to accept school textbooks for free from the *patronato scolastico*:

> "She was illiterate and thus she cared a lot about our education. She worked in order to be able to buy school textbooks, pencils, pens, everything we needed. We were never short of school stationery".

There was in her mother's attitude a consciousness of the importance of being socially accepted in the school environment. Not only did she buy school stationery and textbooks with her own money, but she did not want her children to stay at school to have the lunch offered by the *patronato*. She most probably did not want her daughters to be stigmatized for making use of a service that Alfonsina defined during the interview as "reserved for indigent families" and that was commonly regarded – as discussed in Chapter 2 – as being overused by Southern parents.

At the same time, Alfonsina's mother was particularly severe about schooling and education:

> "I went to school even when I was sick; school was the most important thing for her".

These memories are in sharp contrast with the stereotypical image of Southern mothers as inattentive to their children's education and only interested in scrounging benefits from school charitable institutions. Moreover, the fact of being illiterate did not prevent her from supervising her daughter's homework:

> "She had never gone to school and she was illiterate, but she knew multiplication tables very well. Every now and again she questioned me!"

Alfonsina's memories regarding her mother's control over her homework changed sharply when it came to the issue of language:

> "My parents could not help me because they only spoke dialect, and I italianized dialect. For instance, I said "little cup" (*coppino*) instead of ladle. My school performance, however, was good. I did it all by myself".

The stigma attached to dialect and its speakers and the desire not to be marked with it still seemed to inform her narrative:

> "I never learned dialect, I really can't speak it even if my mother still speaks Neapolitan. I always talked in Italian. We were so many children speaking so many different dialects and we needed to understand each other. At home my parents talked to me in dialect but I answered in Italian."

Overall, however, Alfonsina remarked that she "had never felt discriminated against because [she] had grown up among Southerners" and that she had always been "proud of being a Southerner". There were some contradictions in her account. She reported, for instance, that she was ashamed of having schoolmates visiting her at home. In the process of composing her life narrative, however, she chose to present herself as a happy child and a successful pupil, never troubled by – but, on the contrary, proud of – her origins.

Immacolata's memories were at odds with those of her sister. About her childhood in the *quadrilatero* she said:

> "When I think about it, I have the impression of remembering another life. After getting married, my parents rented a house in the *quadrilatero*, the area where all the Southerners went to live. Now it is a nice area, but it was completely different at that time. Houses were insalubrious, full of insects, rats, cockroaches. There was everything under the sun. Our place had only one room without a bathroom. We shared it with other families living on the same floor. It was a *casa di ringhiera*[60]. We were on the third floor with five or six other families. You can imagine what it was like."

Her first school memory was of the nursery run by nuns that she attended from the age of three. It was not a pleasant memory:

> "There were two nurseries, one next to the other. One was private and really expensive. Children wore beautiful and always clean uniforms. We went to the other instead, run by nuns, which was for poor children and we were treated badly, badly, really badly to the extent that even

today I cannot stand nuns. They beat us up. Some were a bit nicer, but others left scars on our bodies even for trivial reasons – if we laughed, for example. We were forced to sleep keeping our heads on the desk. I could not sleep and I used to ask to dry cutlery in order to avoid the nap. If I think about it now, I am shocked. It is something I never allowed my daughters to do at that age, but I did it and I was very little. We were poor and they made us feel guilty. We were Southerners and they made us feel even more guilty. They always checked us to see if we had lice. I was really scared because if you had them you were put in the corner. It took me years to accept all this"

As for primary school, it is worth remarking that Immacolata's account shared with that of her sister the same concept of "discrimination". She reported that "things changed at primary school", owing – in her view – to her good performance and willingness to learn: "I liked school. I learnt quickly, I really liked it". She attended the same school as her sister, "a school for Southern immigrants" – she said – "even though we were not completely ghettoized since there also were a few Piedmontese children". One of these children, Margherita, whose mother was a teacher in that school, was Immacolata's classmate and best friend:

"I still remember her and her family. They were kind and welcoming. They never made me feel discriminated against because I achieved more than Margherita"

Both Alfonsina and Immacolata expressed the belief that they had not felt discriminated against as Southerners because of their school attainment. In their self-narratives, merit seems to act as an antidote to what they themselves refer to as "discrimination". They thus seem to conceive the latter not as a collective matter but as a private one, directly caused by individual underachievement rather than by more intricate social and cultural issues.

Unlike Alfonsina, however, Immacolata was more critical of certain practices related to the merit system, such as the awarding of medals to particularly successful pupils. She declared herself satisfied that these practices had been abandoned in more recent time, as she had had the opportunity to note when her daughters attended primary school. The sense of frustration and anger she remembered feeling when, as a child, she had seen her teacher awarding the medal to a Piedmontese and richer girl still marked her memory:

"I was so upset when the medal was awarded to Bianchi. She was Piedmontese and rich. She looked perfect. Her family ran a furniture shop which was just in front of our school. She always wore beautiful aprons, with small bows. Our aprons were always the same from the first to the last grade. Her socks were long and white, mine were short and ugly. She was just a grind and the teacher had a preference for her."

The experience of seeing that girl taking medals just because she was rich and Piedmontese symbolized for Immacolata the starting point for the discovery of her own 'otherness'. This process was far from being easy or painless. It took the form of a long journey through her lack of self-esteem and her shame because of herself and her family:

> "I thought it was unfair. I was really angry. I know, teachers are human beings, but I think that her attitude had a great influence on me, on my lack of self-esteem, on my approach to work. I understood that I was different. Once out of the protective shell of the building where I lived with my family, where we all were equals, I realized that I was different"

Such feelings characterized not only her school memories but also those related to other sites of sociability, such as shops:

> "I remember when I went to the market with my mother. We were among Southerners and we felt at ease, but if we got into a shop it was different. We were treated like strangers. It hurt me so much. My mother spoke dialect and her Italian was not good, I don't know why she has never learnt it. They treated her very badly. They were very rude. I felt ashamed"

Immacolata recalled how shame split her life into two separate compartments. There was the life of the neighbourhood, of the building, of the family, and there was another life, far away from the first, in which she did not want to be pointed at as "different" by her peers. In order to achieve this goal, she adopted some camouflaging strategies: her closest friends were always Piedmontese but she did not invite them to her place. "I only allowed those who were in the same situation as mine to come and see me at my place, but I never allowed all the others. I was ashamed of the place where I lived", she said.

Already ashamed of her house, neighbourhood and family when she was attending primary school, Immacolata was even more ashamed during the years of middle school. She chose to attend a renowned school located in an elegant area of Turin because "all the people [she] admired went there". Her hopes to feel like them, however, were going to be dashed. All the Southerners were indeed grouped in the same classes. Their teachers were always provisional. Immacolata reported not having had the same Maths teacher for more than a couple of months, for instance. Her class was most probably a *classe differenziale*. However, when I asked her if she had ever heard of these classes, she answered negatively. She did not even know what it was. I told her what the *classi differenziali* were and how in Turin they had become classes for migrants. Her answer then changed:

> "Well, I was in a *classe differenziale* then even though I have never heard of this word. Not only were we all Southerners, but many of my classmates had been failed many times and were extremely disruptive. My primary school classmate, Pedretti, had ended up in our class at the beginning. She immediately asked to be moved to another class and after fifteen days she was no longer with us"

Immacolata's attitude towards her parents was, unlike that of her sister, critical. She blamed her own and her classmates' parents for not demanding a different treatment for their children owing to their conservative conception of education:

> "It was impossible not to realize that we had all been placed in the same class on purpose. Nobody protested, however. Our parents never protested. They were only interested in our marks. If they were good we could continue to go to school, otherwise we had to get a job."

Her parents' indifference as well as all the "traumas" she had to go through during her first eight years of school were indicated by Immacolata as the main reasons for her subsequent bad life choices. She dreamt of being a teacher, but she did not pursue this career path in the end. The words she used to describe these events were the words of defeat:

> "I gave up. I would have liked to attend the *liceo*, but I went for vocational training instead. I gave up. I followed my sister's path, I thought that at least I would have got a job. But I did not do what I liked."

Immacolata currently runs her own business with her husband in an area mostly populated by the new Turin migrants. She told me that the memory of the way in which her mother was treated by shopkeepers when she was a child has an impact on her attitude towards her customers:

> "I always remember what I went through and I always try to be kind with everybody. Even if they cannot speak, I try to understand. I don't do what Piedmontese shopkeepers did with us"

To return to the above-mentioned Isabelle Bertaux-Wiame's argument, in this case, both sisters managed to improve their social and economic condition. Born to a working-class family, they can currently be classified as middle class. Although both have been socially successful, they approach their pasts in completely different ways. This may suggest that when it comes to explain how people deal with their childhood memories, their social position is not enough. Their narratives can indeed be influenced by other elements – more personal and circumstantial – that the researcher may miss.

4.3.2 Gender and class

Traditional categories such as those of gender and class are, however, of utmost importance for the analysis of childhood and school narratives. In this respect, the cases of Angela and Rosario are particularly telling.

Angela moved to Turin with her family in 1955. She was four years old. She was born in a small town not far from Salerno, in Campania. Her father was a tailor. "There were too many tailors in our town, though", she told me in explanation of the reasons why her parents had decided to go to Turin. The first to arrive had been her father, along with three friends. They were young and they wanted to try their luck:

> "There was this myth of Turin as the city of the factories then, where it was not difficult to get a job. So my father and his friends decided to give it a try".

As soon as the three arrived, however, things started to get difficult. Angela's father only managed to rent a small metal hut where he could hardly have accommodated his family. He was asked to pay a year's deposit in advance in order to rent a proper house. He consequently sold a piece of land he owned and was finally able to bring his family to Turin.

After many years, Angela still remembered her arrival. The first impression of Turin was not a positive one:

> "It was September and we went to stay at the place belonging to one of my father's friends. I was a bit upset because these people lived in a single room apartment with a curtain in the middle while we used to live in a real house, with more than one room".

Soon after their arrival, Angela's sister, only a month old, fell seriously ill. Her father did not have a permit to stay because of the anti-urbanism laws and he preferred not to take the baby to a public hospital. He thus had to pay for a private doctor. At the same time, he had paid the deposit. The family was left with no money:

> "It was a really difficult time. My parents told me years later that we had to eat at a neighbour's place, since we did not have money to buy food".

Angela started primary school when she was five-and-a-half years old. The school was in the same peripheral neighbourhood where she lived. At school, Angela remembered feeling – in her own words – "discriminated against". She said she realized that she belonged to the category of "immigrants". The sense of being a second-class pupil was instilled in her by her teacher through certain practices. Migrant children, for example, were never seated in the first row of desks, even if they were quite short and could only barely see the blackboard from the back of the classroom – as was the case for Angela. At the end of each week, children were given coloured ribbons if they had behaved well. Angela remembered those given to her or to other migrant children as being "less bright and new" than those given to the others. Children could take books from the class library. Angela remembered always ending up with damaged and old books:

> "These things may seem stupid now, but they really hurt me then. They never gave us new hardbound books with beautiful pictures because they thought that we would damage them at home, that we did not look after them. To me it was a great discrimination. They told me: 'No, that book is not for you'. We could not choose the books we wanted. I remember that once I wanted to read a book – it was *Little Women* maybe. It had wonderful drawings. I really wanted to read it, but the teacher said I could not take it and my father bought it for me as a Christmas present"

Angela is now a primary school teacher and as such, she has rethought her pupil experience from an inside perspective which has enabled her to notice and critically analyse *ex post* certain issues which other interviewees did not dispute. At the same time, the memory of her experience as a Southern migrant child offered her the opportunity to criticize current educational policies. This was the case with aprons, for example. In 2008, the then Minister of Public Instruction, Maria Stella Gelmini, decided that primary school children had to wear school aprons in order to make social inequalities less visible. The idea on which this decision was based – according to the Minister – was that wearing the same apron would reduce social and economic differences between rich and poor children. Angela's view – based on her own experience – was completely different:

> "I only had one apron and sometimes it was dirty. There weren't ballpoint pens then, we had the inkwell. It was very easy to have big ink stains on your apron which could not be washed during the week. I came back from school at noon and it had to be washed and ironed by the following day. My mum did her best but sometimes the apron was not ready. It was a problem. When I became a primary school teacher I did not want my pupils to wear aprons precisely to avoid discrimination. I told parents that children had to wear old dresses because they had to work with pens, colours and so on. A handsome apron is much more expensive than an old dress and many parents

can hardly afford it or are forced to buy one or more aprons instead of a book or pencils."

One episode, in particular, was impressed on Angela's mind and still represented a trauma that marked her childhood. Her parents worked together as tailors and they often got second-hand toys from one of their customers, who was far richer than they were and had children. He once gave them a pencil box which Angela took to school the following day. Her teacher, however, accused her of having stolen it. Angela still remembered in detail that shameful scene which she looked upon as particularly telling of her status as a Southern migrant:

> "I still remember the pencil box very well. It was green and incredibly tasteless, but I liked it a lot, you know. I was only a child. It was a bit damaged, but my mother had repaired it. I was so happy to bring it to school. I put it on my desk. I was very proud. I wanted all my classmates to see it. All of a sudden my teacher said 'Whose is that pencil box? Where have you stolen it from?". I was ashamed. My parents had taught me what stealing was, so I was aware of what she was accusing me. I knew what a thief was. I was so ashamed. She opened it and saw that it had been repaired and, luckily, she understood that it was mine, that I hadn't stolen it, but I understood very well that she thought that a Southern migrant could not do anything but steal"

Angela told her parents what had happened. They decided, however, not to take action against the teacher:

> "My parents knew of this prejudice against Southerners, but they followed this rule: 'Do not care about what people say, just prove that you aren't a thief'. For them, it was up to the people to understand"

High school was even harder, in Angela's view. She attended a Teacher Training School (*istituto magistrale*), which, unlike primary and middle school, was far from the neighbourhood where she lived. She had felt a stranger, an outsider, especially in comparison with her classmates:

> "I remember that one of my classmates was the grand-daughter of a prominent politician. Her dresses were always wonderful. You know the *istituto magistrale* was then a school for well-off girls. I felt quite lonely. I only had two friends: one was a Southerner like me and the other was an anarchist, her father was an anarchist. And that's it"

Angela recalled the case of one of her friends, Clara, which had particularly struck her. Clara, born to a Southern family, had been one of her closest friends from childhood and, after middle school, had chosen to attend the *liceo classico*. "She was really clever and she really wanted to go to that school", Angela said. After two years, however, Clara decided to leave school:

> "It was impossible for a Southern migrant to go to the *liceo classico*. One had to wear certain dresses and certain shoes. She felt marginalized and she dropped out. The impact of the world outside the neighbourhood had been more tragic for her than for me. It was a pity"

Angela's school experience is likely to be linked with her lack of self-confidence, still persisting in adulthood. In spite of her successful career as a graduate primary school teacher, during the interview she declared herself convinced of not being "able to speak Italian properly". When talking about high school, she kept saying that she had "never been good with Italian". The memory of having felt a second-class pupil was still very much alive and influenced the perception of her adult self.

Rosario's school career had been objectively more troubled than that of Angela. He had been failed three times, for example. Moreover, unlike Angela, he had not used education as a means to move up the social ladder. Still, his school and childhood memories reflected a completely different sense of self. The way in which he composed his narrative, as well as its content and even his tone of voice, were far from those of Angela. His view of his past was not characterized by traumas and bad memories. On the contrary, he remembered a happy childhood and a school experience free of worries.

Born in Caltanissetta in the early 1950s, Rosario had moved to Turin at the age of three. His father was a civil servant and his mother a housewife. During the first few years they lived in the *quadrilatero*. Then they moved to what is now a suburban neighbourhood but which then was on the border between the city and the countryside. In Rosario's first childhood memories, Turin was an immense countryside:

> "There were some flats reserved for civil servants, a few other building and nothing else. I remember the fields. There were no buses, no shops. From the 1960s, however, the fields started to disappear. In front of the building where we lived there were sheep. Then one morning I saw the cranes; and where the grass was are big buildings[61]"

Rosario is currently a civil servant and a freelance historian. He is the author of some local history books and one of the founding members of an association promoting micro-history research on Turin and its dissemination among the general public. The way in which he talked about his past was influenced by his role as historian. His narrative was not anecdotal, but, on the contrary, tended to focus on the historical dynamics in which his personal experiences had taken place.

"I do not remember rivalry between Piedmontese and Southerners, nor exclusion. There was a form of exclusion but it was related to the gangs. In my neighbourhood there was the 'gang of the paper mill'. The difference was between those who lived close to the paper mill and all the others. The first to live at the paper mill in the 1930s were immigrants from Veneto. After the war, and above all in the 1950s, there arrived the Southerners. Probably, but I am not sure, there were some people who had fled from Polesine after the floods of 1951 as a result of the links with first immigration from the Veneto, but unfortunately there is no archive where we could obtain more information"

Gender played an important role in shaping Rosario's memory and to make it different from that of Angela. When I asked him to be more specific about what the 'paper mill gang' was his account moved to the fights with them:

"They were the bad boys, so our teachers said. Some of them were in the same class as me. Sometimes we argued, I mean, I was not a saint, we fought"

As for his school performance, Rosario, as well as other male interviewees, talked about his underachievement without regret but, on the contrary, with a pinch of satisfaction:

"I always sought the maximum result with the minimum effort [...] In the fifth grade I did nothing, I really enjoyed myself"

Another male interviewee, Lorenzo, was proud of his poor school results and clearly represented himself as an indomitable urchin:

"I was the only child in Italy to play truant from the first grade. Every Thursday I did not go to school. I played truant with my brother and some other friends. We hid ourselves under the cars when our teacher passed by looking for truant children. We made pranks"

According to Carolyn Jackson, boys tend to construct themselves as "'laddish'" to feel protected from the fear of failure and of appearing feminine. By "'laddishness'", she refers to a set of behaviours such as "going out or 'hanging around' with mates; playing sport (mainly football); wearing the 'right sort' of clothes; and not being seen to work hard at schoolwork such as there was a consensus that it is not cool to work".[62] Working hard at school is seen as 'feminine' in dominant discourses on masculinity, Jackson maintains. For boys, appearing 'laddish' is a way to affirm their masculinity. At the same time, it enables them to transform school failure into an instrument to preserve their privileged position.[63]

It was also, however, social class that marked the difference between Angela's and Rosario's memories. The latter was the son of middle-class parents. "We were not rich", he stated. They were certainly better off than Angela and her family, though. It is not by chance that Rosario talked extensively during the interview about his toys: they did not trigger memories of trauma, as was the case for Angela. On the contrary, in his narrative, toys and food symbolized what he assumed to be the difference between the Northern Italian economic and social situation and that of Sicily:

> "In the summer we went back to Sicily. That world was totally absurd to me. Maybe it was because I perceived the difference between living here and in Sicily. In the middle of the 1960s in Sicily one could see shoeless children or kids wearing one brace only. I perceived the difference between them and us. They did not have our ice-creams. Going out for dinner was terrible. They did not even know what a yoghurt was"

Emotions, such as embarrassment, shame, or disgust, and their memories are class-based. By relying on Raymond Williams' concept of "structure of feeling", the sociologist Sandi Kawecka Nenga has analysed the differences characterizing working-class and middle-class women's childhood memories and, particularly, those related to clothing, food, and leisure.[64] As for clothing, the majority of working-class women "recounted stories of how their clothing violated norms [and] reported feeling shame, anger and anxiety".[65] This was also the case for Angela, whose current teaching practice is still influenced by the frustrating memory of her dirty school apron. Rosario, on the contrary, referred to Sicilian food with the same distrust and disgust which Kawecka Nenga's middle-class interviewees had expressed in relation to "food that was associated with ethnic groups or poor people".[66]

4.3.3 A lapse of memory

This chapter has so far been devoted to the analysis of what interviewees remembered and decided to share with me. The last section will instead focus on a case of oblivion concerning a man, Marcello.

I knew Marcello through his sister, Chiara. She was the friend of a friend of mine and, having heard of my research and being the daughter of Southern parents, she had contacted me. She did not want to be interviewed, though, but offered to introduce me to her brother Marcello because, so she said, "I am sure he has something interesting to tell you".

I met the two of them at Chiara's place. Marcello was extremely friendly and agreed to be interviewed.

> "I was born in Turin in 1964 [...] but I ran the risk of being born in Naples or in Milan or elsewhere. My father told me that he had some contacts in different parts of Italy and it was only by chance that he

eventually chose to move to Turin to work in one of its many factories. He considered Germany too. Before coming to Turin, he had been
for three years there and his plan was to come back to his village
[in Apulia] and convince my mum to move to Germany, but maybe
Germany was a bit too far for her, so they preferred Northern Italy."

Marcello's narrative revealed that he had been thinking about his parents'
experience, comparing it with the most common representations of migrations from the South to the North:

"My father was a peasant, his parents were peasants, but they were
land-owners. That's something nobody says. Many migrants were
peasants, but they owned their land, they were young, they had dreams,
that's why they moved and my father was one of them. He was really
proud of being a factory worker, though"

Marcello's mum had worked as a factory worker as well, until her son was
born. She then decided to work at home as a housewife. The family lived
in one of Turin's most working-class suburbs. Marcello attended primary
school there:

"My primary school teacher was about 40 years old. She was from
Sicily. She had a strong Sicilian accent. She was like a mum. She was
tender, she used to hug me. Sometimes she was harsh, though, especially with some of my classmates. She had a ring, a big ring with a
crown on the top and when she slapped us she turned the ring so that
the crown was on her hand palm and the slap hurt even more. These
things were not uncommon then"

Marcello went to primary school between 1970 and 1975. As has been
discussed in Chapter 3, Italian education was changing rapidly at that time.
The wind of renewal was blowing. Old teaching methods, like those used
by Marcello's primary school teachers, were being replaced by new ones.
During his first year at middle school, in 1976, Marcello was involved in
a project organized by his teacher of Italian. Each student had to share
something with the class – a poem or a song, for example – in his or her
own dialect. The project was aimed at raising the status of dialects and
had been probably conceived in the wake of the GISCEL's Ten Theses for
Democratic Language Education published in 1975.[67] In spite of his teacher's good intentions, Marcello was not fond of the project. He refused to
take part in it. The conflict with his teacher reached a point of no return
and his parents decided to send him to another school:

"We were all Southerners here, it was natural to hear different dialects.
You did not feel different. I felt at home here, I was born here. So it

was at least at primary school. When I was at middle school, something changed. I started to perceive words, insinuations which I hadn't noticed when I was a child, because when you are a child you think only of play. So I started to understand that being from the South had been a problem for many people and that the issue was very much alive. My teacher of Italian asked us to translate some words or sentences from Italian into our own dialect – if you were from Apulia, like me, into Apulian, if you were from Sicily into Sicilian, and so on. It was nothing bad, those were years of change in schools. We were not given marks, so retrospectively I can see what my teacher's aim was, but then I did not like taking part in the project. I perceived a discrimination, or a risk of discrimination, and I refused to participate. This thing caused a lot of trouble because I did not want anything to do with the project and with the teacher. I did not want to go to school. The only solution was to go to another school. I do not know why, maybe I had felt something I had not liked and I shut myself away"

The episode reported by Marcello raises some important questions: how were 1970s pupils, especially the children of migrants, affected by the changes taking place in the education system and particularly in the day-to-day school practice? Were pupils involved in decision-making or were they simply considered passive recipients? The answer is not obvious. Marcello, for example, would have preferred not to talk about his origins. He was born in Northern Italy and, sensing an unpleasant attitude towards the Southerners, he would probably have preferred to pass for a Turinese. He adopted a strategy of social mimesis, whose success was put at risk by the project.[68]

Marcello remembered having been upset by the comments of those who "came from other parts of Italy and believed, for this reason, that they were better than you". As a child, he was sensitive to his parents' difficulties:

"They told me that when they had arrived it had been really difficult to find a house. Nobody wanted to rent to Southerners. They were discriminated against. It was a trauma for them"

He described himself as sympathetic towards his parents but, at the same time, ashamed of them and other members of the family. His relatives and their dialect forced Marcello to deal with his origins, something he did not want to do:

"My grandma lived with us here . It really upset me that she spoke in dialect in the streets, in the shops. I did not like it. She was not the only one to do that and every time I felt so upset, believe me! [...] I did not like to feel different. That's probably the reason why I did not want to take part in the school project. It was as if I was trying to say 'I'm here, it doesn't matter where I am from'"

During the interview, Marcello was reticent about the episode of the project and his feelings towards his family. I had already asked him if the fact of being born to Southern parents had ever been a source of difficulty for him and he had replied with a convinced "No". His sister, however, had interrupted him saying, "Why don't you tell her about your first year at middle school?" It was only after his sister had raised the issue that Marcello started to talk about it. Even if he agreed that his refusal to participate in the project had had a huge impact on his life – he had refused to continue to go to the same school and was sent to a different one – he kept saying that his memories were "not clear [and] really confused". They were indeed influenced by what Alistair Thomson has referred to as "'strategies of containment', [that is] the methods we use to deal with frustration, failure, loss and pain", including reticence and forgetfulness.[69] These strategies are at work at an individual and a social level. Marcello's difficulty in coming to terms with an important part of his life is not dissimilar to the embarrassment and the ambiguity towards publicly defining as racist the attitude towards Southern Italian migrants in Northern Italy in the 1960s and 1970s and even now.

Notes

1 The book was first published in France as *L'Enfant et la vie familiale sous l'ancien regime*, Paris: Librairie Plon, 1960. It was translated in English as *Centuries of Childhood*, London: J. Cape, 1962. The fiftieth anniversary of its publication has been widely celebrated. See Heywood, C., "Centuries of Childhood: An anniversary – and an epitaph?", *Journal of the History of Childhood and Youth*, 3, 3, 2010, pp. 343–65.

2 Hendrick, H., "The Child as a Social Actor in Historical Sources. Problems of Identification and Interpretation", in Monrad Christensen, P., Allison, J., (eds), *Research with children. Perspective and practices*, London: Routledge, 2000, p. 41.

3 Idem, p. 42.

4 Mintz, Steven, *Huck's Raft. A History of American Childhood*, Cambridge: Harvard University Press, 2004, p. vii.

5 Garrison, J., "The Unequal Status of Children in American Educational History. Historiographical Reflections and Theorethical Possibilities", in Meyers, D., Miller, B., (eds), *Inequality in education. Historical Perspectives*, Plymouth: Lexington Books, 2009, p. 24.

6 Meda, J., "Tra le sudate carte...Guida ragionata ai fondi di quaderni ed elaborati didattici in Italia", *Biblioteche Oggi*, 2004, pp. 51–6.

7 Meda, J., Montino, D., Sani, R., *Exercise books for a History of the Approach to Schooling and Education in the 19th and 20th Centuries*, Florence: Polistampa, 2010.

8 https://www.indire.it/lucabas/lkmw_file/archivio_storico/Fondo_MariaMaltoni.pdf [last time accessed 5/11/2022] See Salotti, B., "Il Fondo Maria Maltoni", in Meda, J., Montino, D., Sani, R., cit., pp. 73–88; See also the catalogue of the exhibition *La maestra e la vita: Maria Maltoni e la scuola di san Gersolè*, Impruneta: Noeedizioni, 2006.

9 Maltoni, M., (ed.) *I quaderni di San Gersolè*, Turin: Einaudi, 1959.

10 Contini, G., *Aristocrazia contadina. Sulla complessità della società contadina. Fattoria, famiglia, individui*, Pistoia: Gli Ori, 2008, p. 19. By the same author see also "Animals, children and peasants in Tuscany. A note on the San Gersolè

archive", in Hussey, S., Thompson, P.R., (eds), *Environmental Consciousness. The Roots of a New Political Agenda*, New Brunswick, 2000 [2004], pp. 55–62.

11 Thompson, P., *The voice of the Past. Oral History*, Oxford: Oxford University Press, 1978, p. 22.

12 Idem, p. 51.

13 Ibidem.

14 Perks, R., Thomson, A., (eds), *The Oral History Reader*, London: Routledge, 1998, p. ix.

15 See Vansina, J., *Living with Africa*, Madison: University of Winsconsin Press, 1994.

16 Portelli, A., "What makes oral history different", in *The Death of Luigi Trastulli and Other Stories. Form and Meaning of Oral History*, Albany: State University of New York Press, 1991, p. 50. The essay was first published as "Sulla specificità della storia orale", *Primo Maggio*, 13, 1979, pp. 54–60.

17 Ibidem.

18 Idem, p. 52.

19 Idem, p. 53.

20 Idem, p. 56.

21 Passerini, L., "Work Ideology and Consensus Under Italian Fascism", *History Workshop Journal*, 8, 1, 1979, p. 84. See also by the same author, *Torino operaia e Fascismo. Una storia orale*, Rome: Laterza, 1984.

22 Ibidem.

23 Ibidem.

24 Idem, p. 25.

25 Ibidem.

26 Ibidem.

27 Abrams, L., *Oral History Theory*, London: Routledge, 2010, p. 163.

28 Ibidem.

29 Sangster, J., "Telling our stories: feminist debates and the use of oral history", *Women's History Review*, 3, 1, 1994, p. 11.

30 Reay, D., "Insider perspectives or stealing the words out of women's mouths: interpretation in the research process", *Feminist Review*, 53, 1996, p. 58.

31 Ibidem.

32 Hale, S., "Feminist Method, Process, and Self-Criticism: Interviewing Sudanese Women", in Gluck, S., Patai, D., (eds) *Women's Words: The Feminist Practice of Oral History*, London: Routledge, 1991, p. 131.

33 Abrams, L. cit., p. 169.

34 Frisch, M., "Oral history and *Hard Times*", in Perks, R., Thomson, A., (eds) cit., p. 33.

35 Idem, p. 35.

36 Abrams, L. cit., p. 109.

37 Barthes, R., "An introduction to the structural analysis of narrative", *New Literary History*, 6, 2, 1975, p. 237.

38 Czarniawska, B., *Narratives in Social Science Research*, London: Routledge, 2004, p. 5.

39 Ibidem.

40 Abrams, L. cit., p. 54.

41 Idem, p. 58.

42 Thomson, A., *ANZAC memories. Living with the Legend*, Melbourne: Oxford University Press, 1994, p. 8.

43 Ibidem.

44 Summerfield, P., "Culture and composure: creating narratives of the gendered self in oral history interviews", *Cultural and Social History*, 1, 2004, p. 69.

45 For privacy reasons all the names have been changed. Interview with the author, Turin, 5 May 2009.
46 Interview with the author, Turin, 11 May 2009.
47 Interview with the author, Turin, 27 May 2009.
48 Interview with the author, Turin, 27 May 2009.
49 Interview with the author, Turin, 20 May 2009.
50 Interview with the author, Turin, 16 May 2009.
51 Interview with the author, Turin, 17 April 2009.
52 Interview with the author, Turin, 5 May 2009.
53 Interview with the author, Turin, 12 May 2009.
54 Interview with the author, Turin, 20 April 2009.
55 Interview with the author, Turin, 30 April 2009.
56 Interview with the author, Turin, 4 May 2009.
57 Bertaux-Wiame, I., "The life history approach to the study of internal migration", *Oral History*, 7, 1, 1979, p. 29.
58 Idem, p. 30.
59 Pitzalis, M., "Hamsters on a wheel? Conflict over the role of school teachers in the primary education state school model", *Italian Journal of Sociology of Education*, 3, 2009, p. 117.
60 A *casa di ringhiera* was a tenement house with an internal courtyard.
61 Interview with the author, Turin, 13 May 2009.
62 Jackson, C., "Motives for 'laddishness' at school: fear of failure and fear of the 'feminine'", *British Educational Research Journal*, 29, 4, 2003, p. 587.
63 See Burke, P.J., "Men and education: masculinities, identification and widening participation", *British Journal of Sociology of Education*, 28, 4, 2007, pp. 411–24.
64 Kawecka Nenga, S., "Social class and structures of feeling in women's childhood memories of clothing, food and leisure", *Journal of Contemporary Ethnography*, 32, 2, 2003, pp. 167–99.
65 Idem, p. 178.
66 Idem, p. 188.
67 https://giscel.it/dieci-tesi-per-leducazione-linguistica-democratica/ [last time accessed 22/9/2021]; see also Chapter 3.4.2
68 For an analysis of the concept see Romania, V., *Farsi passare per italiani. Strategie di mimetismo sociale*, Rome: Carocci, 2004.
69 Thomson, A., cit., p. 237.

Conclusions

In 1971, a pamphlet entitled *How the West Indian Child is Made Educationally Subnormal in British Schools* by the Grenadian scholar and activist Bernard Coard was published in the UK, sparking a heated debate. Coard denounced how a disproportionate number of children born to West Indian families were referred to schools for Educationally Sub-Normal (ESN) pupils.[1] More than any other group, West Indian pupils were deemed less gifted owing to the poor results they scored in culturally biased IQ tests.

The issue had already been raised by migrants' associations in the late 1960s. The Black Supplementary School (BSS) movement was the response of the black community to the racist attitude towards their children in post-war British schools. Independent schools run by parents and voluntary teachers were created throughout the country. As Jessica Gerrard has remarked, the BSS movement was also part of the wider reaction of the black community to the racism experienced during the 1950s and 1960s.[2]

This reaction was made possible by the existence of a syncretic, transnational culture bridging Britain, Africa, and the Americas to which Paul Gilroy has referred to as the "black Atlantic".[3] The figure of Claudia Jones is particularly significant in this respect. Born in Trinidad, she moved with her family to the United States. Expelled because of her affiliation to the Communist Party, in 1955 she arrived in London where, within a few years, she founded the *West Indian Gazette* and initiated what was going to become the Notting Hill Carnival. Both the *Gazette* and the Carnival became symbols of the affirmation of West Indian identity in Britain and, according to Bill Schwarz, of the role they played in the decolonization of British culture.[4]

In spite of the relevance of the issue of migration in post-war British schools, the topic has been neglected by historians. The same can be said of other European countries. Kevin Myers has defined the silence of historians of education on the presence of migrants and minorities in post-war Europe "puzzling and rather disturbing". It is puzzling that such an important phenomenon which changed the face of the continent and challenged the education systems of the affected countries has not been investigated.

DOI: 10.4324/9781003100546-6

It is disturbing because, in Myers' words, "it may be taken as a sign that historical studies on education are failing to illuminate or, to speak to, the most important issues of the day".[5]

This book contributes to fill the gap in this field of research with a specific focus on Italy. The similarities between the British and the Italian case are striking. Southern Italian pupils attending Turin primary schools between the 1950s and the 1960s were constructed as a burden and referred in large numbers to the *classi differenziali*. In the 1970s, in the wake of protest movements, this practice was harshly criticized to the extent that the *differenziali* were suppressed. West Indian children moving to the UK in the same period were perceived as a major problem in British schools. As Ian Grosvenor's study on the case of Birmingham shows, West Indian pupils were "the main problem for the education system" and many of them, as denounced by Coard, ended up in ESN schools.[6] As Grosvenor has pointed out, education was crucial for the "racialization" of the West Indians.[7]

One may wonder if a similar process was at work in post-war Italy. The answer should take into account the difficulties faced by the country in coming to terms with the history of its racism. There is indeed a myth haunting Italy. The myth of the good-natured Italian, unable to commit bad actions and immune to racism.[8] The Italians were benign in their African colonies, to whose progress they contributed with their hard work. Italian colonialism was different from that of other European countries. Italy was poor and overcrowded. It needed new territories for its surplus population. Its colonialism thus had a human face unlike that of Great Britain or France, craving power and riches. Italians did not take part in the persecution and extermination of the Jews between the 1930s and the 1940s. Italians did not commit war crimes. Italian soldiers were friendly with the populations of the countries they invaded during the Second World War.

The existence of an Italian colonial history is a recent discovery for post-war Italians. It took many years for scholars – initially very few – to gain access to archives and documents and shed light on the atrocities committed by the Italian occupiers. The same can be said of the racism against the Jews. When, in the 1980s, racism against foreign migrants manifested itself very clearly, the most common reaction was general surprise and difficulty in seeing the phenomenon for what it really was. And even now, there is a certain scepticism about the possibility that the general attitude towards the migrants living in the peninsula might be racist.

If the word racism is not enunciated very often as far as former colonial subjects, Jews or migrants are concerned, it is used even less in reference to the South. Anti-southernism (*anti-meridionalismo*) is a far more common term, even among scholars. To date only Enrica Capussotti and Michele Nani have explicitly applied the category of racism to the history of the relations between the *Mezzogiorno* and the rest of the country.[9]

Nani points out that in order to understand whether or not something can be called racist, one should first clarify what racism is. If for example, it is assumed that there cannot be racism without any reference to the existence of races or to strictly biological features, except for the theories of the school of criminal anthropology, it is not possible to consider the post-unification discourse on the South as racist. If racism is assumed to be characterized by institutional violence, apart perhaps from the post-unification war against brigandage, it is not possible to say that Southerners were ever the object of racism. However, Nani asks, is it possible to accept these definitions of racism? His answer is negative. An acceptable definition of racism, in his view, should refer to the Gramscian concept of common sense. Gramsci – Nani notes – proposed a "denaturalization of common sense" and recognized its "sociological definiteness [and] historical variability".[10] Common sense was for Gramsci linked to hegemony. The stereotypical image offered by the late nineteenth century press – Nani argues – contributed to the further dissemination of an idea of the South and its inhabitants as irreducibly 'other' and of a language through which the *Mezzogiorno* was made sense of.

Capussotti has analysed post-war Southern migrations towards the industrial triangle "through the lens of racism which historically has produced not only the attitude of the 'Northerners' towards the 'Southerners', and vice versa, but the contents making these entities meaningful by naturalizing in cultural terms spatial and geographical differences". The post-war racialization of Southern migrants – she argues – thus was not based on "presumed 'bio-zoological differences'" in line with the continuously central role that "cultural characteristics and their essentialization" have played in the history of Italian racism.[11]

Nani's and Capussotti's reflections are useful in answering our question about the possibility that what Southern pupils experienced in post-war Turin primary schools can be defined racism. Depicted in the dominant discourse as 'different' and inferior, Southern migrants were represented as a threat to the social and cultural integrity of the Piedmontese capital. One of the most powerful symbols of this threat were their children, described in the press as poor, dangerous, and less clever and made the object of scientific studies aimed at understanding and solving the presumed problem of their maladjustment.

Primary schoolteachers used these discursive constructions in a strategic way. Their post-war working conditions were difficult. Not only had they to supervise overcrowded classes in often inadequate buildings, but they were strictly controlled by their superiors, particularly by heads of school. The latter inspected classes, checked class registers, and, above all, assessed teachers using children's preparation as a yardstick. The marks assigned by heads of school influenced teachers' careers and their prestige in the school community. This tense situation led teachers to draw on the repertoire of stereotypes of Southern families and their children to justify their work and educational choices. The use of sources such as class registers does not allow us to discern what teachers really thought of their Southern pupils. Class registers were official documents regularly checked by heads of school and other superiors. What is certainly true is that the distinctive traits attributed to Southerners, for example, by the general press were reproduced in the account of the classroom activities and pupils' descriptions offered by teachers in the registers. It is also true that the same stereotypes informed the treatment of the issue of Southern pupils by educational periodicals.

The increasing demand for instruction by subaltern classes had not been matched in the post-war period by substantial changes to educational institutions. The education system continued to be based on rigid selection. At the same time, the growing school population served as a privileged observation point for experts – such as psychiatrists and psychologists – to study the social changes occurring at the time. Experts identified one of the main features of post-war Italy in what they referred to as the educational and social maladjustment of children and particularly of those born to Southern families living in North-Western cities, including Turin. These studies provided the breeding ground for teachers to ease the pressure within their classes. Especially between the 1960s and the 1970s, an increasing number of Southern pupils were sent to special education classes, called *classi differenziali*. These classes had existed since the early twentieth century and their history, as well as that of Italian special education, is still to be written. It is important to remark, though, that they were not set up specifically to solve the problem represented by Southern children. They already existed and were numerous in other areas of the country. In Turin, however, they were meant to be 'classes for immigrants', as they were sometimes openly identified. From the early 1970s, the *classi differenziali* were strongly criticized by the progressive forces forming around primary schools. Things started to change at a higher level through the introduction of new arrangements for educational activities. This did not mean, however, that the stereotypical view of Southern children and their families disappeared.

It cannot be said that any reference to the biological features of Southern pupils was made by teachers or heads of school or psychiatrists. Nor were they mentioned in educational journals or newspapers or magazines. In addition, the practice of referring them, as suggested by some of the experts, to the *classi differenziali* was very common, but it was not a rule. Were Southern children the object of racism? The answer is yes if we consider the peculiarity of Italian racism that Capussotti mentions. Southern pupils were defined as educationally and socially maladjusted, underachieving, and less clever than their North-Western peers as a result of their culture. The *classi differenziali* were indicative of the alleged impossibility of reconciling the culture of Southern pupils and their families with the dominant one.

The problem with applying the category of racism to this case may arise when it comes to the way in which the subjects themselves make sense of their experience. The interviews analysed in this book seem to show that school and childhood narratives of grown-up Southern children living in Turin are not unequivocal. Some of them reported feeling discriminated against. Others offered a positive reading of their experience. Categories, such as gender and class, influenced the way in which their memories were organized.[12] In addition, it does not seem that any form of collective response resembling that of black supplementary schools in the UK took place. A wider and more detailed analysis of this kind of memories would be a fruitful area for future work.

Notes

1 Coard, B., *How the West Indian Child is Made Educationally Subnormal in British Schools*, London: New Beacon Books, 1971.
2 Gerrard, J., "Self-help and protest: the emergence of black supplementary schooling in England", *Race, Ethnicity and Education*, 16, 1, 2013, pp. 32–58. See also Kehinde Andrews, *Resisting Racism: The Black supplementary school movement*, London: Institute of Education Press, 2013.
3 Gilroy, P., *The Black Atlantic. Modernity and Double-Counsciousness*, London: Verso, 1993.
4 Schwarz, B., "'Claudia Jones and the *West Indian Gazette*': reflections on the emergence of post-colonial Britain", *Twentieth Century British History*, 14, 3, 2003, pp. 264–85. On Claudia Jones see also Boyce Davis, C., *Left of Karl Marx. The Political Life of Black Communist Claudia Jones*, Durham: Duke University Press, 2008.
5 Myers, K. "Immigrants and ethnic minorities in the history of education", *Paedagogica Historica*, 45, 6, 2009, p. 802.
6 Grosvenor, I., *Assimilating Identities. Racism and Educational Policy in Post-1945 Britain*, London: Lawrence & Wishart, 1997, p. 121.
7 Idem, p. 185.
8 Bidussa, D., *Il mito del bravo italiano*, Milan: Il Saggiatore, 1994; Schwartz, G., "On myth making and nation building: the genesis of the 'myth of the good Italian' 1943–1947", *Telos*, 164, 2013, pp. 11–43.
9 Capussotti, E., "*Nordisti contro Sudisti*": Internal Migrations and Racism in Turin, Italy: 1950s and 1960s", *Italian Culture*, XVIII, 2, 2010, pp. 121–38; Nani, M., *Ai confini della nazione. Stampa e razzismo nell'Italia di fine Ottocento*, Rome: Carocci, 2006.
10 Nani, M., cit., p. 241.
11 Capussotti, E., "Migrazioni interne, razzismo e inclusione differenziale nel secondo dopoguerra a Torino", in Curcio, A., Mellino, M., (eds), *La razza al lavoro*, Rome: Manifestolibri, 2012, pp. 143–4. On the entanglement between biologism and culturalism in the history of Italian racism see Cassata, F., *Molti, Sani e Forti* cit.
12 For an analysis of the influence of social class over the perception of foreign migrants in late twentieth century Italy see Cole, J., *The New Racism in Europe. A Sicilian Ethnography*, Cambridge: Cambridge University Press, 1997.

Bibliography

Archives

Central State Archive
Turin State Archive
Archive of Turin City Council
Archive of the *Istituto Piemontese per la Storia della Resistenza e della Società Contemporanea*
Archive of the Primary School "Antonino Parato"
Archive of the Primary School "Aristide Gabelli"
Archive of the Primary School "Gian Enrico Pestalozzi"
Archive of the Primary School "Margherita di Savoia"

Books

L'Associazione nazionale per gli interessi del Mezzogiorno d'Italia nei suoi primi cinquant'anni di vita, Roma: Collezione Meridionale, 1960

Atti del Convegno Internazionale di Studio su Immigrazione, Lavoro e Patologia Mentale: Milano, 23–24 marzo 1963, Milan: Zanolla, 1963

Atti Parlamentari, Disegni di legge, Camera dei Deputati, V Legislatura, Rome: 1970

Abrams, L., *Oral History Theory*, London: Routledge, 2010

Alasia, F., Montaldi, D., *Milano, Corea. Inchiesta sugli immigrati*, Milan: Feltrinelli, 1960

Ambrosoli, L., *La scuola in Italia dal dopoguerra ad oggi*, Bologna: Il Mulino, 1982

Aries, P., *Centuries of Childhood*, London: J. Cape, 1962

Arzenati, P.M., *La Rivista 'L'Infanzia anormale' (1911–1925)*, Unpublished MA Dissertation, Faculty of Letters and Philosophy, University of Milan, 2005–2006

Aschcroft, B., *On Post-Colonial Futures: Transformations of Colonial Culture*, London: Continuum, 2001

Associazione per la lotta contro le malattie mentali (sezione autonoma di Torino), *La fabbrica della follia*, Turin: Einaudi, 1971

Babini, V.P., *La questione dei frenastenici. Alle origini della psicologia scientifica in Italia (1870–1910)*, Milan: Angeli, 1996

Babini, V., Lama, L., *Una donna nuova. Il femminismo scientifico di Maria Montessori*. Milan: Angeli, 2003

Bacigalupi, M., Fossati, P., *Da plebe a popolo. L'educazione popolare nei libri di scuola dall'Unità alla Repubblica*, Florence: La Nuova Italia, 1986

Badino, A., *Tutte a casa? Donne tra migrazione e lavoro nella Torino degli anni Sessanta*, Rome: Viella, 2008

Barbagallo, F., (ed.), *Storia dell'Italia Repubblicana*, Turin: Einaudi, 1995

Barbagli, M., *Educating for Unemployment. Politics, Labor Markets, and the School System. Italy, 1859–1973*, New York, NY: Columbia University Press, 1982

Baroni, M.R., *Il linguaggio trasparente. Indagine socio-linguistica su chi parla e chi ascolta*, Bologna: Il Mulino, 1983

Bermani, C., *Una storia cantata, 1962–1997. Trentacinque anni di attività del Nuovo Canzoniere Italiano*, Milan: Jaca Book, 1997

Bernardi, B., Poni, C., Triulzi, A., (eds), *Fonti orali: antropologia e storia*, Milan: Angeli, 1978

Bernini, S., *Family Life and Individual Welfare in Post-war Europe. Britain and Italy Compared*, Basingstoke: Palgrave, 2008

Bertolini, P., *Delinquenza e disadattamento minorile. Esperienze rieducative*, Bari: Laterza, 1964

Bevilacqua, P., De Clementi, A., Franzina, E., (eds), *Storia dell'emigrazione italiana*, Vol. I, *Partenze*, Rome: Carocci, 2001; *Storia dell'emigrazione italiana*, Vol. II, *Arrivi*, Rome: Carocci, 2002

Bidussa, D., *Il mito del bravo italiano*, Milan: Il Saggiatore, 1994

Bollati, G., Bertelli, C., (eds), *Storia d'Italia, Annali 2, L'immagine fotografica 1845–1945*, Turin: Einaudi, 1979

Bollea, G., (ed.), *Disadattati e minorati. Ricerca sulla scuola e la società italiana in trasformazione*, Rome: Laterza, 1964

Bonetta, G. *Scuola e socializzazione in Italia fra '800 e '900*, Milan: Angeli, 1989

Bonetta, G., *Corpo e Nazione. L'educazione ginnastica, igienica e sessuale nell'Italia liberale*, Milan: Angeli, 1990

Borghi, L., Finocchiaro, B., (eds), *Opere di Gaetano Salvemini. Scritti sulla scuola*, Milan: Feltrinelli, 1966

Boyce Davis, C., *Left of Karl Marx. The Political Life of Black Communist Claudia Jones*, Durham, NC: Duke University Press, 2008

Boussion, S., Gardet, M., Ruchat, M., *L'internationale des républiques d'enfants (1939–1955)*, Paris: Anamosa, 2020

Bravo, A., Bruzzone, A.M., *In guerra senz'armi. Storie di donne. 1940–1945*, Rome: Laterza, 1995

Broccoli, A., *Educazione e politica nel Mezzogiorno d'Italia, 1767–1860*, Florence: La Nuova Italia, 1968

Burke, P., Porter, R., (eds), *The Social History of Language*, Cambridge: Cambridge University Press, 1987

Canestri, G., Ricuperati, G., *La scuola in Italia dalla legge Casati ad oggi*, Turin: Loescher, 1976

Caroli, D., *Day Nurseries and Childcare in Europe, 1800–1939*, London: Palgrave, 2017

Cassata F., *Molti, sani e forti. L'eugenetica in Italia*. Turin: Bollati Boringhieri, 2006

Casti, E., Turco, A. (eds), *Culture dell'alterità. Il territorio africano e le sue rappresentazioni*, Milan: Unicopli, 1998

Castronovo, V., Tranfaglia, N. (eds), *La Stampa italiana del neocapitalismo*, Rome: Laterza, 1976

Castrovilli, A., Seminara, C., *Storia della Barriera di Milano*, Torino: Associazione culturale Officina della memoria, 2004.

Centro Furio Jesi, (ed.), *La menzogna della razza. Documenti e immagini del razzismo e dell'anti-semitismo fascista*, Bologna: Grafis, 1994

Chabod, F., *L'Italia contemporanea (1918–1948)*, Turin: Einaudi, 1961 [2002]

Chabod, F., *Italian Foreign Policy*, Princeton, NJ: Princeton University Press, 1996

Chauvière, M., *Enfance inadaptée, l'héritage de Vichy*, Paris: Éditions Ovrière, 1980 [L'Harmanattan, 2009]

Chianese, G., *Quando uscimmo dai rifugi. Il Mezzogiorno tra guerra e dopoguerra (1943–1946)*, Rome: Carocci, 2004

Chianese, G., Crainz, G., Da Vela, M., Gribaudi, G., (eds), *Italia 1945–1950. Conflitti e trasformazioni sociali*, Milan: Angeli, 1985

Ciampani, A., (ed.), *L'Amministrazione per gli aiuti internazionali. La ricostruzione dell'Italia tra dinamiche internazionali e attività assistenziali*, Milan: Angeli, 2002.

Cimino, G., Dazzi, N., (eds), *La psicologia in Italia. I protagonisti e i problemi scientifici, filosofici e istituzionali (1870–1945)*, Milan: LED, 1998

Cimino, G., Lombardo, G.P., (eds), *Sante De Sanctis tra psicologia generale e psicologia applicata*, Milan: Angeli, 2004

Città di Torino-Assessorato all'Istruzione, *Atti del dibattito sulla validità delle classi differenziali nella scuola dell'obbligo*, Turin, 1970

Cives, G., (ed.), *La scuola italiana dall'Unità ai giorni nostri*, Scandicci: La Nuova Italia, 1990

Clemente, P., Meoni, M.L., Squillacciotti, M., (eds), *Il dibattito sul folklore in Italia*, Milan: Edizioni di Cultura Popolare, 1976

Codignola, T., *Nascita e morte di un piano. Tre anni di battaglia per la scuola pubblica*, Florence: La Nuova Italia, 1962

Cole, J., *The New Racism in Europe. A Sicilian Ethnography*, Cambridge: Cambridge University Press, 1997

Colucci, M., *Lavoro in movimento. L'emigrazione italiana in Europa 1945–57*, Rome: Donzelli, 2008

Conrad, P., *The Medicalization of Society: On the Transformation of Human Conditions into Treatable Disorders*, Baltimore, MD: John Hopkins University Press, 2007

Cooter, R., (ed.), *In the Name of the Child. Health and Welfare 1880–1940*, London: Routledge, 1992

Contini, G., *Aristocrazia contadina. Sulla complessità della società contadina. Fattoria, famiglia, individui*, Pistoia: Gli Ori, 2008

Cornis, I., Waters, S., *Memories of 1968. International Perspectives*, Bern: Peter Lang, 2010

Cortellazzo, M., (ed.), *Guida ai dialetti veneti*, Padua: CLUEP, 1981

Cortellazzo, M., *Italiano d'oggi*, Padua: Esedra, 2000

Crainz, G., *Il paese mancato. Dal miracolo economico agli anni Ottanta*, Rome: Donzelli, 2003

Crainz, G., *Il paese mancato. Dal miracolo economico agli anni Ottanta*, Rome: Donzelli, 2005

Cunningham, H., *Children and Childhood in Western Society since 1500*, London: Longman, 1995

Curcio, A., Mellino, M., (eds), *La razza al lavoro*, Rome: Manifestolibri, 2012

Czarniawska, B., *Narratives in Social Science Research*, London: Routledge, 2004

D'Alessandro V., *Gino Ferretti e il rinnovamento della pedagogia*, Florence: La Nuova Italia, 1959

Depaepe, M., (ed.), *Order in Progress. Everyday Educational Practice in Primary Schools, Belgium, 1880–1970*, Leuven: Leuven University Press, 2000

De Fort, E., *Scuola e analfabetismo nell'Italia del Novecento*, Bologna: Il Mulino, 1995

Id., *La scuola elementare dall'Unità alla caduta del Fascismo*, Bologna: Il Mulino, 1996

De Grazia, V., *How Fascism Ruled Women: Italy, 1922–1945*, Berkeley: University of California Press, 1992

Dei, M., *Colletto bianco, grembiule nero. Gli insegnanti elementari italiani dall'inizio del secolo al secondo dopoguerra*, Bologna: Il Mulino, 1994

Dei, M., Barbagli, M., *Le vestali della classe media. Ricerca sociologica sugli insegnanti*, Bologna: Il Mulino, 1969

Del Boca, A., *Gli Italiani in Libia. Tripoli bel suol d'amore 1860–1922*, Rome: Laterza, 1986 [Milan: Mondadori, 1993]

Del Boca, A., (ed.), *Adua. Le ragioni di una sconfitta*, Rome: Laterza, 1997

De Martino, E., *Sud e magia*, Milan: Feltrinelli, 1959

De Mauro, T., *Storia linguistica dell'Italia unita*, Rome: Laterza, 1963 [1984]

De Palma, G., *Surviving without Governing. The Italian Parties in the Parliament*, Berkeley: University of California Press, 1977

Dickie, J., *Darkest Italy. The Nation and Stereotypes of the Mezzogiorno, 1860–1900*, Basingstoke: Macmillan, 1999

Dickie, J., *Una catastrofe patriottica. 1908: il terremoto di Messina*, Rome: Laterza, 2008

Douglas, M., *Purity and Danger. An Analysis of the Concepts of Pollution and Taboo*, London: Routledge, 1991

Duggan, C., Wagstaff, C., (eds), *Italy in the Cold War: Politics, Culture and Society, 1948–1958*, Washington, DC: Berg, 1995

Ericsson, K., Simonsen, E., *Children of World War Two: The Hidden Enemy Legacy*, Oxford: Berg, 2005

Fadiga Zanatta, A.L., *Il sistema scolastico italiano*, Bologna: Il Mulino, 1971

Faeta, F., *Questioni italiane. Demologia, antropologia, critica culturale*, Turin: Bollati Boringhieri, 2005

Ferrio, C., *La psiche e i nervi: introduzione storica ad ogni studio di psicologia, neurologia e psichiatria*, Turin: UTET, 1948

Fofi, G., *L'immigrazione meridionale a Torino*, Milan: Feltrinelli, 1964

Foot, J., *Milan Since the Miracle. City, Culture and Identity*, Oxford: Berg, 2001

Forgacs, D., Gundle, S., *Mass Culture and Italian Society from Fascism to the Cold War*, Bloomington: Indiana University Press, 2007

Fornaca, R., *I problemi della scuola italiana dal 1943 alla Costituente*, Roma: Armando, 1972

Frigessi Castelnuovo, D., Risso, M., *A mezza parete. Emigrazione, nostalgia, malattia mentale*, Turin: Einaudi, 1982

Fuhrmann, I., Montanari, G., *Scuola, storia e memoria del sindacalismo torinese. Negli anni di movimento Sessanta e Settanta*, Turin: Angolo Manzoni, 2005

Gabaccia, D., *Italy's Many Diasporas*, London: University College of London Press, 2000

Gagliani, D., Salvati, M., *La sfera pubblica femminile. Percorsi di storia delle donne in età contemporanea*, Bologna: Clueb, 1992

Gayre, G., R., *Italy in transition*, London: Faber and Faber, 1946

Galfré, M., *Una riforma alla prova. La scuola media di Gentile e il fascismo*, Milan: Angeli, 2000

Galfré, M., *Tutti a scuola! L'istruzione nell'Italia del Novecento*, Rome: Carocci, 2017

Gallerano, N. (ed.), *L'altro dopoguerra. Roma e il Sud 1943–1945*, Milan: Angeli, 1985

Galli de Paratesi, N., *Lingua toscana in bocca ambrosiana. Tendenze verso l'italiano standard: un'inchiesta sociolinguistica*, Bologna: Il Mulino, 1984

Gallo, S., *Il commissariato per le migrazioni e la colonizzazione interna (1930–1940). Per una storia della politica migratoria del Fascismo*, Foligno: Editoriale Umbra, 2015

Gambino, A., *Storia del dopoguerra. Dalla liberazione al potere DC*, Rome: Laterza, 1975

Garbero, C., *La scuola medico-pedagogica "Padre Agostino Gemelli" di Torino*, Turin, 1967

Giarrizzo, G., *Mezzogiorno senza meridionalismo. La Sicilia, lo sviluppo, il potere*, Venice: Marsilio, 1992

Gibelli, A., *L'officina della guerra. La Grande Guerra e le trasformazioni del mondo mentale*, Turin: Bollati Boringhieri, 1991

Gibson, M., *Prostitution and the State in Italy, 1860–1915*, New Brunswick: Rutgers University Press, 1986

Gibson, M., *Born to Crime. Cesare Lombroso and the Origins of Biological Criminology*, Westport, CT: Praeger, 2002

Gilroy, P., *The Black Atlantic. Modernity and Double-Counsciousness*, London: Verso, 1993

Ginsborg, P., *A History of Contemporary Italy. 1943–1980*, London: Penguin, 1990

Gluck, S., Patai, D., (eds), *Women's Words: The Feminist Practice of Oral History*, London: Routledge, 1991

Gonella, G., *Cinque anni al Ministero della Pubblica Istruzione*, Vol. 2, *Libertà della scuola e nuovi ordinamenti scolastici*, Milan: Giuffrè, 1981

Goretti, L., *I 'neri bianchi'. Mezzadri di Greve in Chianti tra lotte sindacali e fuga dalle campagne (1945–1950)*, Rome: Odradek, 2008

Graff, H.J., *The literacy myth. Literacy and Social Structure in the Nineteenth Century*, New York, NY: Academic Press, 1979

Graziano, L., Tarrow, S., *La crisi italiana*, Vol. 2, *Sistema politico e istituzioni*, Turin: Einaudi, 1979

Gribaudi, G., (ed.), *Terra bruciata. Le stragi naziste sul fronte meridionale*, Naples: L'Ancora del Mediterraneo, 2003

Id., *Guerra Totale. Tra bombe alleate e violenze naziste. Napoli e il fronte meridionale 1940–44*, Turin: Bollati Boringhieri, 2005

Grosvenor, I., *Assimilating Identities. Racism and Educational Policy in Post-1945 Britain*, London: Lawrence & Wishart, 199

Grosvenor, I., Lawn, M., Rousmaniere, K., *Silences and Images: The Social History of the Classroom*, New York, NY: Peter Lang, 1999

Gundle, S., *Between Hollywood and Moscow. The Italian Communists and the Challenge of Mass Culture, 1943–1991*, Durham, NC: Duke University Press, 2000

Hall, S., (ed.), *Representation. Cultural Representations and Signifying Practices*, London: Sage, 1997

Hobsbawm, E., *Nations and Nationalism since 1870. Programme, Myth and Reality*, Cambridge: Cambridge University Press, 1992

Hussey, S., Thompson, P.R., (eds), *Environmental Consciousness. The Roots of a New Political Agenda*, New Brunswick, 2000 [2004]

Inzerillo, G., *Storia della politica scolastica in Italia: da Casati a Gentile*, Rome: Editori Riuniti, 1974

Ipsen, C., *Dictating Demography. The Problem of Population in Fascist Italy*, Cambridge: Cambridge University Press, 1996

Jackson, J.P., *Science for Segregation: Race, Law and the Case against Brown v Board of Education*, New York, NY : New York University Press, 2005

Jackson, M., (ed.), *Health and the Modern Home*, London: Routledge, 2007

Kehinde Andrews, *Resisting Racism: The Black Supplementary School Movement*, London: Institute of Education Press, 2013

Klein, G., *La politica linguistica del fascismo*, Bologna: Il Mulino, 1986

Lepre, A., *Storia della prima Repubblica: l'Italia dal 1943 al 1998*, Bologna: Il Mulino, 1999

Levi, C., *Christ stopped at Eboli*, London: Penguin, 1948 [2000]

Levi, F., Maida, B., (eds), *La città e lo sviluppo. Crescita e disordine a Torino, 1945–1970*, Milan: Angeli, 2002

Lombroso, C., *Criminal Man*. Translated and with a new introduction by Mary Gibson and Nicole Hahn Rafter, Durham, NC: Duke University Press, 2006

Lorenzetto, A., *Alfabeto e analfabetismo*, Rome: Armando, 1962

Lumley, R., *States of Emergency: Cultures of Revolt in Italy from 1968 to 1978*, London: Verso, 1990

Lumley, R., Foot, J., (eds), *Italian Citiscapes. Culture and Urban Change in Contemporary Italy*, Exeter: University of Exeter Press, 2004

Lumley, R., Morris, J., (eds), *The New History of the Italian South. The Mezzogiorno Revisited*, Exeter: University of Exeter Press, 1997

Maida, B., *I treni dell'accoglienza. Infanzia, povertà e solidarietà nell'Italia del dopoguerra, 1945–1948*, Turin: Einaudi, 2020.

Malaparte, C., *La pelle*, Rome: Aria d'Italia, 1949 [Milan: Adelphi, 2010]

Maltoni, M., (ed.), *I quaderni di San Gersolè*, Turin: Einaudi, 1959

Malvezzi, G., Zanotti Bianco, U., *L'Aspromonte occidentale*, Milan: Libreria Editrice Milanese, 1910

Mantovani, C., *Rigenerare la società. L'eugenetica in Italia dalle origini ottocentesche agli anni Trenta*, Soveria Mannelli: Rubettino, 2004

Marland, H., Gijswijt-Hofstra, M., (eds), *Cultures of Child Health in Britain and the Netherlands in the Twentieth Century*, Amsterdam: Rodopi, 2003

McClintock, A., *Imperial Leather: Race, Gender and Sexuality in the Colonial Context*, London: Routledge, 1995

McGauley, P., *Matera, 1945–1960. The History of a 'National Disgrace'*, Oxford: Peter Lang, 2019

Meda, J., Montino, D., Sani, R., *Exercise Books for a History of the Approach to Schooling and Education in the 19th and 20th Centuries*, Florence: Polistampa, 2010

Medici, G., *Introduzione al piano di sviluppo della scuola,* Rome: Istituto Poligrafico dello Stato, 1959

Meyers, D., Miller, B., (eds), *Inequality in Education. Historical Perspectives,* Plymouth: Lexington Books, 2009

Miletto, E., *Con il mare negli occhi. Storia, luoghi e memorie dell'esodo istriano a Torino*, Milan: Franco Angeli, 2005

Minella, A., Spano, A., Terranova, F., *Cari bambini, vi aspettiamo con gioia. Il movimento di solidarietà popolare per la salvezza dell'infanzia nel dopoguerra,* Milan: Teti, 1980

Minesso, M., *Stato e infanzia nell'Italia contemporanea: origini, sviluppo e fine dell'ONMI, 1925–1975*, Bologna: Il Mulino, 2007

Ministero della Pubblica Istruzione, *Relazione della commissione d'indagine sullo stato e sullo sviluppo della pubblica istruzione in Italia*, Rome, 1963

Mintz, Steven, *Huck's Raft. A History of American Childhood*, Cambridge: Harvard University Press, 2004

Moe, N., *The View from the Vesuvius. Italian Culture and the Southern Question*, Berkeley: University of California Press, 2002

Molinari, A., *Le navi di Lazzaro. Aspetti sanitari dell'emigrazione transoceanica italiana: il viaggio per mare*, Milan: Angeli, 1988

Monrad Christensen, P., Allison, J., (eds), *Research with Children. Perspectives and Practices*, London: Routledge, 2000

Montaldo, S., Tappero, P., (eds), *Cesare Lombroso cento anni dopo*, Turin: UTET, 2009

Montaldo, S. (ed.), *Cesare Lombroso. Gli scienziati e la nuova Italia*, Bologna: Il Mulino, 2011

Motti, L., Caponeri Rossi, M., (eds), *Accademiste a Orvieto. Donne ed educazione fisica nell'Italia fascista, 1932–1943*, Ponte San Giovanni: Quattroemme, 1996

Murialdi, P., *La stampa italiana dal dopoguerra ad oggi, 1943–1972*, Rome: Laterza, 1973

Nani, M., *Ai confini della nazione. Stampa e razzismo nell'Italia di fine Ottocento*, Rome: Carocci, 2006

Palma, S., *L'Italia coloniale*, Rome: Editori Riuniti, 1999

Papuzzi, A., *Portami su quello che canta: processo a uno psichiatra*, Turin: Einaudi, 1977

Pasquinelli, C., *Antropologia e questione meridionale. Ernesto De Martino e il dibattito sul mondo popolare subalterno negli anni 1948–1955*, Florence: La Nuova Italia, 1977

Passerini, L., *Torino operaia e Fascismo. Una storia orale*, Rome: Laterza, 1984

Patanè, L. (ed.), *Gino Ferretti*, Catania: Trincale, 1983

Patriarca, S., *Race in Post-Fascist Italy 'War Children' and the Color of the Nation*, Cambridge: Cambridge University Press, 2022.

Pavone, C., *Alle origini della Repubblica. Scritti su fascismo, antifascismo e continuità dello Stato*, Turin: Bollati Boringhieri, 1995

Perks, R., Thomson, A., (eds), *The Oral History Reader*, London: Routledge, 1998

Petraccone, C., *Le due civiltà. Settentrionali e meridionali nella storia d'Italia*, Rome: Laterza, 2000

Petraccone, C., *Le 'due Italie'. La questione meridionale tra realtà e rappresentazione*, Rome: Laterza, 2005

Petrusewicz, M., *Come il Meridione divenne una Questione*, Soveria Mannelli: Rubettino, 1998

Pick, D., *Faces of Degeneration. A European Disorder, c. 1848-c. 1918*, Cambridge: Cambridge University Press, 1999

Pinna, G., *Due problemi della Sardegna. Analfabetismo e delinquenza*, Sassari: Gallizzi, 1955

Pistolesi, E., (ed.), *Lingua, scuola e società. I nuovi bisogni comunicativi nelle classi multiculturali*, Trieste: Istituto Gramsci, 2007

Pivato, S., *La storia leggera. L'uso pubblico della storia nella canzone italiana*, Bologna: Il Mulino, 2002

Portelli, A., *The Death of Luigi Trastulli and Other Stories. Form and Meaning of Oral History*, Albany, NY: State University of New York Press, 1991

Quine, M.S., *Italy's Social Revolution: Charity and Welfare from Liberalism to Fascism*, London: Palgrave, 2002

Raponi, N., (ed.) *Scuola e Resistenza. Atti del convegno promosso dalla Regione Emilia-Romagna per il XXX della Resistenza: Parma, 19–21 maggio 1977*, Parma: La Pilotta, 1978

Reineri, M., *Cattolici e Fascismo a Torino. 1925–1943*, Milan: Feltrinelli, 1978

Richardson, T., *The Century of the Child. The Mental Hygiene Movement and Social Policy in the United States and Canada*, Albany, NY: State University of New York Press, 1989

Rinauro, S., *Il cammino della speranza. L'emigrazione clandestina degli italiani nel secondo dopoguerra*, Turin: Einaudi, 2009

Romania, V., *Farsi passare per italiani. Strategie di mimetismo sociale*, Rome: Carocci, 2004

Romano, R., Vivanti, C., (eds), *Storia d'Italia*, Vol. V, *I documenti*, Turin: Einaudi, 1973

Ruffino, G., *L'indialetto ha la faccia scura. Giudizi e pregiudizi linguistici dei bambini italiani*, Palermo: Sellerio, 2006

Salotti, B., *La maestra e la vita: Maria Maltoni e la scuola di san Gersolé*, Impruneta: Noè, 2006

Salvadori, M.L., *Il mito del buongoverno. La questione meridionale da Cavour a Gramsci*, Turin: Einaudi, 1963

Sanfilippo, M., *Problemi di storiografia dell'emigrazione italiana*, Viterbo: Sette città, 2003

Sani, R., Corsi, M., *L'educazione alla democrazia tra passato e presente*, Milan: V&P strumenti, 2004

Sani, R., Pazzaglia, L., (eds), *Scuola e società nell'Italia unita. Dalla legge Casati al centro-sinistra*, Brescia: La Scuola, 2001

Santoni Rugiu, *Il professore nella scuola italiana*, Florence: La Nuova Italia, 1968

Santoni Rugiu, A., *Storia sociale dell'educazione*, Milan: Principato, 1987

Sarracino, V., Piazza, R., *La ripresa: scuola e cultura in Italia (1943–1946)*, Lecce: Pensa Multimedia, 1998

Scartabellati, A., *Intellettuali nel conflitto. Alienisti e patologie attraverso la Grande Guerra (1909–1921)*, Bagnaria Arsa: Edizioni Goliardiche, 2003

Schneider, J.C., Schneider, P.T., *Festival of the Poor. Fertility Decline and the Ideology of Class in Italy, 1860–1980*, Tucson, AZ: University of Arizona Press, 1996.

Scuola di Barbiana, *Lettera a una professoressa*, Florence: Libreria Editrice Fiorentina, 1967

Semelin, J., *Unarmed Against Hitler. Civilian Resistance in Europe, 1939–1943*, Westport, CT: Praeger, 1993

Semeraro, A., *Il mito della riforma. La parabola laica nella storia educativa della Repubblica*, Scandicci: La Nuova Italia, 1993

Signorelli, A., (ed.), *Cultura popolare a Napoli e in Campania nel Novecento*, Naples: Edizioni del Millennio, 2002

Spurr, D., *The Rhetoric of the Empire: Colonial Discourse in Journalism, Travel Writing and Imperial Administration*, Durham, NC: Duke University Press, 1993

Soddu, P., *L'Italia del dopoguerra. 1947–1953: una democrazia precaria*, Rome: Editori Riuniti, 1998

Soldani, S., (ed.), *L'educazione delle donne: scuole e modelli di vita femminile nell'Italia dell'Ottocento*, Milan: Angeli, 1989

Soldani, S., Turi, G., (eds), *Fare gli italiani. Scuola e cultura nell'Italia contemporanea*, Bologna: Il Mulino, 1993

Stella, G.A., *L'orda. Quando gli albanesi eravamo noi*, Milan: Rizzoli, 2002

Id., *Il maestro magro*, Milan: Rizzoli, 2005

Street, B.V., *Literacy in Theory and Practice*, Cambridge: Cambridge University Press, 1984

SVIMEZ, *Mutamenti nella struttura professionale e ruolo della scuola. Previsioni per il prossimo quindicennio*, Rome: Giuffrè, 1961

SVIMEZ, *Trasformazioni sociali e culturali in Italia e loro riflessi sulla scuola*, Rome: Giuffrè, 1962

Taruffi, D., De Nobili, L., Lori, C., *La questione agraria e l'emigrazione in Calabria*, Florence: Barbera, 1908

Id., *Trasformazioni sociali e culturali in Italia e loro riflessi sulla scuola*, Rome: Giuffrè, 1962

Teti, V., *Il senso dei luoghi: memoria e storia dei paesi abbandonati*, Roma, Donzelli, 2004

Thompson, P., *The Voice of the Past. Oral History*, Oxford: Oxford University Press, 1978

Thomson, A., *ANZAC Memories. Living with the Legend*, Melbourne: Oxford University Press, 1994

Tomasi, T., *La scuola italiana dalla dittatura alla Repubblica 1943–1948*, Milan: ER, 1976

Tomasi, T., (ed.), *L'istruzione di base in Italia. 1859–1977*, Florence: Vallecchi, 1978

Tornesello, M.L., *Il sogno di una scuola. Lotte ed esperienze didattiche negli anni Settanta: controscuola, tempo pieno, 150 ore*, Pistoia: Petit Plaisance, 2006

Tosi, A., *Language and Society in a Changing Italy*, Clevedon: Multilingual Matters, 2001

Tranfaglia, N., *Mafia, politica e affari nell'Italia repubblicana, 1943–1991*, Rome: Laterza, 1992

Tranfaglia, N., (ed.), *Storia di Torino. Gli anni della Repubblica*, Turin: Einaudi, 1999

Tranfaglia, N., Novelli, D., *Vite sospese: le generazioni del terrorismo*, Milan: Baldini Castoldi Dalai, 2007

Treves, A., *Le migrazioni interne nell'Italia fascista*, Turin: Einaudi, 1976

Tucker, W., H., *The Funding of Scientific Racism: Wickliffe Draper and the Pioneer Fund*, Urbana, IL: University of Illinois Press, 2002

Vansina, J., *Living with Africa*, Madison, WI: Univerity of Winsconsin Press, 1994

Villari, P., *Le lettere meridionali e altri scritti sulla questione sociale in Italia*, Naples: Guida, 1979

Weindling, P., (ed.), *International Health Organizations and Movements, 1918–1939*, Cambridge: Cambridge University Press, 1995

Wong, A.S., *Race and the Nation in Liberal Italy 1861–1911. Meridionalism, Empire and Diaspora*, Basingstoke: Palgrave, 2006

Zanotti Bianco, U., *Il martirio della scuola in Calabria*, Florence, Vallecchi, 1925

Zanobini, L., *Raccolta delle circolari della Pubblica Istruzione. Vol. I, Istruzione Primaria*, Milan, Giuffrè, 1965

Articles and pamphlets

"Le finalità scientifiche e i mezzi d'indagine dell'Istituto Biotipologico di Genova", *Annali dell'Istruzione Elementare*, V, 3–4, 1930, pp. 18–53

"L'insuccesso dell'alunno nella scuola primaria", *Scuola di Base*, 1958, pp. 1–6

"Il 'Tempo Pieno' a Torino", *Vita Nostra*, XIV, October 1971, p. 1

"Presentazione", *Meridiana*, I, 1, 1987, pp. 9–15

Atti del primo simposio nazionale sul recupero dei bambini ritardati e difficili. Quaderni di Infanzia anormale, 2, 1962

Alfieri, F., "Le cose difficili da far accettare anche alle famiglie operaie", *Cooperazione Educativa*, XXII, 8, August 1973, pp. 23–25

Arcamone, G., "L'Istituto biotipologico-ortogenetico di Genova", *Annali dell'Istruzione Elementare*, V, 2, 1930, pp. 35–49

Barrera, G., *Dangerous Liaisons: Colonial Concubinage in Eritrea, 1890–1941*, PAS Working Papers No. 1, Program of African Studies, Northwestern University, 1996

Barthes, R., "An Introduction to the Structural Analysis of Narrative", *New Literary History*, 6, 2, 1975, pp. 237–272

Benigno, F., Lupo, S., "Mezzogiorno in idea: a mo' di introduzione", *Meridiana*, 47–48, 2003, pp. 9–21

Bernini, S., "Natural mothers: teaching morals and parental crafts in Italy, 1945–60", *Modern Italy*, IX, 1, 2004, pp. 21–33.

Berteaux-Wiame, I., "The life history approach to the study of internal migration", *Oral History*, 7, 1, 1979, pp. 20–27

Bhabha, H., "The other question. Homi K Bhabha reconsiders the stereotype and colonial discourse", *Screen*, 24, 6, 1983, pp. 18–36

Bisiach, G., "I dibattiti televisivi: i meridionali al Nord", *Vie Assistenziali*, X, October 1966, pp. 44–48

Bollea, G., "La selezione scolastica. Principi teorici e organizzazione pratica", *Infanzia anormale*,n. 6, 1954, pp. 218–227

Bollea, G., "Evoluzione storica e attualità della neuropsichiatria infantile", *Infanzia anormale*, 37, 1960, pp. 141–163

Bollea G., "Il medico scolastico come psico-igienista", *Igiene mentale*, 1962, pp. 414–421

Bollea, G., "Le pedagogie speciali nelle scuole elementari. Problematiche del 'depistage' e del trattamento dei disadattati", *Annali della pubblica istruzione*, n. 12–13, 1964, pp. 285–296

Bravo, A., "Armed and unarmed: struggles without weapons in Europe and Italy", *Journal of Modern Italian Studies*, X, 4, 2005, pp. 468–484

Burke, P.J., "Men and education: masculinities, identification and widening participation", *British Journal of Sociology of Education*, 28, 4, 2007, pp. 411–424

Caldwell, L., "Courses for Women: The example of the 150 hours in Italy", *Feminist Review*, 14, 1983, pp. 71–83

Cannella, S., Poletti, M., Cattani, L., "La scuola e l'igiene mentale", *Riforma della scuola*, XV, 10, 1969, pp. 33–35

Capussotti, E., "Sognando *Lamerica*. Memorie dell'emigrazione italiana e processi identitari in un'epoca di migrazioni globali", *Contemporanea*, 4, 2007, pp. 633–646

Capussotti, E., "*Nordisti contro Sudisti:* Internal Migrations and Racism in Turin, Italy: 1950s and 1960s", *Italian Culture*, XVIII, 2, 2010, pp. 121–138

Capussotti, E., "'Arretrati per civiltà'. L'identità italiana alla prova delle migrazioni interne", *Zapruder*, 28, 2012, pp. 40–56

Cecchini, M., "Ritardo e differenziali", *Riforma della Scuola*, XVI, 6–7, 1970, pp. 9–16

Ciari, B., "La grande disadattata", *Riforma della Scuola*, XVI, 4, 1970, pp. 16–22

Coard, B., *How the West Indian Child is Made Educationally Subnormal in British Schools*, London: New Beacon Books, 1971

Comitato per la salvezza dei bambini di Napoli, *Aiutiamo i bambini di Napoli*, Naples, 1946

Coveri, L., "Dialetto e scuola nell'Italia unita", *Rivista Italiana di Dialettologia*, 5–6, 1981–82, pp. 77–97

De Fort, E., "L'associazionismo degli insegnanti elementari dall'età giolittiana al fascismo", *Movimento operaio e socialista*, IV, 4, 1981, pp. 375–404

Id., "I maestri elementari italiani dai primi del Novecento alla caduta del Fascismo", *Nuova Rivista Storica*, 68, 1984, pp. 527-576.

De Franco, F., "Per una legislazione organica in materia di igiene mentale infantile", *Igiene Mentale*, 1962, pp.285–307

De Sanctis, C. "Il Comitato Italiano per la Psichiatria Infantile", *Infanzia Anormale*, 1, 1953, pp. 15–29

Dei, M., "Le elezioni magistrali dal 1909 al 1924: un approccio sociologico", *Rivista di storia contemporanea*, XIV, 4, 1985, p. 554–586

Dei, M., "Travaglio e apoteosi del movimento cattolico magistrale: 1924–1948", *Rivista di storia contemporanea*, XVI, 1, 1987, p. 85–115

Deva, F., Pepe, M., "L'adattamento dei ragazzi immigrati nella scuola elementare", *Scuola e Città*, XIV, 7, 1963, pp. 340–6

Di Tullio, B., "L'opera del medico nella lotta contro la criminalità", *La Scuola Positiva*, 1964, pp. 389–402

Faustini, G., "La programmazione dei 'depistages' nella scuola dell'obbligo in una prospettiva scolastica di sanità mentale e di educazione alla società", *Ragazzi d'oggi*, XIII, 4, 1962, pp. 9–20

Faustini, G., Conte, M.T., "La delinquenza minorile in Italia dal 1958 al 1963", *Esperienze di Rieducazione*, XI, December 1964, pp. 42–65

Fiorani, M., "Giovanni Bollea (1913–2011). Per una storia della neuropsichiatria infantile in Italia", *Medicina&Storia*, 21–22, 2011, pp. 251–276

Fusco, M., "L'Associazione nazionale per gli interessi del Mezzogiorno nella lotta contro l'analfabetismo (1910–1928)", Estratto da *Archivio storico per le provincie napoletane*, XX, 1981

Gerrard, J., "Self-help and protest: the emergence of black supplementary schooling in England", *Race, Ethnicity and Education*, 16, 1, 2013, pp. 32–58

Giaccone, E., "Il servizio sociale nella scuola", *Ragazzi d'oggi*, IV, 4, 1953, pp. 3–6

Ginsborg, P., "The Communist Party and the Agrarian Question in Southern Italy, 1943–1948", *History Workshop Journal*, 17, 1984, pp. 81–101

Giordano, G.G., "Significato e Funzioni del Centro Medico-Psico-Pedagogico", *Infanzia Anormale*, 6, 1954, pp. 207–218

Gonella, G., *Salviamo il fanciullo. Discorso tenuto in Campidoglio per l'inaugurazione del convegno nazionale dell'Ente per la protezione morale del fanciullo*, Rome: Istituto poligrafico dello Stato, 1946

Groppelli, A., "I centri-medico-psico-pedagogici e la scuola", *Ragazzi d'oggi*, VI, 6, 1955, pp. 6–9

Gruppo Torinese, "Lavoro di Quartiere alle Vallette-S. Caterina", *Cooperazione Educativa*, XIX, 6, June 1970, pp. 6–8

Gualco, S., "Forme di crescenza accertate e curate nella scuola in un quinquennio", *Annali dell'istruzione elementare*, XI, 4–5, 1936, pp. 134–161

Gualco, S., "Il controllo della crescenza ad uso degli educatori", *Annali dell'istruzione elementare*, XI, 4–5–6, 1936, pp. 224–233

Guarnieri, P., "E la mamma dov'è? Medici, donne e bambini nell'Ottocento", *Bollettino di demografia storica*, 30–31, 1999, pp. 95–117

Guarnieri, P., "Un piccolo essere perverso. Il bambino nella cultura scientifica italiana tra Otto e Novecento", *Contemporanea*, IX, 2, 2006, pp. 253–284

Jackson, C., "Motives for 'laddishness' at school: fear of failure and fear of the 'feminine'", *British Educational Research Journal*, 29, 4, 2003, pp. 583–598

Jerrard, J., "Self-help and protest: the emergence of black supplementary schooling in England", *Race, Ethnicity and Education*, 16, 1, 2013, pp. 32–58

Kawecka Nenga, S., "Social class and structures of feeling in women's childhood memories of clothing, food and leisure", *Journal of Contemporary Ethnography*, 32, 2, 2003, pp. 167–199

Lasagno, D., "Il falò delle cinghie. Lotte nei manicomi a Torino nel 1968–1969", *Zapruder*, 16, 2008, pp. 24–37

Liguori, M., "Fenomeni migratori e sociologia. La letteratura sociologica sulle migrazioni interne nel Triangolo industriale (1958–1968)", *Rassegna Italiana di sociologia*, XX, 1, 1979, pp. 109–146

Lorenzetto, A., "La lotta contro l'analfabetismo e l'educazione degli adulti", *Il Ponte*, VI, . 5, 1950, p. 455–470

Lupo, S., "Storia del Mezzogiorno, questione meridionale, meridionalismo", *Meridiana*, 32, 1998, pp. 17–52

Macchiaroli, G., *Un'esperienza popolare del dopoguerra per la salvezza dei bambini di Napoli*, Naples, 1979

Maderna, A., Leone, B., "Interferenze affettive nel disadattamento di scolari immigrati da zone depresse", *Igiene Mentale*, 1962, pp. 1190–1196

Maderna, A., Valseschini, S., "Alcuni aspetti della situazione scolastica dei figli degli immigrati", *Minerva Medicopsicologica*, V, 4, 1964, pp. 235–238

Massucco Costa, A., "La dimensione storica nella formazione della coscienza individuale e sociale: Nord e Sud", *Rivista di Psicologia Sociale*, VIII, 2, 1961, pp. 127–154

Massucco Costa, A., "Lo stereotipo del meridionale", *Rivista di Psicologia Sociale*, XI, 1, 1964, pp. 53–62

Massucco Costa, A., "Ragazzi immigrati nelle scuole di Torino", *Riforma della Scuola*, XV, 6–7, 1969, pp. 43–45

Massucco Costa, A., Rizzo, G., "Condizioni oggettive e moventi soggettivi nelle migrazioni interne", *Rivista di Psicologia Sociale*, XVI, IV, 1969, pp. 295–312

Meda, J., "Tra le sudate carte. Guida ragionata ai fondi di quaderni ed elaborati didattici in Italia", *Biblioteche Oggi*, 2004, pp. 51–56

Medea, E., "Igiene Mentale e Scuola", *Scuola e Città*, XIII, 9, 1962, pp. 334–339

Melis, G., "Apparati di stato e democrazia repubblicana", *Quale Stato*, 4, 2006, pp. 393–405

Minicucci, M., "Antropologi e Mezzogiorno", *Meridiana*, 47–48, 2003, pp. 139–174

Misiani, S., "Educazione e tutela del paesaggio nell'azione meridionalista di Umberto Zanotti Bianco", *Meridiana*, 46, 2003, pp. 213–240

Montesano, G., "La S.I.A.M.E.", *Infanzia Anormale*, 2, 1953, pp. 131–138

Moraglio, M., "Dentro e fuori il manicomio. L'assistenza psichiatrica in Italia tra le due guerre", *Contemporanea*, 1, 2006, pp. 15–34

Myers, K. "Immigrants and ethnic minorities in the history of education", *Paedagogica Historica*, 45, 6, 2009, pp. 801–816

Oneto, R., "Fanciullezza in difficoltà", *Scuola e Città*, XI, 12, 1960, pp. 471–473

Oneto, R., "Per la gioventù disadattata", *Scuola e Città*, XII, 2, 1961, pp. 62–64

Palma, S., "Fotografia di una colonia. L'Eritrea di Luigi Naretti (1885–1900)", *Quaderni Storici*, 109, 2002, pp. 83-147

Parente, G., "Un fanciullo e l'ambiente", *I diritti della scuola*, a. LXII, n. 16, 1 June 1962, pp. 24–25

Parmentola, A., "Giovani immigrati a Torino", *Esperienze di Rieducazione*, IX, March 1962, pp. 21–33

Parmentola, A., "Fenomeni degenerativi dell'immigrazione a Torino", *Esperienze di Rieducazione*, IX, May 1962, pp. 34–51

Passalacqua, C., "Il 'Pieno Tempo': una soluzione per una scuola migliore", *Vita Nostra*, XIII, October 1970, p. 4

Passerini, L., "Work Ideology and Consensus Under Italian Fascism", *History Workshop Journal*, 8, 1, 1979, pp. 82–108

Passione, R., "Il Sud di Cesare Lombroso tra scienza e politica", *Il Risorgimento*, LII, 1, 2000, pp. 133–154

Patriarca, S., "Italian neopatriotism: debating National identities in the 1990s", *Modern Italy*, 6, 1, 2001, pp. 21–34

Petrina, S., "The Medicalization of education: A historiographic synthesis", *History of Education Quarterly*, XLVI, 4, 2006, pp. 503–531

Pigliaru, A., "Scuola e banditismo in Sardegna", *I problemi della pedagogia*, 1, 4, 1955, pp. 80–111

Pitzalis, M., "Hamsters on a wheel? Conflict over the role of school teachers in the primary education state school model", *Italian Journal of Sociology of Education*, 3, 2009, pp. 116–135

Pizzolato, N., "'Una situazione sadomasochistica ad incastro'. Il dibattito scientifico sull'immigrazione meridionale", *Quaderni Storici*, 118, 2005, pp. 97–120

Pontrelli, E., "Immigrazione e dissocialità minorile", *Minerva Medicolegale*, LXXXV, 5, 1965, pp. 29–38

Porta V., "Migrazione interna ed igiene mentale. Quadro psicologico e psicopatologico", *Igiene Mentale*, 1962, pp.728–750

Reay, D., "Insider Perspectives or Stealing the Words out of Women's Mouths: Interpretation in the Research Process", *Feminist Review*, 53, 1996, pp. 57–73

Rotondo, F., "Infanzia e migrazioni interne", *I diritti della scuola*, LXIII, 4, 15 November 1962, pp. 11–12

Rovigatti, M.T., "Le classi differenziali", *Ragazzi d'oggi*, III, 11–12, 1952, pp. 6–9

Rovigatti, M.T., "Le classi differenziali in Italia", *Infanzia Anormale*, XXIV, 5, 1954, pp. 65–82

Rovigatti, M.T., "La classe differenziale", in *Infanzia Anormale*, 6, 1954, pp. 233–42

Ruocco, E., "Incidenza dell'ambiente sull'inadattamento sociale dei giovani, 1", in *Ragazzi d'oggi*, III, 3, 1952, pp. 7–8

Ruocco, E., "Incidenza dell'ambiente sull'inadattamento sociale dei giovani, 2", in *Ragazzi d'oggi*, III, 5, pp. 7–8

Sangster, J., "Telling our stories: feminist debates and the use of oral history", *Women's History Review*, 3, 1, 1994, pp. 5–28

Saunders, R., "'Critical Ethnocentrism' and the Ethnology of Ernesto De Martino", *American Anthropologist*, VC, 4, 1993, pp. 875–893

Sauro, M., "Valutazione della subnormalità", *I Diritti della Scuola*, LXV, 9, 1st February 1965, pp. 15–16

Scarcella, M., "Igiene mentale delle migrazioni interne", *Minerva Medicopsicologica*, II, 1, 1961, pp. 9–12

Scarcella, M., "Rilievi su una proposta di classi differenziali per i figli di meridionali emigrati nel Nord", *Infanzia anormale*, 1, 1965, pp. 88–94

Schwartz, G., "On myth making and nation building: the genesis of the 'myth of the good Italian', 1943–1947", Telos, 164, 2013, pp. 11–43

Schwarz, B., "'Claudia Jones and the *West Indian Gazette*': reflections on the emergence of post-colonial Britain", *Twentieth Century British History*, 14, 3, 2003, pp. 264–285

Scotellaro, R., "Scuole di Basilicata –I", *Nord e Sud*, I, 1, 1954, pp. 67–95

Scotellaro, R., "Scuole di Basilicata – II", *Nord e Sud*, II, 2, 1955, pp. 73–101

Segrue, B., "Un coraggioso esperimento di lotta contro la delinquenza minorile", *Scuola e Città*, XII, 9, 1961, p. 357

Semeraro, A., "Educazione e sviluppo nel Mezzogiorno. Momenti di un dibattito del dopoguerra", *Studi Storici*, 31, 4, 1990, pp. 899–918

Stagnoli, G., "Aspetti educativi dell'assistenza scolastica", *Notiziario dell'Ufficio provinciale Attività assistenziali italiane e internazionali di Roma. Atti incontro di studio sull'assistenza scolastica organizzato dall'Attività assistenziali italiane e internazionali e dalla Associazione dei patronati scolastici. Lido di Roma, 24–25 Aprile 1955*, 29, July 1955, pp. 39–40

Stewart John, "The scientific claims of British Child Guidance, 1918–1945", *British Journal for the History of Science*, 42, 3, 2009, pp. 407–432

Summerfield, P., "Culture and Composure: Creating Narratives of the Gendered Self in Oral History Interviews", *Cultural and Social History*, 1, 2004, pp. 65–93

Tannozzini, F., "Scuola e urbanesimo. Inchiesta sull'emigrazione dal Sud al Nord", *I diritti della scuola*, LXIII, 13, 15 April 1963, pp. 10–12

Tannozzini, F., "Scuola e urbanesimo. Inchiesta sull'emigrazione dal Sud al Nord. Cfr. n. 13", *I diritti della scuola*, LXIII, 14, 1 May 1963, pp. 11–12

Tomasi, T., "Mezzo secolo di attività dell'Associazione per gli interessi del Mezzogiorno d'Italia", *Scuola e città*, XII, 6, 1961, pp. 227–233

Tornatore, L., "Scuola media per tutti", *Scuola e città*, XV, 1, 1964, pp. 6–14

Trainito, G., "Il dibattito parlamentare sul problema degli handicappati", *Annali della pubblica istruzione*, XXII, 2, 1976, pp. 219–223

Van Pelt, T., "Otherness", *Postmodern Culture*, 10, 2, 2000

Van Drenth, A., (ed.), *History of Education. Special Issue on the History of Special Education*, XXIV, 2, 2005

Zanotti Bianco, U., "Tra la perduta gente (Africo)", *Il Ponte*, II, 5, 1946, pp. 405–414

Zanotti Bianco, U., "Tra la perduta gente (Africo)", *Il Ponte*, II, 6, 1946, pp. 509–519

Zanotti Bianco, U., "Tra la perduta gente. Continuazione e fine", *Il Ponte*, II, 7–8, 1946, pp. 642–648

Zanotti Bianco, U., "Il problema della scuola", *Il Ponte*, VI, 9–10, 1950, pp. 1149–54

Zappella, M., "Un paese di deficienti?", *Riforma della Scuola*, XV, 12, 1969, pp. 21–23

Newspapers and magazine articles

"In 24 anni la popolazione è aumentata solo per l'arrivo di immigrati", *La Stampa*, 2 March 1955

"Il foglio di via obbligatorio per gli immigrati irregolari", *La Stampa*, 23 October 1955

"In nove mesi sono giunti circa 40 mila immigrati", *La Stampa*, 23 October 1955

"Siamo un po' tutti responsabili", *La Stampa*, 1 February 1956

"La corsa al Nord", *La Stampa*, 5 February 1956

"In un anno 56 mila immigrati a Torino da ogni parte d'Italia", *La Stampa*, 13 June 1956

"Un ambulante uccide con sei rivoltellate il compaesano che corteggia sua sorella", *La Stampa*, 19 July 1956

"L'Africa in casa", *L'Espresso*, V, 17, 26 April 1959

"Le quattro casbah di Palermo", *L'Espresso*, V, 18, 3 May 1959

"Il cielo non si mangia", *L'Espresso*, V, 19, 10 May 1959

"Le tribù dell'Aspromonte", *L'Espresso*, V, 20, 17 May 1959

"Gli stregoni di Valsinni", *L'Espresso*, V, 22, 31 May 1959

"Ragazzo di 15 anni respinto a scuola lascia uscire i familiari e si impicca", *La Stampa*, 13 June 1972

"Un'insegnante dello studente: 'Lo ha ucciso lo scontro con la città che lo respingeva", *La Stampa*, 13 June 1972

"Il pastorello pugliese era uno sradicato forse la scuola avrebbe potuto aiutarlo", *La Stampa*, 14 June 1972

"Ora ci si domanda: di chi la colpa?", *La Stampa*, 14 June 1972

"Quel che dicono della vittima il preside, le insegnanti di lettere e di francese", *La Stampa*, 14th June 1972

"Questi teppisti della Pacinotti", *La Stampa*, 15 June 1972

"La madre: quando andavo a parlare del figlio mi mandavano via", *La Stampa*, 15 June 1972

"Cerchiamo di non scordare perché è morto", *La Stampa*, 16 June 1972

Besozzi, T., "Alla mensa dei bimbi poveri i genitori stanno a guardare", *L'Europeo*, IV, 8, 22 February 1948

Besozzi, T., "I bambini di Napoli non mangiano sole", *L'Europeo*, IV, 10, 7 March 1948

Besozzi, T., "L'errore del vescovo di Mileto", *L'Europeo*, IV, 11, 14 March 1948

Cravero, R., "I problemi di Torino sono aggravate dal continuo flusso immigratorio", *La Stampa*, 11 October 1956

Fallaci, N., "I ragazzi che la scuola perde", *Oggi*, 1 July 1972

Gatto, A., Pietzsch, P.M., "Il miracolo del Gargano", *Epoca*, I, 11, 23 December 1950

Gatto, A., Pietzsch, P.M., "Matera, la città dei sassi", *Epoca*, II, 15, 20 January 1951

Ghirotti, G., "I calabresi della Riviera condannano il ratto solo perché eseguito con le armi", *La Stampa*, 18 November 1956

Grifoni, C., "Infanzia alle porte della civiltà", *La Stampa*, 11 February 1969

Mussa, C., "Il piatto di minestra sotto l'albero di Natale", *Gazzetta del Popolo*, 21 December 1971

Natoli, V., "Sono 'meno intelligenti' i bambini figli di poveri immigrati a Torino", *Gazzetta del Popolo*, 26 September 1969

Patellani, F., "Le scuole impossibili", *Epoca*, 28 giugno 1952

Perotti, C., "Alla conquista di una soffitta", *Gazzetta del Popolo*, 15 July 1962

Perotti, C., "Mezza Corleone si è trasferita a Borgaro", *Gazzetta del Popolo*, 9 September, 1962

Ronchey, A., "C'è un milione di analfabeti adulti che si possono recuperare con trenta miliardi", *La Stampa*, 4 March 1962

Ronchey, A., "La scuola media unica è una necessità urgente e chiara nell'Italia 'del miracolo'", *La Stampa*, 14 March 1962

Ronchey, A., "Il sole di Napoli non giunge nelle aule ricavate da rifugi di fortuna", *La Stampa*, 23 March 1962

Ronchey, A., "Sulla scuola della cintura di Torino si ripercuotono gli angosciosi problemi del Sud", *La Stampa*, 31 March 1962

Songs

Della Mea, I., "Ballata per Ciriaco Saldutto", originally in the LP album *La Balorda* (Dischi dello Zodiaco VPA 8165, 1971) reprinted in Ivan Della Mea *Venne Maggio* (1969–1971 integral and critical rerelease of *Il rosso è diventato giallo* and *La Balorda* - NOTA BN 2CD594, 2019) ISBN 9788861631939

Interviews

Alfonsina, Turin, 1955, accountant. Interview with the author, Turin, 20 April 2009

Angela, Salerno, 1951, teacher. Interview with the author, Turin, 20 May 2009

Assunta, Turin, 1955, civil servant. Interview with the author, Turin, 12 May 2009

Giovanna, Turin, 1954, retired. Interview with the author, Turin, 5 May 2009

Immacolata, Turin, 1958, business owner. Interview with the author, Turin, 16 May 2009

Lorenzo, Turin,1954, factory worker. Interview with the author, Turin, 5 May 2009

Marcello, Turin, 1964, entrepreneur. Interview with the author, Turin, 30 April 2009

Mauro, Crotone, 1964, caretaker. Interview with the author, Turin, 27 May 2009

Michele, Turin, 1948, teacher. Interview with the author, Turin, 17 April 2009

Monica, Troia – Apulia, 1957, housewife. Interview with the author, Turin, 11 May 2009

Pasquale, Palermo, 1959, postman. Interview with the author, Turin, 27 May 2009

Roberto, Turin, 1947, factory worker. Interview with the author, Turin, 4 May 2009

Rosario, Caltanissetta, 1953, civil servant and free-lance historian. Interview with the author, 13 May 2009

Websites

Camera dei Deputati: http://www.camera.it November 2022

GISCEL: http://giscel.it November 2022

Official Vatican Website: http://www.vatican.va November 2022

Newspaper *La Repubblica:* http://www.repubblica.it November 2022

Rizzoli: http://www.speakers-corner.it/rizzoli/ November 2022

Index

Note: Page numbers followed by "n" denote endnotes.